LANGUAGE, EDUCATION AND SOCIAL
PROCESSES IN A GAELIC COMMUNITY

route

direct editions

LANGUAGE, EDUCATION AND SOCIAL PROCESSES IN A GAELIC COMMUNITY

KENNETH MACKINNON
Department of Psychological and Social Studies
Hatfield Polytechnic

WITHDRAWN
UNIVERSITY LIBRARY NOTTINGHAM

ROUTLEDGE DIRECT EDITIONS

ROUTLEDGE & KEGAN PAUL
London, Henley and Boston

First published in 1977
by Routledge & Kegan Paul Ltd
39 Store Street,
London WC1E 7DD,
Broadway House,
Newtown Road,
Henley-on-Thames,
Oxon RG9 1EN and
9 Park Street,
Boston, Mass. 02108, USA

Printed and bound in Great Britain
by Unwin Brothers Limited,
The Gresham Press, Old Woking, Surrey
member of the Staples Printing Group

© Kenneth MacKinnon 1977

No part of this book may be reproduced in
any form without permission from the
publisher, except for the quotation of brief
passages in criticism

ISBN 0 7100 8466 8

Do'm dheagh chàirdean
anns a' Chòmhlan Chruinn
agus gu h-àraidh dhaibh-san
a chuidich leam ann an
iomadach dòigh rè
sgrìobhadh an leabhair seo

CONTENTS

FOREWORD

We have witnessed in the study of the social features of language
the development of a distinction between socio-linguistics and the
sociology of language. I believe Fishman first drew attention to
this fragmentation. Socio-linguistics appears to concern itself
with contextualised studies of speech in inter-actional settings.
To a very great extent this field is dominated by linguists rather
than sociologists, although it is true that ethnomethodologists
have contributed to these contextualised studies by drawing attention to the rules and indexical features of talk whereby we impli-
citly create situated order in on-going inter-actions. Fishman
argues that the major function of socio-linguistics has been to
enlarge the horizons of linguistics 'beyond the phrase, beyond the
utterance, to the speech act and the speech occasion'. As a consequence, the final success of socio-linguistics may well be its
ultimate incorporation with linguistics. On the whole, it is
empirically the case that there are few theories in the field of
socio-linguistics which establish explicit conceptual relationships
with institutional features of language (political, economic, religious) in the context of the formation, maintenance and reproduc-
tion of the values, communication networks and referential systems
of social groups. Dr MacKinnon's book should be seen from this
perspective.

Dr MacKinnon has combined a number of methods in his research,
but I am sure he will agree that the crucial experience was the
year he spent with the people of the Isle of Harris. His book is
likely to become a basic text not solely because of the sensitive
and systematic analysis of the central issue, but because of his
treatment of the wider problems his research raises.

Basil Bernstein

University of London
Institute of Education

ix

PREFACE AND ACKNOWLEDGMENTS

This book is an abridgement of a Ph.D. thesis accepted in 1975 by
the Faculty of Education, University of London. The fuller work,
containing an extensive review of relevant literature, full texts of
the questionnaires and speech samples used, and appendices containing
further analyses of economic and onomastic data, is available from
the Senate House and Institute of Education libraries, London
University.

The fieldwork for this study was made possible by the award of a
Senior Research Fellowship by the Social Science Research Council
and by the generosity of Dr William and Catherine MacKenzie for the
loan of their Harris home during 1972-4; their confidence in my work
is very gratefully acknowledged. I am most greatly indebted to
Professor Basil Bernstein for his interest in and encouragement of my
work, from and including my master's dissertation, and sustained over
the years beyond the completion of the present study. I greatly appreciate his practical assistance, helpful criticism, insights and ideas.

I am greatly indebted to many people for their hospitality, help-
fulness, time, energies and thought on my behalf, especially Finlay
Macleod, Anne Morrison, John Murdo Morrison, Roy and Jenny Pedersen,
Colin and Jess Spencer, Frank and Margaret Thompson together with the
educational officials, head teachers, staff and pupils of Inverness-
shire and Harris schools, and the people of Harris who assisted me as
helpers and informants, whose interest, hospitality and kindness
greatly sustained me in my work.

I wish to thank Lewis Grant who deputised in my post of Head of
Department of General and Social Studies, Barking College of Techno-
logy and who rendered, as did Pamela Bradbury of Hatfield Polytechnic,
invaluable statistical advice and assistance. I am most grateful to
my present colleagues for generous and practical support and help in
the later stages of my work.

Finally I wish most gratefully to acknowledge the support and fore-
bearance of my wife, son and daughter during my protracted absences
and involvement in these studies, and I express much gratitude to
Robina Jo Roberton, Redbridge Technical College, for the devotion of
much time and energy to the production of the original typescripts.

Kenneth MacKinnon

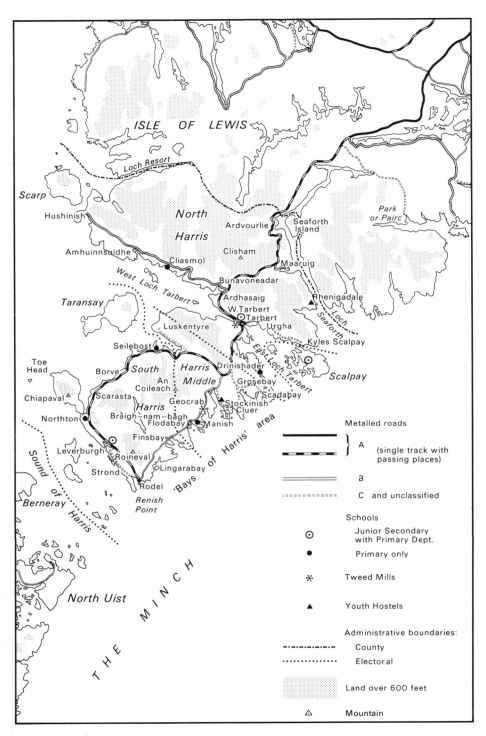

ISLE OF LEWIS

Loch Resort

Scarp

Hushinish

North

Harris

Ardvourlie   Seaforth
                  Island   Park
                                            or Pairc

Amhuinnsuidhe   Clisham
            Cliasmol   △

                                Maaruig
West Loch Tarbert   Bunavoneadar

Taransay   Ardhasaig   Rhenigadale
                      W.Tarbert ⊙ Tarbert
                           ✳   Urgha
                  Luskentyre   Kyles Scalpay

            Seilebost   Scalpay
Toe   Drinishader
Head   South   Harris
        Borve   Middle   Grosebay
              An   Scadabay
Chiapaval △   Coileach △   Geocrab Stockinish
        Scarasta   Harris   Cluer
Northton   Bràigh–nam–bàgh ▲
              Flodabay ● Manish
         Finsbay
Leverburgh ⊙   Roineval   'Bays of Harris' area
        Strond △   Lingarabay

              Rodel
Berneray   Renish
              Point

North Uist

THE MINCH

Metalled roads

────────── ⎫ A
─ ─ ─ ─ ─   ⎭ (single track with
                 passing places)

═══════════   B

============   C and unclassified

Schools

⊙   Junior Secondary
     with Primary Dept.

●   Primary only

✳   Tweed Mills

▲   Youth Hostels

Administrative boundaries:

─·─·─·─·─   County

··········   Electoral

              Land over 600 feet

△   Mountain

The Isle of Harris

Chapter 1

INTRODUCTION: SCOTTISH GAELIC STUDIES - SOCIOLOGICAL PERSPECTIVES

The cultivation of Gaelic studies in Scotland has witnessed a century of development. Although the Education Act (Scotland) passed in 1872 effectively transferred responsibility for public education in the Highlands from Gaelic Society schools and church schools (which by then were using Gaelic as a teaching medium), the Act conceived no specific reference to Gaelic and public authority schools in Gaelic Scotland initially accorded scant place to Gaelic either as a teaching medium or as a subject of specific study in its own right.(1)

The activities of the Gaelic Society of Inverness (established in 1871), together with the efforts of the Gaelic Society of London (founded in 1777), were in large measure instrumental in securing the establishment of the first professorial chair of Celtic studies in a Scottish university. In 1882 Donald MacKinnon was elected first professor of Celtic languages, literature, history and antiquities at Edinburgh University.(2) In 1891 the Highland Association, An Comunn Gàidhealach, was founded and it rapidly came to lead the language-loyalty movement — although essentially within a Lowland context. It may be forgotten today that the end of the nineteenth century was, within the Highlands, a time of political agitation and unrest. The Highland Land League (utilising popular Gaelic poets such as Mary MacPherson, Skye) were securing successes such as the election of Crofter Party MPs and the passing of the first Crofters' Acts.(3) The early 1890s also witnessed the secession of the Free Presbyterian Church. Thus the specifically cultural and language-loyalist Gaelic societies formed during this period strove conspicuously to avoid sectarian and political entanglement. This tradition has remained so to the present day until long after the religious and political tumult has died away. The language 'cause' has perpetuated its political quietism and it may be that its active membership and leadership has tended to come, if not from political neutrals, then very definitely from the politically non-activist. No doubt the neutral stance of the Gaelic movement at the turn of the century provided its strength. By the later twentieth century neutralism very definitely proved to be its weakness.

1

In Ireland, the Gaelic League, Conradh na Gaelige, founded in 1893, combined the functions separately undertaken in Scotland by the Highland Land League, An Comunn Gàidhealach and the precursors of the Scottish National Party. In Wales the Welsh language continued to enjoy a public identification as an essential component of Welsh national life. In Scotland, Gaelic had long ceased to be similarly identified. It would seem the politics of the Scottish Reformation severed the previously acknowledged identification of Gaelic as being the original language of the Scottish people.(4) Early in the twentieth century attempts were made to reassert the significance of Gaelic as the Scottish language with the development of a nationalist party in Scotland. These moves were thwarted by the predominating Lowland and English-speaking element of the Scottish people who had come to identify the Scottish Lowland dialect of English as 'Scots' and so comprising the essential linguistic expression of the core society of modern Scotland and the linguistic marker of the predominating concept of Scottish nationality.(5) So today there is virtually no 'language-dimension' to Scottish politics in contrast to Wales - or even Ireland. Scottish accents and Scotticisms in common usage are not felt to be under attrition from English influence in the same way as the Welsh language is felt by Welsh nationalists and language-loyalists to be in course of erosion by the use of English in public administration and institutions in Welsh society today.

In 1968 the Scottish National Party adopted a policy of cultivation of Gaelic in the conference resolution to set up a 'Gaelic Secretariat'. But only in 1974 was a resolution adopted to formulate a detailed policy for Gaelic.

Without the stimulus of a political movement and an associated ideology behind it, Gaelic in Scotland has not enjoyed the status of being an 'election issue'. In Wales the seminal thought of Saunders Lewis articulated a pro-Welsh language ideology and provided a nomenclature for the political discussion of the problem. His broadcast talk in 1962 'Tynged yr Iaith' ('The Fate of the Language') galvanised the Welsh-language community and especially its youth to a conscious and overt activism.(6) Nothing like this has ever occurred with respect to Gaelic in Scotland, although an organisation was constituted in 1971 (Comunn na Canain Albannaich) taking as its conscious model Cymdeithas yr Iaith Gymraeg in Wales.

Over 80 years of activity in the cultural field, An Comunn Gàidhealach has successfully promoted cultural festivals, the National and Provincial Mòds (on the lines of the Welsh Eisteddfodau), stimulated publishing and exerted a certain influence on educational affairs. It has been very guarded with respect to pronouncements concerning Gaelic in public affairs. It has taken very strictly and seriously its royal patronage and its non-political and non-sectarian constitution. By the mid-century it became very clear that the academic cultivation of Gaelic in the universities, the admission of Gaelic as a subject into the schools, the literary and cultural cultivation of Gaelic by voluntary associations, were seemingly of little effect in safeguarding the maintenance of Gaelic as a community language. In the 1950s Gaelic was scarcely recognised in any way by public administration. At this time the BBC was broadcasting only some 1¾ hours in Gaelic

weekly. Publishing in Gaelic was at its lowest ebb ever and one of
the few signs of encouragement was the establishment of the all-
Gaelic quarterly 'Gairm' in 1952.

The leading Gaelic organisation, An Comunn Gàidhealach, very
slowly rethought its role in the post-war period. However, in
1965 it appointed a professional director, Donald J. MacKay, who
brought an essential contemporary spirit into its work. By 1967
he extended its aims to include 'the social and economic welfare of
the Highlands and Islands of Scotland', and called for the appointment of a Gaelic-speaking Highlander to the Highlands and Islands
Development Board, the encouragement of sociological research into
language and community life, and for association branches to tackle
practical projects and the Comunn to act more vigorously as a
pressure group.

The later 1960s were a time of increasing activity within the
Gaelic movement. The Comunn was successful in stimulating interest
in its new policies. For the first time offices were established
within the Highlands and Hebrides, government grants secured and
further full-time staff appointed. Despite some setbacks the
broadcasting media provided more time for Gaelic. In 1966 a
government grant enabled Glasgow University to commence work for a
Historical Dictionary of Scottish Gaelic, and further grants from
1969 established the Gaelic Books Council. These modest advances
were the slow-to-ripen fruits of much work undertaken largely out
of public sight. During the 1920s and 1930s An Comunn Gàidhealach
had convened conferences on Gaelic in education. Its report of
1936 called for improved school time for Gaelic, improved teacher
qualifications and inspection, better provision of textbooks,
curricular reform and attention to the needs of learners and adult
students. Many of its recommendations were reiterated in later
county and official reports.

During the 1950s and 1960s the Committee on Bilingualism of the
Scottish Council for Research in Education developed concern for
Gaelic, publishing Christina Smith's study of mental testing of
Lewis children in 1948, the study 'Gaelic-Speaking Children in
Highland Schools' in 1961, and a collection of children's rhymes
and lore for use in schools, 'Aithris is Oideas', in 1966. Con-
ferences concerned with Gaelic in education had been convened during
this period, stimulating the 1961 report and new policies for Gaelic
in Inverness-shire and Ross-shire. As a precursor of the Gaelic
Books Council, a committee for Gaelic school texts was founded, and
together with an increasing output of publications of Aberdeen and
Glasgow Universities, the 'Gairm' imprimatur and the Scottish
Gaelic Texts Society, the output of Gaelic texts improved greatly
during the 1960s — even more so after the Gaelic Books Council and
Club Leabhar got under way in the early 1970s. Improved arrangements for school examinations in Gaelic for natives and learners
also occurred — unfortunately as yet not providing a range of
subjects examinable through Gaelic.

Although concerned with Gaelic in education and the provision
of Gaelic literature, Gaelic scholarship has until recently lacked
specific concern with sociological or sociolinguistic perspectives.
Gaelic studies as pursued in the university departments of 'Celtic'
have in the past been concerned with such themes as comparative

philology, historical linguistics, dialectology, folklore, and
literary criticism and have been criticised for antiquarianism and
a divorce of concern from present-day conditions affecting the
Gaelic community. Recent years, though, have seen a stronger
awareness of the importance of such aspects of Celtic studies as
the social history of the Highlands. Such leading figures in
Gaelic scholarship as Professor Derick Thomson have approached the
study of Gaelic literature from the point of view of the social
processes whereby this literature has been generated. His work
also shows a concern to examine the social milieu of the producers
of literature and the social condition of its public. Something of
a sociological awareness has entered the study of Gaelic literature.
   So far a sociological study of language as such has not yet been
attempted on any extensive scale in respect of Gaelic and its
speakers. Development of the sociolinguistic study of Gaelic in
Scotland has been hindered by the social situation of Celtic and
sociological studies themselves in Scottish academic life. As we
have seen, Celtic studies have chiefly recruited their students and
exponents from the 'pool' of native Gaelic speakers in the Gaelic
homelands, or from those within the general academic tradition of
philology and structural linguistics. Only recently has socio-
linguistics started to enter this field in Scotland. As Carter has
pointed out,(7) the pattern of development of academic sociology in
Britain has been such that
     Scotland is *terra incognita* for British sociology. Little work
     has been done by sociologists on Scotland, rather than in
     Scotland. This situation is to be explained by a number of
     factors. The first is that departments of sociology are of
     relatively recent growth in Scottish universities. Consequently,
     the vast majority of sociologists working in Scotland today were
     neither born nor trained in the country. A second factor is the
     marked centripetal tendency among British sociologists; English
     conurbations, and above all London, draw them inexorably . . . .
     A third factor . . . is an assumption of British homogeneity
     . . . there is no point in going to distant parts to do research
     that could be done . . . within a fifteen-mile radius of
     Hampstead.
Thus, suggests Carter, 'sociologists have either ignored Scotland or
they have misunderstood Scotland'. It was certainly true of Aberdeen University, from whence Carter was writing, that with scarcely
one exception (an Orcadian) no member of the sociology department
was a native-reared Scot.
   For such reasons as the foregoing, and the fact that the Gaelic-
speaking community in Scotland is small and peripheral, it has not
attracted a great deal of sociological study. Such a small and
atypical community might not seem to provide enough scope for the
study of 'problems of the middle range'.(8) Yet this is surely mistaken on a number of counts. First, the Gaelic speech-community may
lack typicality within modern Britain, yet it may have close
parallels with situations very commonly found within the 'third
world'. Its geographical closeness to the core society of modern
Britain (although a little outside Carter's fifteen-mile radius of
Hampstead) makes it a conveniently close instance of an autochthonous ethnic group within a larger and ethnically differentiated

polity.(9)   Second, the size of the community renders it capable of
being readily compassed by the methods of social science as currently
practised.   It is of manageable dimensions.   This fact should enable
the development of theories which bridge the gap between micro- and
macro-level approaches, which should enable phenomena at these differing levels to be coherently related together - to provide in
fact 'theories of the middle range' as suggested by Merton.
   Considerations of the 'Gaelic Problem' whether by language-
loyalist and activist movements, practising educators or the academic establishment have each tended to skirt round a piece of
unexplored territory.   Language associations have tended to operate
outside the Gaelic-speaking areas and to cater for the exile, the
dilettanti, and those seeking the provision of entertainment and
culture in the language.   Considerations of social problems by
Gaelic societies such as An Comunn have until recently been avoided
— as has an active presence in the Gaelic homelands — for these
concerns may have been seen as conducive to political and sectarian
internal strife.   Practising educators have until 1958 generally
taken the spirit of the 1872 — and the 1918 — Education Acts as
the 'official line' to do very little in, or for, Gaelic language
and culture.   Academic Celtic studies have until very recently concentrated upon philological, historical, literary and structural
linguistic aspects of Gaelic.   Academic sociology has ignored this
community in large measure since it is small and out of the way and
until very recently sociology has not returned again to one of its
earlier considerations: the problem of language.   Similarly the
Gaelic community had little political weight in the twentieth century.   Until recently it sat upon few valuable economic resources.
Although public administration left much to be desired there were
no outrageous public scandals and outcries.   (But then neither were
there any such at the height of the notorious Sutherland evictions
in the early nineteenth century!)(10)   The Gaelic speech-community
was thus perceived as providing neither major social problems
requiring substantial political attention, neither was it perceived
as providing important and interesting sociological problems requiring scientific investigation.
   The continued existence of the Gaelic community into the last
third of the twentieth century is a problem requiring explanation.
Sociologically its mere existence and persistence is very interesting.   A previous study has sketched in something of the history of
the Gaelic language in Scotland and has attempted to look sociologically at the situation of its speakers over time and at the
present day.(11)
   As the result of clearance of population, lack of economic
development and consequential continued high outward migration,
tacit policies inimical to the language in education and public
life, it is surprising that there should be anyone at all alive
today who can speak the Gaelic language.   Yet Gaelic remains the
everyday community speech throughout most of the Hebrides — and
still in one or two mainland enclaves today.   It remains for sociology rather than any other of the fields of endeavour cited above to
explain this phenomenon.   The persistence of Gaelic speech has to be
explained in terms of language-maintenance rather than in terms of
overt activist language-loyalty.   As the language of folk life

rather than of national or official institutions, Gaelic probably
possesses certain significances within the sub-culture of its
speakers. For them it probably conveys particular meanings of
importance to their value system. There are large numbers of
studies of language in culture and in society for communities of
this size and scale in the 'third' and 'fourth' worlds. The findings of these studies are interesting and suggestive but one may
not infer that because, say, Gumperz has elucidated certain relationships and processes in northern Norway or northern India(12)
that they necessarily pertain or indeed are to be found at all in
the Hebrides. Similarly the speech of black ghetto children in
Harlem may be perceived by Labov to possess certain characteristics.(13) This is not to say that we should necessarily expect to
find them in the speech of Gaelic-speaking children in small rural
schools. Fischer discovered structural differences between the
language of the adjacent Pacific islands of Truk and Ponape. He
also cited parallel differences between the culture and social
relations within the respective island communities.(14) There are
structural differences between Gaelic and English. Whether or not
cultural and social differences should be expected between Gaelic-
speaking and English-speaking communities is problematical.

But the size of the Gaelic-speaking community is such that it
should be possible readily to elucidate its actual sociolinguistic
characteristics, which may or may not parallel research findings
in ostensibly similar situations elsewhere.

The Isle of Harris appeared to be an appropriate community to
study in order to explicate the relationships between social processes and sociolinguistic phenomena for a number of reasons, such
as its size, homogeneity and central position in the present-day
Gaelic-speaking area, and the availability of previous studies,(15)
thus providing an example of a 'crucial case' for the present
purpose.

It was proposed then to build up a societal model of such an
ideal-typical Gaelic speech-community at the present time by setting
out to examine the place that the Gaelic language has within the
local culture. It was hoped to explore the functions of language by
the use of such concepts as 'dominance configuration'.(16) In this
way one could attempt to map out the nature of Gaelic-English bilingualism and differentiation of usage. The study proposed to
derive a model of the various domains of usage and the social
patternings which influence the choice of language used in typical
situations. It was hoped that to use such variables as class,
status and occupation and that these explorations would throw light
upon the operation of power and further illuminate aspects of cultural cleavage.

It was intended to develop hypotheses explanatory of such phenomena as language-shift, stability and instability of societal bilingualism as regards the persistence of Gaelic as a community
language and the development of language-loyalty towards Gaelic.

The school appears to play a key role within the socioeconomic
processes of communities like Harris, and has an important function
as an agency of social control. The study of the language and
culture of the school is essential to an analysis of the relationship of local culture and society to that of the mainstream

culture and mass society of modern Britain.

At the inception of the study, the Gaelic community had not developed the self-conscious activist type of language-loyalty movement that had come into being, for example, during the 1960s in Wales, where issues of nationalism and nationality are more closely associated with issues of language. Language-maintenance rather than language-loyalty seems to be the more important aspect of language-conservation in communities like Harris. The local language is conserved more at the level of folk-life than through the 'high' culture, official patronage or overtly-organised activism. Such developments may be incipient in Harris — as during the period of the study a more activist and self-regarding posture was developing with regard to Gaelic in southern Skye. However, owing to the size, social situation and isolated character of Gaelic-speaking communities, such developments within the Gaelic-speaking population as a whole may be inhibited.

Such a society as Harris may provide, close to mainstream British society, an example of societal processes very closely parallel with increasingly common situations in the 'third world' both with respect to the increasingly numerous instances of bilingual situations affecting educational programmes, as well as the phenomenon of incorporation of lingual minorities within plural-ethnic polities. The conclusions may be valuable in considering administrative and political problems in such situations.

At the outset, I had visited Harris for varying periods annually over a few years and I had the opportunity to reside for the greater part of a year on the island, commencing in the autumn of 1972, and attended the National Mòd in Inverness, the principal annual cultural event of Scottish Gaeldom. During the early stages of the fieldwork I took the opportunity to visit almost all the island schools and to spend some time observing play, lessons and talking to teachers. I was also able to attend meetings of the district council and island education sub-committee, church services and weekday prayer meetings, committee meetings of the Council of Social Service, local development association, public entertainments and dances, the initial meetings during the formation of a craft guild and other public events. I was also able to develop discussions with local people in their own homes, and my own, in hotels, shops, public transport and so forth. Amongst community leaders I made contacts with ministers, council members, village bards, teachers and officers of local associations.

From observation of community life and discussions with local people, a number of lines of approach seemed appropriate to me. First, to focus interest upon the school as a key institution in the social structure. As education might be one of the principally operative processes whereby children are selected and sponsored for differential access to the occupational and career structure of wider society, then it would be important to monitor the passage of children through it, into local employment, selective secondary education away from the island, further and higher education and the career structure beyond Harris. As the school may be said actively to operate the allocation of life-chances to local children, it must surely comprise an important agency or mechanism for the influencing of the social and demographic structure of the

community. In addition to its significance in socialisation and
the influence of the societal value-system, the school may be
hypothesised as having an important physical function in regulating
the size and internal structure of the local community, whether at
manifest or latent levels. It would not be so important to consider
whether or not the school were *consciously* used as a deliberate
agency for ensuring that such a remote locality as Harris never
again became a 'congested district', as to consider whether despite
official policy to the contrary the school system was *in practice*
actually underdeveloping local society and the local economy.

Accordingly a number of studies of the education system were
undertaken early in 1973.

1. A study of the use of Gaelic and English in the initial stages
of schooling: with beginners primary classes I and II. Recordings
of class teaching and individual tuition were undertaken. Behind
this exercise were the questions, for what purpose is Gaelic now
utilised within the schools? How is English introduced to Gaelic-
speaking children? How do the two languages function within the
primary school?

2. An important study of Gaelic-speaking children in Highland
schools was undertaken in 1957-9.(17) This focused particularly on
years primary I and II and secondary I. A useful amount of factual
and statistical material was published for Harris. Although the
methodology of this study might, after 15 years be improved in
certain respects(18) it provided a useful base or datum-level which
was capable of being updated a decade and a half later to yield a
useful indication of the rate of change over time. Its questionnaires were reproduced and reissued to the Harris schools.

3. In order to fill out a bare factual and statistical sample
of two stages of schooling (beginners in primary and secondary
stages), a further questionnaire was prepared for use among senior
secondary pupils (SIII - VI inclusive). This was intended to explore such factors as media-variance(19) and ability in Gaelic
(understanding, speaking, reading and writing), where these abilities were acquired, attitudes to Gaelic and Gaelic studies, news
and entertainment media, knowledge of Gaelic organisation, language-
loyalty(20) and activism. In order to explore secondary-aged
children's attitudes to language-varieties an experiment was
devised of pre-recording four typical speech-varieties (two in
Gaelic, two in English) in common use in Harris and inviting respondents to check upon a pro-forma their reactions to them. Almost
all the SIII - VI children, whether on or away from the island, were
contacted and undertook these exercises.

4. Harris students at colleges of further education were traced
and undertook these two exercises.

5. Discussions were undertaken with all these older Harris
children at local schools, at hostels in schools elsewhere and at
colleges of further education. These were open-ended, free ranging
over the problems raised in the questionnaires, and were recorded.

6. Contacts were made with Highland education authorities and
the colleges of education in Scotland, the Scottish Education
Department and the Scottish universities in order to gain factual
and detailed information regarding the flow of children from Highland communities into and around the education system and out of it

into employment, further and higher education, professional training and careers. It would be useful to substantiate claims sometimes advanced that Highland children showed a marked regional or
cultural bias towards higher education and entry into higher-graded
jobs and the professions. Information was also sought regarding
recruiting and staffing policies for the remote and Gaelic-speaking
areas and the extent to which awareness existed of desirability of
teacher education not merely for teaching Gaelic as a subject but
of Gaelic-speaking children as such. I also attempted to trace
career details of Harris former pupils through their school and local
authority records.

Subsequently in 1973 I was able unobtrusively to record Gaelic as
used in committee meetings, church services and in everyday conversations.

In mid-1973 I transferred my principal focus of interest to the
significance of Gaelic within the culture of the general or adult
population. I undertook a 5 per cent sample survey (which produced
a better than 4 per cent final sample) throughout the whole of the
registered 18+ adult population. The issues explored by this study
comprised media-variance and ability in Gaelic (understanding, speaking, reading and writing), dominance-configuration(21) — the use of
Gaelic or English in a variety of sociolinguistic domains of usage,
(22) use of second-person pronouns in address, attitudes to authority, attitudes to Gaelic, and the way in which Gaelic is associated with the value system, socialisation and childrearing, and
the interpenetration of the home community by outsiders and outside
influences.

Becoming interested in naming practices as a feature of the local
culture I collected from three south Harris villages a complete
collection of patronymics and hypercoristics for the entire adult
population. I also extracted from the local register of births,
marriages and deaths, statistics on given names as well as vital
statistics since 1858.

In 1974 I returned for a short period in order to undertake an
exploration of code in the Gaelic and English of the younger primary-aged children (6, 7 and 8 years of age) and to update the 1973
survey of secondary I pupils.

Previous studies of Gaelic speech-communities have been few and
have approached the problem chiefly from the perspectives of
linguistics, literary criticism and social history, e.g. in the
studies by John Lorne Campbell of Canna, Professor Derick Thomson
and Charles Dunn. A more specifically sociological approach is
developed by the more recent work of Campbell and MacLean and Karl
Deutsch.

J.L. Campbell's study of 1945, 'Gaelic in Scottish Education and
Life'(23) provided for many years virtually the only available study
of Gaelic in its social situation. Over history Gaeldom is seen in
particular forms of power relationship with its surrounding society:
autonomous, sectarian, utilitarian and bureaucratic phases. The
study is valuable for its carefully garnered information regarding
Gaelic in Scottish life in the mid-twentieth century. Many of his
recommendations have been achieved over the years but it has become clear that improvements of the 'status' alone of the language
will be insufficient to perpetuated Gaelic as the community

language of an ever contracting *Gàidhealtachd*. Campbell's study
of Gaelic in Canada,(24) based on work in eastern Nova Scotia and
Prince Edward Island, is interesting for its claim that Gaelic was
at that time being maintained inter-generationally (in some contrast
to Scotland). Although in both cases the Gaelic communities were
culturally dependent upon an English-speaking society, a more pene-
trating sociological analysis would have been valuable, as Campbell
recorded the last generation of tradition-bearers in the Hebrides
and experienced a live Gaelic situation in Canada - in both cases
crucial periods of community history.

Dunn has provided in 'Highland Settler: a Portrait of the
Scottish Gael in Nova Scotia'(25) a particularly well-documented
social history of the Gaelic community illustrated from its own
internal sources of Gaelic folk-poetry. Dunn has vividly drawn an
account of the transplantation, transmutation and cultural attrition of the Gaelic folk-culture in its Canadian setting. He draws
very interesting accounts of the perpetuation of naming practises
even surviving societal language-shift. A recent account of this
community, 'Beyond the Atlantic Roar: A Study of the Nova Scotia
Scots' by Dougal Campbell and Ray MacLean is disappointing in terms
of its sociological approach.(26) It is a most valuable social
history of the Gaelic settlements and their fortunes, utilising both
oral and written sources, but its sociolinguistic perspectives are
unfortunately thin, relying upon the explanatory models of Hertzler
and Barker developed from Mexican-American and 'Old Family' Spanish
social situations. That of the Gaelic diaspora is markedly different — and Campbell and MacLean provide a valuable account of the
presentday culture (and an interesting perspective upon the summer
visitor culture of returning exiles). By the 1970s effective transmission of Gaelic had ceased amongst the sixth generation immigrants. J.L. Campbell had found cultural transmission effective up
to the preceding generation, leaving us an intriguing sociolinguistic problem, for there had evidently been little change in
power relationships, cultural arrangements, values or populations.
There is surprisingly no discussion of such issues as 'third generation interest' and 'return', 'diglossia' or 'language function',
despite recognition in education and multiculturalism and 'a few
optimists who see revival on the horizon . . . . For Gaelic, it is
perhaps too late.'(27)

The corpus of work developed in Scotland by Derick Thomson is
valuable for its social awareness. Developed within the tradition
of academic 'Celtic Studies' it is not specifically sociological.
His studies of medieval learned orders and of the remarkable
MacMhuirich bardic family(28) (ante 1139 in Ireland to post 1800
in Canada) draw attention to the underpinning of kinship in the
development and transmission of the Gaelic high culture. In his
study of The Role of the Writer in a Minority Culture and Literature
and the Arts in 'The Future of the Highlands',(29) Thomson draws
attention to the intimate relationship between economic development, the symbolic value-system, language and literature, and
emphasises the way in which the 'high', 'folk' and 'metropolitan'
traditions of Gaelic literary production have stemmed from the
structure of Gaelic society and its economic strength. Thomson
sees Gaelic culture as a whole or 'of the same piece'. He calls for

a regeneration of Highland society not merely economically in terms
of development, but also socially and culturally. The writer has
an important role as literature provides insights into the world
view of the society 'from the inside', into social forces shaping
society 'from the outside' and realigning it internally. There is
a relationship between community morale, access to and transmission
of the culture, the social functions of language as used both by
the writer and the native speaker.

Karl Deutsch provides a sociological analysis of the Gaelic
speech community as one of his typifying cases in his study 'Nationalism and Social Communication'.(30) The essential model of this
work is in viewing society as a vehicle for the transmission of
culture. He sees society essentially as process rather than structure and is concerned with the internal and external dynamics of
nationalities, speech-communities and language-groups. A national
society is defined as a network for communication of the elements of
a common culture. Social change may be introduced in various forms:
migration, industrialisation, urbanisation, etc. With such change
'mobilisation' of a population may occur. If this is rapid, as with
the Czechs and the Finns, a minority culture may socially develop
so as to dominate a communication network of its own. A 'lift-
pump' effect or 'social updraft' attracts thousands, and eventually
millions into new settlements, occupations and patterns of social
intercourse. Social learning is rapid in that outsiders rapidly
become assimilated to new ways. Unlike Czechoslovakia or Finland,
the process of modernisation was unable to Gaelicise urban Scotland,
despite the influx of a large, mobilised Gaelic population, as the
rate could not be sustained and the bottom of the barrel was reached
well before the end of the nineteenth century. However, Deutsch's
model implies that a small speech-community may through greater
relative mobilisation maintain effective political power and promote
its speech as standard for the polity as a whole. Its hegemony may
be usurped if a larger speech-community mobilises more rapidly than
processes of assimilation can cope with. Thus the dynamics of
language-shift are to be sought not merely in terms of power relations, cultural diffusion, culture-lag and culture contact, but in
an assessment of the place that language has within the culture of
the groups in contact: the meaning that language has *per se* as a
symbol of group life and its place in the value-system. Thus understood, Deutsch's analysis may be over-deterministic, underestimating
even the role of ideology in sociolinguistic processes.

This disparate literature indicates something of the lack of
development of a sociolinguistic approach to Scottish Gaelic studies
as well as comprising a particular case of the general lack of focus
on specific Scottish problems in academic sociology. On the other
hand these diverse contributions do indicate something of the
variety of insights which can be utilised in the study of social
processes operating within the present-day Scottish Gaelic speech-
community.

Chapter 2

LANGUAGE-FUNCTION AND SOCIAL CONSTRAINT

This chapter discusses the concept of the social functions of language and the various ways in which this has been understood, and attempts to relate these ideas to aspects of social behaviour involving language within the Harris community and to the dynamics of language-shift within the Gaelic speech-community as a societal whole.

Language as one of the principal distinguishing features of human behaviour was an early concern of sociology. In eighteenth-century Scotland Monboddo and Ferguson explored the origins and social function of speech and the comparison of cultures. In the early twentieth century French sociology focused interest in language as a social phenomenon with the work of Durkheim and Mauss.(1) The development of these interests subsequently have dropped out of the central ground of sociological concern. Yet the theme has never been entirely absent. There was Mead's idea of the self as a social production of the exchange of a significant gesture, language, between the 'I', the 'me' and the 'generalised other'. In his study of the Chinese literati, Weber regarded the organisation of education, administration, class relations and the social functions of the vernaculars and literary languages as stemming from the characteristics of Chinese language and script.(2) C. Wright Mills was similarly aware of the differences between Chinese and European languages and saw language as the link between the inner world of ideas and the external reality of social structure: 'By acquiring categories, we acquire the structured 'ways' of a group - and the value-implicates of those ways.'(3)

The ideas of Sapir and Whorf of course stand in some contrast to those of Durkheim and Mauss. For the latter the characteristics and categories within language are a reflection of the social structure, whereas for Whorf the semantic grid of language disposes the speakers to particular ways of habitual thought, images of reality, social behaviour and cultural practices. Whether these views represent irreconcilable approaches to the sociology of language or are merely contrasted processes, reversible under certain social conditions, remains a fascinating sociological problem.

Until the issues of language in society returned to mainstream sociology in the recent work of Bernstein, Fishman, Bourdieu and

the ethnomethodologists, phenomenologists and cognitive sociologists, the problem was principally left to the anthropologists,
philosophers, literary critics, social psychologists and linguists.
We shall briefly consider some of these approaches.

Halliday has recently drawn attention to the 'false equation' of
language 'function' with 'use'.(4) Allied to this has been the
problem of 'domain'. It clearly follows from Halliday's analysis
that a description of this problem is likely to result in typologies
of infinite length: as many types of function as there are uses or
users of language. Moreover, he adds, 'people . . . nearly always
seem to be using language in more than one "function" at once.'(5)
The discussion of the problem of domain, which Fishman has attempted
to explicate in terms of emic significance within the dynamics of
the speech-community, involving the topic, locale and role-rela-
tionship of the speaker,(6) forms one line of approach which enables
the sociologist of language to avoid the sterile problem of how
many and what are the domains of usage or of social functioning of
language within society. The problem remains within the impressive
descriptive sociology of language developed by Fishman of formulating hypotheses of the social processes which generate the pattern
of internally significant domains and the patterns of constraint of
bilingual usage within them.

Within the various disciplines contributing to these problems,
taxonomies of language function have ranged from the simple (mere
dichotomies) to the highly complex. An early approach was the distinction by Ogden and Richards of the 'symbolic' function of the
scientific use of language for the disinterested transmission of
fact with the 'evocative' function of exclamation and oath (with
mixed functions subsisting in rhetoric, orders, commands and
threats).(7) The level of explanation is pre-sociological: a
psychological contrast between denotative and connotative speech.
Malinowski, in his appendix to the above work provided an important
insight into speech-function in his concept of 'phatic communion'.
(8) Neither a true exclamation nor an oath, a meaningless utterance
such as 'How do you do?' evokes solely the sentiment of the shared
social bond: a symbol of social solidarity, 'one of the bedrock
aspects of man's nature in society'.(9) 'Are words in phatic
communion . . . to convey meaning? Certainly not! . . . language
here does not function as a means of transmission of thought.'(10)

Within the field of literary studies Britton also has advanced
a simple taxonomy of language use but has subsequently complicated
it.(11) Britton develops Harding's sociologically weak concepts of
participant and spectator role relating to an individual's involvement in or externality to a given occurrence, contrasting a 'language
to get things done' with a 'language of being and becoming': transactional as compared with poetic language. An intermediate 'expressive' speech links speaker and listener intimately (as does
Malinowski's phatic communion) in 'our principal means of exchanging
opinions, attitudes and beliefs . . . far more important . . . for
social action than any sermon, political speech, pamphlet, mani-
festo . . .'(12) The social roles of those involved in expressive
speech are vague and left undeveloped as Britton's taxonomy is con-
flated with a scheme devised by Moffett(13) comprising an analysis
of the relation between a speaker and his topic, recording, reporting,

generalising, theorising, and 'tautologic of transformation' (abstracted theory concerning phenomena). Both in Britton's adaptation and in Moffett's original schema, categories do not always appear to be consistently distinguished. The methodological weakness of these approaches is that of a cumbersome system ending up with almost as many subcategories as actual speech events studied (Figure 2.1).

1 TRANSACTIONAL	2 EXPRESSIVE	3 POETIC
Informative	Conative	Poetic (conative)
Record	Regulative	Poetic (informative)
Report	Persuasive	Poetic (expressive)
Generalised narrative (descriptive information)		
Analogic (low level of generalisation)		
Analogic		
Speculative		
Tautologic		

FIGURE 2.1   Forms of language use (after Britton)(14)

   Anthropological approaches have also resulted in schemes of increasing complexity. Hymes, for example, provides a sevenfold taxonomy of language functions: expressive (emotive), directive (conative, pragmatic, rhetorical, persuasive), poetic, contact, meta-linguistic, referential, contextual (situational).(15)   Again it is not always clear precisely what are the consistent criteria distinguishing all of these. However, the contribution of Hymes to this problem is important for the contribution of his concept of the ethnography of speaking. The various functions ascribed to language do not hold good between all societies — some do not pertain within all societies — and these facts provide insightful means of analysing societal differences. There are no 'primitive' languages defective of the means of expressing any given thought, but it is quite definitely the case that languages will vary widely in the ways of expression. Societies differ regarding the topics they discuss and their speechways indicate whether or not or to what extent a community articulates within given fields of interest. Hymes observes(16) that it is usual to ask, 'what does a language contribute to the maintenance of personality, society and culture?' but it may be more revealing of language-function in cultural change to ask instead, 'what does a personality, society or culture contribute to the maintenance of a language?'(17)   In the case of the Gaelic community of Harris this type of approach would seem the more valuable in explaining Gaelic language-maintenance in terms of the associations and warm affective tone Gaelic might possess for its speakers and the ways in which Gaelic functions as a component of the folk culture.
   In terms of a more sociological approach, Hasan recognises the multitude of dimensions along which language-variation occurs.(18) Moreover, she also draws attention to the problematical nature of where the boundaries occur not merely geographically as between dialects but also socially as between sociolects, registers and codes. Code is to be seen as stemming from particular forms of

social relationship: linguistic features become linked to behavioural codes as social roles are achieved under different forms
of social solidarity, mechanical and organic. Hasan locates these
processes within Bernstein's four contexts of socialisation: regulative (moral), instructional, imaginative, and interpersonal
(affective). The later work of Halliday(19) is also to be understood in terms of the development of this line of exploration. He
conceptualises some eight dimensions of language-function (which
are not intended as separable categories between unidimensional
extremes) — instrumental, regulatory, interactional, personal,
heuristic, imaginative, representational and ritual. Halliday
emphasises that language in use necessarily subserves more than one
given social function — and in the above scheme he certainly under-
plays the importance of the ritual function. The scheme is intended
however as explicative of the development of children's speech
within an homogenous speech-situation. Adult speechways may be
understood as being subsumed under three 'macro-functions': ideational ('processes of the external world, including material, mental
and abstract processes of every kind');(20) interpersonal (embody-
ing 'all use of language to express social and personal relations');
and textuality ('distinguishing a living message from a mere entry
in a grammar or dictionary', giving it operational relevance in a
real context).(21) Although Halliday's system is fundamentally
linguistic in purpose its intention is to treat language as a social
semiotic, for in analysing language function he is concerned to
describe how people use language and how language varies in use.
These comprise the key to how language is acquired and organised.
Contained within the everyday use of language are the processes
whereby social structure, values, systems of knowledge and culture
are transmitted. Acknowledged here is the work of Bernstein, 'whose
theories of cultural transmission and social change are unique in
this respect, that language is built into them as an essential element in social processes'.(22) Apposite to our present purpose is
Halliday's view that the representational function of language may
become 'the only model of language that many adults have'(23) — a
very common case in English-only speech communities. The ritual
function of language as a social marker may become very important in
contact-situations where languages function as symbols of ethnicity,
allegiance or groupness. (Conducting visitors onto the Isle of
Scalpay, Harris, I was once called after in Gaelic by children
clearly using Gaelic as a symbol of group identity.)
     Although Halliday locates aspects of language function in linguis-
tic phenomena (grammar, style, etc.), sociologically it is as
important concerning what language does as an institution of social
life, as much as how the internal system of language is affected by
social use. For example, a bilingual community like Harris may show
very sharply how language is used to differentiate the character of
social relationships in the way in which language is typically used
by members of the speech-community. Later chapters explore the ways
in which the two languages enter into social behaviour patterns. But
it may be pertinent to consider here the ways in which language
features or usages, say, in Gaelic, may affect aspects of social
life. In this connection we may consider briefly a number of such
problems: the Whorfian position whereby linguistic features may

affect culture and social life, forms of address, naming practices
and folk-taxonomies.

THE CONSTRAINT OF GAELIC UPON THOUGHT AND CULTURE

The work of Benjamin Lee Whorf has the clear implication that where
a language and a culture have been associated together over a long
period of time, we should expect to find correspondences between the
two. Of course the processes outlined above might proceed in either
direction: language influencing thought, behaviour, social structure
and culture; or culture, etc. influencing language — but for Whorf
the coercive character of language upon thought, behaviour and
culture was dominant:

   How does such a network of language, culture and behaviour come
   about historically? Which was first: the language patterns or
   the cultural norms? In the main they have grown up together,
   constantly influencing each other. But in this partnership the
   nature of the language is the factor that limits free plasticity
   and rigidifies channels of development in the more autocratic
   way. This is so because a language is a system, not just an
   assemblage of norms. Large systemic outlines can change to
   something new only very slowly, while many other cultural innovations are made with comparative quickness — language thus
   represents the mass mind: it is affected by inventions and
   innovations but affected little and slowly, whereas to inventors
   and innovators it legislates with the decree immediate.(24)

   At the level of deep structure (Whorf's 'cryptotypes') language
is very resistant to change. At the lexical level it is not.
Languages adopt neologisms as readily as Whorf regards culture as
adapting to changing circumstance. Perhaps Whorf here neglects the
underlying deep structuring of culture. At this level culture may
be as resistant to change — and as externally coercive upon the
individual — as language is for Whorf. It would be possible to
interpret the history of the Gaelic-speaking peoples as adaption to
induced change from outside accompanied by the retention of deeply
structured linguistic and cultural features (persisting in some
instances after societal language-shift to English and after incorporation of the folk-community into modern mass-society).

   As a European language, Scottish Gaelic has many features which
mark it off from Whorf's 'Standard Average European'.(25) So far
as one such difference is concerned, the basic sentence pattern is
for example formulated: verb, subject, object, rest of predicate.

   Fischer, in a study of two neighbouring Pacific islands, Truk
and Ponape,(26) has attempted to associate differences in social
behaviour and cultural traits with variations in the language.
Greenberg has discussed the implication for culture of variation of
structure of the noun phrase.(27) Fischer feels that the ordering
of basic sentence divisions is more significant than the internal
ordering of noun phrases. This implies that in terms of suspense-
fulness and directness of speech the order subject-object-verb (as
in Japanese) is the most suspenseful, English intermediately so with
its order, subject-verb-object, and the other extreme order, verb-
subject-object, as in Gaelic, the most direct and least suspenseful

of the three. This quality should presume for Gaelic a slackness of linguistic etiquette in that inference of meaning becomes easier and interruption of a speaker or his failure to complete a sentence becomes more likely. Such an argument would be highly doubtful. There is an etiquette amongst Gaelic-speakers to hear the other person out — and indeed to pause and consider one's reply before making it. At times this means that conversations may be punctuated by silences as others wait for the speaker whose turn it is to articulate his thoughts. Silence amongst friends and within conversing groups is certainly more tolerated than in English or American society — reminiscent of Basso's Western Apache who value silence in such circumstances as 'meeting strangers', 'children coming home', 'being with people who are sad'.(28)

The verb is Gaelic is scarcely declined for person, although prepositions are. There are only ten irregular verbs. Relative conjunctions and pronouns are typically absorbed into verbal particles. There are two verbs 'to be' — one is used to form continuous tenses for other verbs. The other is defective and assertive: existing only in the present-future tense and in the simple past. As in the other Celtic languages, declension of the noun and adjective is moribund but the mutation of initial consonants (aspiration) is a device which is used to convey a wide range of syntactic and semantic distinctions. These unusual features for a speaker of English — or Whorf's 'SAE' — have caused Gaelic to be regarded as a 'difficult' language by those familiar only with other Indo-European languages. What is, of course, difficult for a learner of Gaelic are the social circumstances under which the learning takes place.

Gaelic has a distinctive range of idioms to convey personal relationships, states of mind, attitudes and possession. These utilise one or other of the verbs 'to be' impersonally in a non-active construction involving an abstract noun, or an adjective together with prepositions, for example:

Gaelic idiom	Literal translation	English equivalent
Tha e agam	It is at-me	I have it
Tha fuath agam ris	Hate is at-me to-him	I hate him
Tha gaol agam ort	Love is at-me on-you	I love you
Tha fios agam air	Information is at-me on-it	I know it
Is leam e	Is with-me it	I possess it
Is miann leam e	Is a wish with-me it	I want it
Is coma leam e	Is indifferent with-me it	I don't mind it
Is fhear leam e	Is better with-me it	I prefer it
Is cuimhne leam e	Is memory with-me it	I remember it
Is aithne dhomh e	Is acquaintanceship to-me him	I know him

Thus Gaelic typically encodes these types of relationship and psychic state into impersonal idioms distinct from the more active type of expression involving a verb, subject and object of the type (in English) 'The man kicked the ball'. Here an action is performed in the physical world by an agent upon a recipient of the action. Although in English such a sentence as 'The man loved the woman' has the same grammatical form — and seems ostensibly to be of the same active type — in actual fact nothing is happening in the physical world. No action is being carried out. In Gaelic a different

idiomatic structure is used: '*Tha guol uig an duine air a'mhnaoi*'
(literally 'There is love at the man on the woman') expressing this
psychic state and relationship in abstract idiomatic form. For in
this instance there is no actual physical activity; merely a mental
state attributed to one person and involving another. Had the man
kissed the woman, '*Phòg e i*' ('He kissed her'), there is in Gaelic
the straightforward verb-subject-object construction of literal
activity. English cannot grammatically distinguish these different
circumstances: both are similarly active in construction.

Whether syntactic patterns such as these in Gaelic dispose its
speakers towards certain patterns of habitual thought and social
behaviour is problematical. Gaelic is, however, well-equipped to
handle abstract ideas in distinctively 'abstract' idioms and it may
be claimed to be a good vehicle for handling abstract concepts.
Although poor in scientific terminology Gaelic is well-equipped
with theological and philosophical terms — though these today will
be found in dictionaries rather than in use. A claim might be sustained for Gaelic that it is a superior conceptual medium for handling abstract thought. Whorf made a similar claim for Hopi as a
tool for thinking about wave-mechanics and electrical vibrations.
(29) The real point is though that for socially quite externally
coercive reasons no one is going to learn Gaelic in order to philo-
sophise, nor Hopi in order to conceptualise the principles of small-
particle physics, however good these languages may be for the purpose.

It would be plausible to attribute the more relaxed tempo of life
in Gaelic communities to habitual thought engendered by the structure
of the language. Whorf regards the English-speaking world as com-
petitive, commercially-organised, progress-oriented, and timetable-
dominated. Whorf regards these characteristics as stemming from
lexical and syntactical categories such as time, duration, tense,
etc.(30) and, we might add, also owing to the active pattern of the
sentence in English, as Whorf himself also seems later to have
realised.(31) In the Gaelic-speaking world the separation of active
sentence patterns to correspond with actual physical events may lend
a more abstract tone to the Gaelic language. Cultural traits such
as the reluctance to exhaust oneself with over-strenuous labour, the
cultivation of religious piety, the lack of competition in the life
of a crofting community, the lack of striving for 'progress', the
lack of precision with regard to time(32) are typically attributed to
Gaelic-speakers, and for a Whorfian would be explicable in terms of
language features. A human geographer might, in contrast, attribute
them to aspects of the physical environment.

Constraint upon everyday social behaviour arising out of language
might perhaps more convincingly be related to other aspects of
language than syntactic forms. A taxonomic system is implicit within
the lexicon and, although never consciously articulated, the categorisation comprising folk-taxonomies may constrain behaviour in
significant ways. Within present-day Gaelic communities three
especially are conspicuous — forms of address, kinship terms and
folk-taxonomies of the environment within which social life and
interaction occurs. In these fields especially the language provides the range of possibilities open to the habitual user and thus
the language disposes the user to certain forms of action rather than
others.

Forms of address

As in many other European languages, Gaelic requires that its
speakers should *tutoyer* and *vousoyer*. It is necessary to choose
between *thu* and *sibh* in second-person address. Unlike German and
Spanish there are no further honorific second-person pronouns
adapted from polite third-person forms (*usted, ustedes; ihr*).
Gaelic thus presents a simpler situation than such languages in
forms of address. The Gaelic-speaker must, however, use *thu* and
sibh correctly. In general, of course, the usual rule of use of
thu to younger persons and *sibh* to older persons pertains, as does
thu for speaking to friends, relatives and acquaintances of similar
age, God and animals and *sibh* for strangers, older relations and
persons of higher status than the speaker. Use of *thu* and *sibh*
was explored amongst adults and fairly consistent results were
obtained so far as usage in regard to parents and older relations
was concerned. The questionnaire on *thu* and *sibh* was daunting to
a few respondents and of the 92 in the final sample only 63 out of
the 85 Gaelic-speakers responded to this section. Typically those
not responding in detail did so because they felt that the only
significant variable here was age. Two respondents also added
'respect', one adding that *sibh* would always be used to a 'public
figure'. One respondent added 'politeness'.
    It is interesting to note, however, that of the 52 respondents
using Gaelic for communications between husband and wife that one
respondent reckoned to use either, 28 (53.8 per cent) to use *thu*
and as many as 23 (44.2 per cent) to use *sibh*. Here sex and age
differences show up considerably (Table 2.1).

TABLE 2.1   Use of V pronoun form in Gaelic between married couples:
Harris 1973

Age group	Husbands using *sibh* to wife (%)	Wives using *sibh* to husband (%)	Totals %
18-39	0.0	28.6	22.2
40-59	50.0	33.3	40.0
60+	61.5	55.5	59.1
Total	52.2	39.3	45.1

(Table excludes one respondent claiming to use both forms: a
woman over 60 years.)

    It may seem surprising that *sibh* should be used at all between
husband and wife. But it would appear to be a practice which is
changing with time. The incidence of use of *sibh* increases with
age. Amongst the younger married couples it is weak. As between
husbands and wives, the usage is non-symmetrical. Husbands use
sibh to wives to a much greater extent than do wives to husbands,
except in the case of the younger marrieds. That V forms rather
than T forms may predominate within the conversations of married

couples may indicate the strength of role-apportioned as compared
with companionate marriages within the culture. In the use of *thu*
and *sibh* between husband and wife, the connotation of the pronoun
used is of course problematical. One would have to assume, on this
hypothesis, that the *sibh* used by the husband is either the *sibh* of
non-solidary peer equality or the *sibh* of politeness or respect.
Does the age-semantic enter into the *sibh* used by the wife? Brown
and Gilman state, 'As yet we have reported no evidence demonstrating
that there exists such a things as personal style in pronoun usage
in the sense of a tendency to make wide or narrow use of T.'(33)

The importance of these results lies not so much in the meanings
which may underline the use of T and V forms between husband and wife
in a Gaelic community, as the fact that there is wider scope for
individual or idiolectal variation within this domain than within any
other which was explored. Moreover, a more societally constrained
pattern which governed older age-groups appears to be breaking down
with time. Marriage, it would seem, is becoming more of a construction of reality negotiated by the partners, than a socially-
given pattern into which the partners must automatically fit. In
this respect, Harris may not be involved in a situation of cultural
lag, but may participate in a general societal transformation of
marriage as an institution. Berger and Kellner have pointed out(34)
how 'marriage and the family used to be firmly embedded in a matrix
of wider community relationships, serving as extensions and parti-
cularisations of the latter's social controls . . .' but that
'. . . in our contemporary society, by contrast, each family consti-
tutes its own segregated sub-world, with its own controls and its
own closed conversation'.(35) The modern pattern of marriage, for
Berger and Kellner, involves a restructuring of reality, the formulation of new joint norms of behaviour through a dialectic of
mutual discussion. Forms of address as used in Harris provide an
interesting insight into such processes at work as a new social
pattern is taken over. If language may serve as an index or as an
unobtrusive measure of institutional change, then we have in this
situation a useful means of indication of the introduction and
success of new cultural norms.

Sex differentiation in form of address used to a Gaelic-speaking
stranger is nil across respondents' age and sex categories. Three
respondents out of the 63, across the age-spectrum, reckoned to
use T to strangers of either sex, two younger respondents reckoned
to use either form, five respondents normally reckoned to address
all strangers in English and 53 respondents maintained the use of
V to all Gaelic-speaking strangers of similar age and either sex.

Respondents maintained a surprisingly high incidence of use of
V to children. Younger respondents generally and middle-aged men
rarely used V to younger children. Older respondents and middle-
aged women reported frequent usage of V to children (incidences
ranging between approximately 25-40 per cent in the various situations explored: explanations to children, reproof when children
misbehaved and conversation regarding religion, the Bible and right
and wrong. Some respondents stated that they always used *sibh* to
children, so that children would get into the habit of using it,
and never misuse *thu* in addressing an elder or superior. A small
number of respondents themselves reckoned to use *sibh* exclusively.

Brown and Gilman draw attention to the overtaking of T forms by V forms in English since the seventeenth century,(36) the *you* of politeness eventually displacing all other forms in general social use. Many respondents felt that standards of usage of T and V were changing and that children were not so careful of this usage as they were — and neither were their parents so careful in inculcating these typical markers of respect. Clearly this peculiar and common usage of *sibh* to younger children indicates a conscious and active determination by the middle-aged and elderly to maintain something of the set of values associated with Gaelic culture. Concerning pronoun usage when talking about religion, the Bible and right and wrong, a 62 per cent incidence of use of *sibh* was claimed by men over 65 in this case).

The importance of the *sibh* of politeness is instanced in high incidence of usage amongst family members other than parent, spouse or children, younger relations, younger people locally, people who co-operate together over croft-work and workmates at place of work.

Highly consistent usage of *sibh* is reported for all the less solidary, and more instrumental, transactional and administrative situations. Variations here are really at a personal level. Departures from the universal norm of politeness are for reasons of personal acquaintance of other individual or idiolectal differences. One respondent said he would be inclined to use *thu* to one of the local girls serving in an island hotel but *sibh* to the barman or a waiter. In a few cases older respondents reckoned to use T with religious, medical and public officials,(37) even when much younger than the speaker. Another respondent reported, for example, 'I always use *thu* with the missionary because I know him. He is a friend of mine.' A further respondent, a middle-aged man, used *sibh* to age-peers, family members and religious office-bearers but always English to the minister. Another middle-aged man reckoned to use *thu* when speaking to local teachers (whose number included a number of younger women) but always *sibh* to the headmaster (although this headmaster was exceptionally young). Most surprising of all were two respondents — ostensibly competent — who stated that they did not distinguish between *thu* and *sibh* or were unaware of differences between them.

Differences in the individual usage of these socially-given norms are useful and interesting in showing the boundaries of constraints, pointers to change in social institutions and something of the social processes whereby the social order is maintained or transformed. Individual differences can be meaningful within an overall study of a particular community or a particular culture. One of the weaknesses of the Brown and Gilman study is its restriction to 107 upper-class and professional students studying abroad drawn from sixteen European countries and cultures. Whilst being suggestive, its perspectives require to be supported by more comprehensive studies of T and V usage within given communities.

Within Gaelic communities, societal bilingualism typically is of the 'co-ordinate' type in which the first or mother tongue is acquired from parents in the home as the sole language of the home. Subsequent language learning of the 'other tongue' is typically acquired at school as the child develops beyond infancy. The Gaelic language carries within its usage of T and V forms an image

or pattern of the system of social status within the society. In
the Gaelic communities, Gaelic is still typically the only language
the infant has, and the young child learns social status with — and
through — the required patterns of language use. Macleod(38)
reports the required deferential respect required by the older from
the young. This behaviour-pattern is realised in the language. If
it may not be said to have its origin within the language, language
as used is certainly strongly supportive of this institutionalisation of social behaviour.

Naming practices

Naming practices in Gaelic communities are highly distinctive and
persistent. Christian names may frequently be constrained by
family tradition, e.g. over a three-generational cycle. Such customs may survive societal language-shift as in east Sutherlandshire
(39) and Nova Scotia.(40) Gaelic naming customs remain functional
in communities where there are considerable incidences of particular
surnames and Christian names, as in the Outer Hebrides. A recent
study of Lewis surnames indicates the stability of the population
both regarding internal migration and immigration.(41) Patterns of
surname distribution persist in Lewis and Harris as the result of
patrilocal marriage.
    The principal Harris surnames (amongst adults) were, in 1972,
MacLeod (20.06 per cent), Morrison (17.70 per cent), and MacDonald
(9.72 per cent) — comprising nearly half the total registered
electorate (47.48 per cent). Together with the MacLennans,
MacKinnons, MacKays and MacSweens, the seven commonest surnames
comprised two-thirds (66.83 per cent) of the total; and three-
quarters (74.94 per cent) of the electorate shared the ten commonest surnames. The commoner male Christian names include: Donald,
John, Murdo, Finlay, Norman, Alexander, Angus, Ewen, Roderick,
Duncan, Kenneth, Calum and Lachlan. There is a greater variety of
female Christian names, including: Mary, Christina, Morag, Marion,
Anne, Margaret, Jane, Flora, Euphemia, Rachel, Johan, Catherine and
Isabella, together with such derivatives as Kirsty, Effie, Maggie,
Peggy, Annie, and Bella. Indicative of the male-dominated character
of local culture are such feminine forms of male names as: Donal-
dina, Dolina, Donalda, Kennethina, Murdina, Finina, Rhoda,
Angusina, Duncanina.
    The high frequencies of a relatively small number of names make
further distinctions necessary. Actually, the Gaelic system of
nomenclature predates the official system presently in use. High-
land surnames are in origin clan-names. The autochthonous system
is patronymic (as in Iceland or Norway). Examples of such patronymics take forms similar to the following: *Niall macLachlainn 'ic
Néill 'ic Iain 'ic Lachlainn* ('Neil the son of Lachlan, the son of
Neil, the son of John the son of Lachlan');(42) *Murchadh 'ic
Dhòmhnaill 'ic Raghnaill á Taransaigh* ('Murdo, son of Donald, son of
Ranald from Taransay');(43) or from present-day Harris usage:
Céiteag Aonghuis Dhomhnaill ('Katie (daughter) of Angus (son of)
Donald'); *Rachag Dhòmhnaill Iain Raghnaill* ('Little Rachel
(daughter of) Donald (son) of John (son) of Ronald').

Names, as recorded on birth certificates, are not in general use amongst Gaelic-speakers in their home communities. The two modern examples, given above, are of women recorded on the electoral roll as 'Katie Morrison' and 'Rachel Maclennan'. These names may be rendered in Gaelic *Céiteag NicGille Mhoire* and *Raonaid NicGhill' Fhinnein* respectively. Gaelic speakers might use such a version of their names on a Gaelic exercise-book at school but unless they undertook such unlikely activities as to write a book, article or letter for publication in Gaelic — or speak or be addressed in Gaelic on a formal public occasion, they would be unlikely ever to use them. In local social usage, their *sloinneadh* or patronymic would be used. The examples given above are somewhat more fulsome than those more commonly used. In practice, two-generational *sloinnidhean* are more commonly used, in addition to or in combination with a hypocoristic or nickname,(e.g. *Nogaidh, Doidean, Loll, Dòmhgan, Diùc* — the 'Duke') or an occupational designation (*am Post* - the postman, *Sàighdear* - soldier, *Greusaiche* - cobbler, *Clachair* - mason) or more rarely a physical feature or location (*Stéisean* — the fishery station). Sometimes an incomer may have to be accommodated within the local system. This is easy for a woman who marries in. She becomes *Bean an . . .*, 'Wife of . . .' and acquires a 'pseudo-sloinneadh'. In a neighbouring village an actual instance occurs *Bean a'Mhogain* 'wife of the Mogan'('*Mogan* - an old soft slipper' - nickname of husband). An incomer man marrying in presents more of a problem — as to some extent all incomers do. The nomenclature system segregates incomers from the local solidary frame of reference — but if you have a local-type name it helps to overcome the difficulty. A story is told of the wife of the man who administers AI to the cows: *Bean an Tairbh* ('The Bull's wife'). The AI man himself was *Tairbh an Aide* ('The Bull with a Hat').

A person's local Gaelic name as used within the community might take the form of a hypocoristic or nickname if he were 'a character', an occupational designation, or more frequently a *sloinneadh* or patronymic. This might strike an English speaker as a presumption across age generational or residential gaps. An English speaker would probably feel reluctance in using Christian names or nicknames in this fashion — but then he would be unlikely to hear or to acquire the knowledge of people's Gaelic names. The use of the naming system is an important reinforcement of community solidarity. (44) Widespread knowledge of people's *sloinnidhean* acts as a constraint upon behaviour — and a form of social control. The *sloinneadh* places a person immediately upon a network of kin-relationships, as the form of the *sloinneadh* is of a skeletal pedigree.

Nancy Dorian reports of east Sutherlandshire that 'Many individuals have both genealogical and descriptive by-names, for instance, or both genealogical and nonsense by-names. The frequency of multiple by-names for one and the same person is the best indication that by-names in east Sutherland have more than a merely utilitarian function',(45) 'They serve as an index of social solidarity and they entertain'.(46) In the case of offensive by-names which 'are capable of causing serious social rupture if used in the wrong company, the actual use of an offensive by-name takes on great social

significance . . . . The user of the by-name indicates his one-
ness with and his confidence in, the people in whose presence he
uses that by-name'.(47) 'It is noticeable too, how rich a stream
of anecdote and incident tends to be released at the mention of
an offensive by-name',(48) and so it is in Harris.

Dorian further observes how the by-name 'may come to overshadow
the official name', many people not even knowing another's surname
(49) and this is no surprise as in terms of continuity of tradition
her 'by-names' are not 'by-names' at all but the original Gaelic
system of nomenclature. Official surnames are in Gaelic communities very late historical innovations. Dorian notes the strength
of the original tradition as it has spread to the incoming English-
speaking community in east Sutherlandshire, as 'the Gaelic language
is nearing extinction on the local scene'.(50)

Folk-taxonomies and social orientation

Kinship terms form an example of a 'folk-taxonomy'. Gaelic uses
fewer separate kinship term elements than does English. There are,
for example, no words as such for 'uncle', 'aunt', 'niece', 'nephew',
'first/second cousin', etc. The relationship is described:
bràthair-mathar ('mother's brother'), mac piuthair-athar ('son of
father's sister') for example. As active geneological knowledge is
a more important component of everyday common-sense usage than is
the case in an English urban setting, this is not really a defi-
ciency in the useability of Gaelic as a community language. The
system of patronymics renders a detailed kinship taxonomy somewhat
superfluous. Vallee reports that on Barra, active family relationship is reckoned as far as the third degree of consanguinity (an
dàrna glùn).(51) This is as far, in fact, as the naming system
might take one without becoming too cumbersome and repetitious of
its elements. Linguistic features thus provide boundaries around
the extended family. In Harris the family could extend to encompass virtually the whole island community. Features contained
within the language constrain the native-speaker to draw the line
somewhere.

In addition to location within the web of personal relationships,
folk-taxonomies provide native-speakers with unquestioned common-
sense classificatory schemata and taken-for-granted segmentations of
the sociogeographical environment of the speech-community. For the
child and the learner, language is externally coercive, and moreover, as Cicourel further observes, 'that a mother's expansion of
a child's speech is more than reading grammar . . . it is providing
the child with the elements of a moral view . . . a developmental
acquisition of social structure'.(52) As language is a social
interpretation, the problem remains whether the categorisations of
language have their origins in social structure or vice versa. The
question cannot be answered but its concern does point to the differences which exist between languages in taxonomic structure.
Sapir believed also that 'Culture is not . . . a "given" at all . . .
but something to be gradually and gropingly discovered . . . elements of culture that come well within the horizon of awareness of
one individual are entirely absent in another individual's land-

scape'.(53) He rejects the crude 'Whorfian' view that language
and cultural categories may reflect one another in 'a simple
correspondence between the form of a language and the form of a
culture of those who speak it. The tendency to see linguistic
categories as directly expressive of overt cultural outlines . . .
should be resisted.'(54) Nevertheless, for Sapir, language was the
key to the understanding of a culture, for '. . . the network of
cultural patterns of a civilisation is indexed in the language'.(55)
     Language is a guide to 'social reality'. . . the 'real world' is
     to a large extent unconsciously built up on the language habits
     of the group. No two languages are ever sufficiently similar
     to be considered as representing the same social reality. The
     worlds in which different societies live are distinct worlds,
     not merely the same world with different labels attached.(56)
     Sapir here overlooks the problem of the language 'cline' —
geographical and social — and the languages of contact. But perhaps the same principle pertains. Language-differentiation, however
slight, arises from or as the result of differentiation, however
slight, in the 'social reality' of the speakers. King has shown
how, in the contact-situation of colonialism, taxonomic structuring
of language has been utilised as a symbolic order: to support the
social structure and value system of the colonisers, to segment the
perceived environment, to allocate native contacts into particular
areas and power relationships and to provide a conceptual scheme
for regarding the situated society surrounding the superposed social
stratum.(57) The marginality of the culture of contact in the present study is not precisely that of colonialism of the Indian pattern such as King described. Nevertheless, the bilinguality of the
speech community provides an arena for the operation of a 'third
culture' distinguishable from the traditional Gaelic system and that
of the incorporating English-speaking mass-society. The asymmetry
of power relations is shown in the 'burden' of bilingualism carried
by almost all of the local population — and the fact that very few
incomers acquire ability in Gaelic.(58) As the bilingual has access
to two languages, it may be argued that he possesses two systems of
categorisation of 'social reality' and these may be differentially
used within the culture.
     The segmentation of the environment involves taxonomies of topo-
graphical terms. Detailed placename studies, using local informants
to augment the detail of ordnance survey large-scale plans have been
undertaken by Harris schools in conjunction with the Linguistic
Survey of Scotland. MacAulay's study of the placename elements as
used in Bernera, Lewis(59) and Fraser's similar study of Illeray on
the adjacent Isle of North Uist(60) provide useful examples of such
topographical taxonomic material — extracted from actual situated
usage and systematically ordered.
     A higher order of aggregation of the folk-taxonomies of space and
place together with the taxonomies of colour, time, living things,
social institutions and so forth, provides the 'joint sociogeographical frame of reference of communities',(61) an inherent model
of the surroundings realised in the language. This abstraction or
model has been treated by various disciplines and variously named a
'perceived environment',(62) a 'behavioural environment',(63) an
'ethnoscience',(64) a 'cognitive map',(65) a 'semantic field',(66)

a 'mental map',(67) and a 'topocosm'.(68)   The last concept is
defined by Gaster, its originator, as comprising not merely the
human community of a given area or locality but the total corporate
unity of all elements, animate and inanimate alike, which together
constitute its distinctive character and 'atmosphere'.   It possesses
a twofold character: at once real and ideal.(69)

Although, in English, terms such as 'village' are used for settlements, the significant segmentation of settlement locally is on the
basis of the crofting townships (*bailtean*).   These are not necessarily in one-to-one correspondence with nucleations or aggrega-
tions of dwelling houses.   A township might include a number of
house-groups — or a large straggle of houses may be divided between
separate townships.

Trefor Owen(70) has provided a useful overall conceptualisation
of the Gaelic topocosm in his study of the crofting township of the
Outer Hebrides.   In its occupance of the land, he describes the
principal segmentation of perceived environmental space of a typical
crofting township as comprising:

cladach	the sea-shore;
machair	the sandy coastal margins and dune land;
talamh-treabhaidh	the mixed black and light soils suitable for arable use;
dubhthalamh	the poorer black soils;
gearraidh	rough grazing no longer cultivated; and
monadh	mountain slopes and moor, used for extensive summer pasture only and for peat-cutting.

These segmentations run in strips parallel to and successively inland
from the sea.   Township settlement is particularly associated with
the *gearraidh* immediately beyond the limit of wind-blown shell-sand.
The island interiors do not appear to be perceived as suitable for
settlement and cultivation.   The interior comprise monotonous peat-
moor (*monadh*), but glacial till exists in places, which with admixture with peat could provide a basis for cultivation.   Such is the
constraint of the perceived pattern of possibilities that these
opportunities are unexploited.   Only at one point in the outer
islands is there an inland settlement and that is in central Lewis
at the significantly named Loch Ganmhaich (meaning 'sandy lake').
Only here is there to be found a topocosm approximating to the typical, littoral, Gaelic settlement-pattern — and hence a perceived
and exploited opportunity for settlement.

The work already cited of White and Gould indicates how persistent and coercive 'mental maps' may be in constraining migration and
settlement choices, for 'people within a fairly uniform group in
any specific place have mental maps that resemble one another.   This
means that one can draw some fairly reliable conclusions about the
images that will affect migration.'(71)

Concerning the folk-taxonomy of colours, terminology in Gaelic
segments the spectrum differently from English.   There are far
fewer colour words, but in the case of the basic colour vocabulary
dearg extends from scarlet towards purple, whereas *ruadh* extends
from crimson towards brown;   *glas* covers an intermediate area
between green, blue and grey.

Regarding the segmentation of time, the unsatisfactory naming of
months in Gaelic points to a now-superseded calendrical system based

upon the phenomena of growth, seed-time, rutting of deer, end of
warm weather, etc., of the 'natural' year. The 'months' were
seemingly of varying duration, and in the highly variable weather
of northwestern Britain the 'months' were regarded as beginning when
the appropriate weather did.(72) The changeover from the old style
calendar to the modern calendar seems to have brought about the
abandonment of the traditional Gaelic year. Today most Gaelic-
speakers use the English names for the months. The modern Western
European calendar today provides the framework for agricultural
practice. Local notes in the local press are much taken up by
concern over the progress or lack of it of agricultural matters
'for the time of year'. Were such months as March (*Mart-na-
curachd,* seed-time), June (*An t-Og-Mhios,* the brood month) and
September (*An Sultuine,* the fat or harvest month) to be regarded
as occurring when the weather rather than where the calendar dic-
tates, much of this anxiety might be obviated.

In such ways Gaelic provides a perceptual grid or cognitive map of
'reality', influencing the social behaviour of its speakers and the
social institutions of its speech-community.
    It would be difficult to sustain a crude determinism of this
analysis. The position attributed to Whorf of linguistic features
affecting the culture and social structure of a speech-community is
capable of being argued either way. In a 'weak' Whorfian sense,
however, it is possible to postulate that language usage (if not
linguistic features) may affect social behaviour and contribute
to the institutionalisation of cultural features. Kinship is
important in Gaelic culture yet the language is restricted in kinship terms compared with English. In social use, Gaelic is rich in
naming patterns compared with English. It is the forms in usage
(nicknames, patronymics, etc.) which reflect the importance of
kinship in Gaelic social relationships, not the degree of complexity
of the folk-taxonomy of kinship terms. Similarly Gaelic colour
terminology is less rich than is English. Here paucity of colour
terms seems to match the paucity of pictorial and representational
art in the indigenous culture, but it is just as likely that lack
of interest in colour and depiction as a cultural feature has affected the language (in the older Gaelic 'high culture' a more developed
colour terminology is to be found than in contemporary Gaelic).
    Linguistic features and language usage are capable of being used
as indices of cultural and social features, but not as a direct,
simplistic attribution. There are relationships but they need to be
unravelled, for the relationships between them are complex and the
correspondences are not necessarily all in the same direction.

LANGUAGE AND POWER IN SOCIAL PROCESS

In their paper on the use of second-person pronouns, Brown and
Gilman (73) illustrate how seemingly aberrant usage of the T and V
pronouns may be explained by the simultaneous operation of the two
sociological principles of power and solidarity. T and V usage
cannot be adequately explained by a 'unitary' concept such as
'social distance'. If there are pronouns of power and solidarity,

in language-contact situations it may be the case that there are
whole languages of power and of solidarity. In Harris, for example,
Gaelic is typically used in such situations as the home, the local
shop and travelling grocery van, the post office, the church and
village entertainments, but English is most used in dealings with
'officialdom', in administrative and educational affairs, the manage-
ment of public services, mass-media of information and entertainment, law enforcement, public affairs and commercial business. A
'power' dimension enters a number of the domains within which Gaelic
is used (e.g. the post office, the church), but in these a 'solidarity' dimension subsists simultaneously. The domains within which
English predominates are those where a power dimension is conspicuously to the fore. Those situations of public life where there is
some extension of the use of Gaelic are those where a solidary group
values are encouraged (club and society meetings).

If language as an institution of social life is used in such a
fashion in a bilingual community such as Harris, some such patterning as the following may be hypothesised:

Characteristics of social relationships	Language used	Exemplifying situations
1 Solidary but not involving power	Gaelic	Home life, shopping, croft work, equivalent work
2 Solidary but involving power	Gaelic	church, post office
3 Not solidary but involving power	English	School, superiors at work, public administration
4 Not solidary and not involving power	Language usages not societally constrained: Gaelic or English	Encounters with strangers

However, there are difficulties in accommodating all speech situations into such a scheme. Further insights into language function as
societally patterned might be gained by the use of a taxonomy of
language-use. The following, comprising four categories, also lends
itself to a two-dimensional schema:

1 Informative: language used to convey information;
2 Normative: language used to effect social control;
3 Expressive: language used to convey affective states;
4 Symbolic: language used to signify group solidarity.

With regard to the underlying operation of the social relationships of power and solidarity it may be taken that with the normative
function power is operative, but not necessarily solidarity; with
the informative function power is not necessarily operative, neither
is solidarity; with the expressive function power is not necessarily
operative, but solidarity is; with the symbolic function both power
and solidarity may be operative. As with Brown and Gilman's dyadic
analysis concerning who effects or attempts to effect power over
whom, use of language as a symbol of groupness may involve the
attempted exercise of power by the solidary group with regard to
others. With the normative use of language, power may be exercised
within the group by one group member over another or power may be
exercised by an outsider upon group members. Power may thus operate
with or without solidarity. In Brown and Gilman's usage, it would
seem that the type of solidarity implied is left open. They do not

organic/mechanical relationships

commit themselves to an analysis in terms of 'mechanical' as contrasted with 'organic' forms of solidarity. Solidarity and power
operating together can be more easily conceptualised as occurring
under conditions of mechanical solidarity where 'individuals share
a common system of beliefs and sentiments which produces a detailed
regulation of conduct'.(74) The linguistic treatment of solidarity
in Brown and Gilman's scheme does not enable it to be too easily
adapted into such an explanatory scheme of language-use.

In terms of a folk-society such as that of Harris, solidary
relationships within the community are chiefly of a mechanical
character whereas solidary relationships with the 'outside' or
mass-society of English-speaking modern Britain are chiefly of the
organic type whereby individuals relate to each other through a
complex interdependence of specialised social function. In the case
of these latter relationships as they intrude into a traditional
society such as that of Harris, a power component is markedly
present. It may be better, then, to modify the conceptual scheme
presented by Brown and Gilman with a more sophisticated concept of
solidarity and to posit not whether solidarity is present or not but
whether the solidary relationship tends towards the mechanical type
or the organic type. Concerning power, it will be helpful to
consider not merely whether it is present or absent, but also who
exercises power upon whom. We may thus arrive at the typs of conceptual scheme, as illustrated in Figure 2.2, where hypothetical
positions are put forward for a number of dyadic relationships where
power may be exercised by one upon another, some under mechanically
solidary conditions, others under organically solidary conditions. It
must be borne in mind that some relationships may be to varying degrees mechanically or organically solidary and that there may be
classes of relationship within which there is very little power component (such as relationships with friends) and others with very
little solidary component (such as relationships with strangers).

		MECHANICAL SOLIDARITY	ORGANIC SOLIDARITY
POWER EXERCISED BY THE INDIVIDUAL		Minister Missionary Church elder Parent Husband Shopper	Policeman Foreman/boss Professional official Public administrator Teacher
Relationships not involving power		Convivial relationships with friends and workmates	Dealings with strangers
POWER EXERCISED UPON THE INDIVIDUAL		Shopkeeper/assistant Wife Child Church member	Pupil Administrated citizen Client Subordinate worker Wrongdoer
LANGUAGE USAGE		Gaelic likely to predominate	English likely to predominate

FIGURE 2.2 Power, solidarity and language-use

We shall view the individual as acquiring these social patternings of language-usage through the processes of his socialisation.
It will be valuable to recall Bernstein's four contexts of socialisation:
1 The regulative contexts: these are the authority relations
   where the child is made aware of the moral order and its
   backings.
2 The instructional contexts: here the child learns about the
   objective nature of objects and acquires various skills.
3 The imaginative or innovating contexts: here the child is
   encouraged to experiment and re-create his world on his own
   terms and in his own way.
4 The interpersonal contexts: here the child is made aware of
   affective states - his own and others.(75)
These contexts are, for Bernstein, in practice inter-dependent, by
which I take to imply that in any given situation of socialisation
aspects of any number or all contexts may be present. Bernstein adds:
'. . . the critical orderings of a culture or sub-culture are made
substantive, are made palpable through the form of its linguistic
realisations of these four contexts - initially in the family.'(76)
    I have suggested above that it may be helpful to look at a rela-
tively simple categorisation of the functions of language in general
social use (normative, informative, expressive, symbolic). Some
such scheme could in a developmental sense be advanced as representing a pattern into which speakers are socialised through
Bernstein's four contexts.
    We should expect to find that a bilingual speech-community, such
as Harris, possesses many of the distinctive attributes of a folk-
society: smallness, isolation, solidarity, co-operation, homogeneity, moral consensus, distinction of the individual in terms of
personality rather than occupation, and social patterning principally operative through kinship.(77) As an example of a late folk-
society, a community such as Harris is certainly no longer at a
'pre-literate' stage. Within the past century the school has ensured
universal literacy, and in any case traditional Gaelic society has
from time immemorial supported literate orders (in ancient and
medieval times the bardic schools and other learned orders, and in
more recent times folk-poets, 'Gaelic scholars' and the modern
clergy). The incorporation of traditional Gaelic folk-societies has
meant also that over recent centuries 'urban' institutions have pene-
trated the older order: the market, the State, modern patterns of
communication and administration, modern education and the mass-
media of communication, and yet something of the cohesiveness and
distinctiveness of a former order remains. As Redfield later says,
'the folk society is that society in which the technical order is
subordinated to the moral order',(78) and on this definition Harris
remains today a folk-society.
    The folk society may be taken into the society of the invading
civilisation as a partner, yet retaining for a long time its
cultural distinctiveness. This is apparently an uncommon outcome.
Toynbee mentions three such cases: the Scottish Highlanders,
the Maoris of New Zealand, the Araucanians of Chile. Such
peoples are more than mere enclaves; they are minority peoples;
they make an adjustment which retains their own traditional

moral order in a considerable degree while yet they take part
in the engulfing society.(79)
The religious life of the Gael is highly distinctive, and as will
later appear, the importance of the place of religion within the
value-system and moral order of the community in Harris cannot be
over-stressed.

Language-use within such a folk-society is distinctively patterned. In general it is the traditional and native institutions
which, as we may expect, are associated with the use of Gaelic, the
community language. Use of English generally symbolises the intrusion of institutions and power-relations from outside. Hence we
find that mechanical solidarity is mediated through Gaelic and
organic solidarity through English. Gaelic is restricted to relationships within the mechanically solidary network. The use of
Gaelic for purposes of organic solidarity (as in the case of Welsh-
language activism), as a symbol of maintenance of group identity, is
rare. But the near-exclusive use of Gaelic within the domestic
system of values and the moral order (as in the church, family
worship and the moral instruction of the young) is very strong
indeed.

Under the influence the division of labour, intrusiveness of
institutions of mass-society and the concomitant form of social
solidarity, we might expect language-use to be highly patterned in
choice of medium. Hence normative functions of language would be
expected to be mediated through English in so far as administrative
requirements were concerned but through Gaelic as regarding religious and personal morality; informative uses would be carried
through English so far as scientific and technological matters were
concerned but through Gaelic for 'recipe knowledge' and information
regarding local conditions; expressive uses might be expected as
being chiefly through Gaelic; and symbolic uses as being virtually
entirely through Gaelic. In terms of the concept code there would
seem to be a marked tendency for 'universalistic' meanings to have
been brought within the range of uses chiefly mediated through
English and the 'particularistic' meanings in the more context-
bound conditions chiefly to comprise those functions mediated
through Gaelic. Robinson has observed of similar contact situations
in East Africa, that Bernstein's linkage of social class and
linguistic code is capable of general application with societies of
similar or more extreme forms of social stratification compared with
modern England.(80) Robinson concludes that 'in multilingual
societies . . . a whole language may function as a restricted
code.'(81)

Such an assumption stated at so simplistic a level may be very
seriously questioned. It remains problematic and it has never
empirically been tested whether this relationship in practice is in
fact true of minority language situations. It is clearly not true
to suggest that a language such as Gaelic fails to generate elaborate
code forms. Quite ordinary people do in fact generate elaborate
spoken Gaelic (for example the extemporary prayer of a congregational member at weekday prayer meeting or the biblical exegesis of
a member speaking at a Communion céisd service). Restricted code
versions of Gaelic and English appear to be generated within the
family situations and peer culture of Gaelic-speaking children.

Through family worship Gaelic-speaking children are habitually
exposed to elaborated forms of Gaelic in the home. What in fact
appears to be the case is that children acquire both elaborated and
restricted varieties of Gaelic and of English and differentiation of
usage opens up between restricted Gaelic and restricted English,
elaborated Gaelic and elaborated English. Thus the socially prescribed patterning of code usage between the languages may be much
more complex than Robinson seems to suggest. Preferences for one
language rather than another, one code rather than another, may
be capable of being made by the speaker in terms of what he sees
as appropriate to the social demands of the setting. (MacLeod's
study of cognitive performance of Lewis schoolchildren in Gaelic
and English, as linked to the concept code, may appropriately be
borne in mind here.(82) His conclusion that the use of Gaelic was
associated with a lower order of cognitive function may be valid
as far as the school setting went within which he undertook his
experiment but it requires supplementation with a study of the
social circumstances and purpose of elaboration of Gaelic in the
settings where this occurs.)
   There are very sharp social discontinuities between traditional
Harris society and the small number of incomers who have settled
on or work on the island. There are similar sharp discontinuities
between the meanings handled through English and those through
Gaelic. A pattern seems to be discernible whereby socialisation
occurs in Bernstein's terms(83) through the 'closed communication
system' of positional-type families. Amongst the 'outsiders' more
of an 'open communication system' within person-oriented family
types seems to pertain. The use of Gaelic is thus giving rise to
access into the 'closed' role and communication network of local
family and community life, whilst the use of English gives access
to 'open' role - and communication networks both to the local and
to the incomer.

LANGUAGE-SHIFT AS A MACROSOCIOLOGICAL PROCESS

We may now consider more widely the problem regarding processes
affecting societal patterns of language usage. The Gaelic speech-
community is often regarded as an example of economic innovation
inducing new patterns of social behaviour and language-use. Contemporary conventional wisdom holds that an inevitable shift from
Gaelic must occur in the face of English as the 'stronger' language
as 'progress' destroys the traditional 'Highland way of life'.
Certainly from the earliest times in Gaelic Scotland economic innovation has been associated with the intrusive use of English.
Despite advanced language-shift, the two languages in societal use
remain intimately bound up with the cultural patterning of behaviour codes. The surface structure of Gaelic linguistic culture
generates from deep structures of traditional norms under increasing influence of intrusive values.
   Sociolinguistic literature presents few studies of the relationships of language and intrusive economic development. Pool
has related per capita gross domestic product with the size of the
largest language community as a percentage of the total population

of some 133 countries.(84)   Pool concludes that there is likely to
be a relationship between economic development and language-use in
that language-diversity hinders economic development.   Diversity
would of necessity seem to reduce as development takes place and
may need to be réduced as a precondition of development occurring.
Pool states that the 'extreme form of economic development with no
homogenisation at all — has never happened'.(85)   This surely
neglects the example of Switzerland — and probably Belgium too.
For in these countries advanced economic development has occurred
concomitant with language-communities which are determined to maintain their territorial integrity and the universality of their
language for all purposes of social life.   The Belgian experience
has been characterised by conflict over the language issue but the
matter has been amicably settled in Switzerland.

In the Gaelic case, language as a symbol of group-loyalty has
never functioned in the overt, activist way that it has in Wales or
Belgium.   As language-shift has occurred throughout the mainland
Gaelic areas from the east and from the south, Gaelic has quietly
faded out of use.   Professor W.J. Watson describes the linguistic
situation in the Easter Ross of his youth (circa 1885) as advanced
language-shift displaced Gaelic as the community-speech.(86)

> When the Gaelic speakers began to take to speaking English, they
> made up their deficiencies in that language by using Gaelic words
> freely instead of the English terms with which they were not yet
> familiar . . . .   As time went on the Gaelic terms became fewer
> . . . but some survive still. . . . From one point of view the
> terms which survive from the earlier language may be said to be
> borrowed into the later, but they are not really loans in the
> ordinary sense — what was borrowed in this case . . . was not
> the Gaelic, but the whole of the English that the people came
> to use.

In another more documented study of social changes in an eastern
Highland parish (Moy and Dalarossie), its minister, the Rev. R.
MacPherson, shows how Gaelic passed from being the community-speech
as the result of 'a widespread change-over in population particularly from 1843 onwards.   The old clan-names virtually disappeared.
It appears that over the years the whole of the population of
original stock left the parish or died out and was replaced by new
tenants or estate-workers.'(87)   MacPherson indicates how the introduction of new economic activities (commercial farming, forestry,
transport services, distilling, catering) involved dislocation of
population as in many other Highland districts, most notoriously
in Sutherlandshire.   It is not altogether easy to apply Pool's perspectives or methods to the results.   In the rhetoric of the time
both the Gaelic language and its speakers were seen as impediments
to the more productive development of lands and resources in the
Scottish Highlands.   The supersession of Gaelic and even of the
people themselves were generally seen by the advocates of economic
development as a necessary prerequisite to progress.   Yet today it
would be difficult to sustain any causal connection or co-occurrence
between language and development in the Highlands.

If a measure of economic development such as rateable value per
head of population is taken in comparison with census returns of
percentage of population able to speak Gaelic aged three years and
over, very poor correlations may result.

In Ross-shire, for example, where Watson describes above the
collapse of Gaelic as community speech in its eastern areas in the
late nineteenth century, the highest and most persistent rates of
language-maintenance for Gaelic are found in its most westerly
districts: especially the Isle of Lewis. *Prima facie*, it might
appear plausible to argue that the more highly-developed east
correlates with earlier language-shift to Gaelic and low rates
of incidence of Gaelic speech in today's population and that high
rates of ability in Gaelic are associated with retarded development
in the west. The correlation for 1961 census data is merely
$r = -0.310$. This indicates that the association is rather weak:
the areas in which societal use of Gaelic is better maintained are,
although only to a rather·modest extent, those in which economic
development relative to the size of population is somewhat low.

If the correlation is undertaken for Ross-shire burghs, the
relationship is even weaker; in the order of $r = -0.020$ (indicating that there is virtually no correlation between per capita
incidence of economic development and extent to which Gaelic is
maintained). It is the case in Ross-shire that the burghs are small
and not particularly well-developed economically. Stornoway on
Lewis is, however, the largest of the burghs and its concentration
of tweed mills produces a high rateable value. It is also quite
strongly Gaelic in comparison with other towns in the county.
Invergordon on the east coast is also unusual. It has a particularly high rateable value owing to the presence of a large naval
base. The service personnel are not enumerated in the returns for
the county divisions, hence the relationship is distorted. If
Invergordon is excluded from the correlation between the districts
of the county, the negative correlation between Gaelic and economic
development reduces considerably: from $r = -0.328$ to $r = -0.055$.
Excluding both Invergordon burgh and district from the correlation
for all county divisions, an overall correlation of $r = -0.310$
reduces to $r = -0.062$.

This result is indicative of there being no direct association
between economic development and shift from Gaelic to English in
this case. Unless there is a massive outside interference, such as
the establishment of a major military base, it would appear to be
the case that the customary scale of economic development in a
Highland county arising as it were *sui generis* has only a very
slight effect in reducing rates of maintenance for Gaelic. Other
factors are most probably of much greater consequence in this
respect.

If the displacement of Gaelic as community-speech is not associated with increasing economic development in a simple linear
relationship, there are alternative hypotheses in the circumstances
outlined above: clearance of population, as in nineteenth-century
Sutherlandshire, and widespread changeover of population, as in the
case of Moy and Dalarossie parish. In circumstances where the
community has not suffered such wholesale physical interference, an
alternative hypothesis is suggested: the interference with the
symbolic value-system of a community operating at a more abstract
level. The distinctively Highland Free Churches owe their existence to a crisis over appointment of parish ministers by landowners, the 'Disruption' of 1843. Gaelic society was convulsed in

a successful bid to defend the integrity of the value-system of
Gaelic society. In the residual Gaelic areas of northwestern
Scotland from the mid-nineteenth century onwards, language-shift
from Gaelic to English seems more to be associated with the more
abstract qualities of social morale, integrity of the system of
values, and confidence in the traditional pattern of socialisation
than in the scale and level of advancement of forms of economic
development as such.

Four models of language-shift are suggested, all of which appear
to have been differentially operative in Scottish Gaeldom:

1 The 'Clearance' model, in which substantial numbers of the
   native population have been through force or other inducement
   removed from an area.
2 The 'Economic Development' model, in which new forms of
   economic organisation bring about cultural changes requiring
   language-shift (e.g. introduction of English as a commercial
   or technical language).
3 The 'Changeover' model operating at the demographic level.
   New people come in to an area to undertake new activities.
   Opportunity for the local population to retain the stability
   of its traditional socio-economic infrastructure diminish and
   the local people die out or leave.
4 The 'Social Morale' model. Changes occur in the power relationship between social groups. The local community loses
   confidence in its system of values, e.g. through religious or
   educational proselytisation. The local language as symbolic
   of superseded local values is shifted in favour of the language in which the new values have been mediated.(88)

By the end of the nineteenth century the passing of the Crofter
Acts, the election of crofter MPs, and the political successes of
the first Highland Land League had ended the operation of the
'clearance model'. There does not seem to be a simple linear relationship between 'economic development' as such and language-shift
(indeed the success of the Harris tweed industry in Lewis and fishery
developments in Harris are undoubtedly strong contributory factors
to the high rates of language-maintenance in rural Lewis and mid-
Harris). The 'changeover' model where economic development is
compounded with differential access for local people to new opportunities has undoubtedly been operative in those areas of the Highlands whose language-shifts were early, sudden and associated with
influxes of new population. With the creation of the Free Church
(1843) and the Free Presbyterian Church (1893) the Highlanders
forged a powerful defensive institution of the symbolic value system
at the religious level. Unfortunately for Gaelic as an institution
in social life, the system of Gaelic-language schools established
in the Highlands chiefly through the charitable efforts of exiled
Gaels were replaced after 1872 by English-language public authority
schools, mediating new values almost exclusively through English.

A fifth model of language-shift requires attention — the model
generally encountered in histories, language maps, census reports,
etc. Recession of Gaelic is shown as an ever-shrinking area, the
Gàidhealtachd, enclosed by an ever-retreating frontier or 'Highland
Line'. The Gaelic 'retreat' is not nearly so tidy on the ground as
on the map: the frontier-zone would need to be the decisive area of

culture-clash. Actually culture-contact is experienced everywhere. As a commentator said of Wales, 'The line of bilingualism
runs down every street in Wales.'(89) In the most Gaelic areas
people — especially men — are widely travelled. Visits between
relations elsewhere are common. Few have not spent considerable
periods outside the Gaelic area. The 'cultural retreat' or
Gàidhealtachd model is the resultant of the combined operation of
the models outlined above.

CONCLUSION

The literature of sociolinguistics and sociology of language has
explored many aspects of language in its social context. The work
of Fishman is useful in the description of the relationships within
which societal bilingualism operates. The work of Bernstein has
provided more dynamic concepts relating the characteristics of
language to processes of cultural transmission. The problem of
language-function has been unsatisfactorily discussed within the
literature owing to confusion between domain, function and use and
insufficient clarity in identifying the principles upon which analysis might be based. In this regard Halliday has gone furthest in
advancing a general theory which may effectively link the social
structure, the medium of language and the forms taken of the socialising of the child. Halliday utilises Bernstein's theories of cultural transmission and social change in the outlining of a theory
of language as a social semiotic.
    The phenomenon of language-shift has not been very well explored
in relationship to economic development. A general theory of
language in society must take account of macro-societal relationships at this level. There are few studies bearing upon this
problem. A number of models treating the relationship between
Gaelic in social use and the social and economic circumstances of
the local speech-community are reviewed. The problem remains for
macrosociolinguistic analysis at this level to be linked dynamically
with the levels of analysis treated by Bernstein and Halliday.

Chapter 3

DIMENSIONS OF AN ISLAND COMMUNITY

ECONOMIC DEVELOPMENT AND COMMUNITY RELATIONS

In common with many remote communities of the Atlantic margins, Harris has shown acutely the phenomena of slow development of the economic infrastructure, high rates of outward migration and attendant ageing of the population structure. From a maximum population of 5,449 recorded in the census of 1911, the population has consistently declined to 3,285 at the 1961 census, 2,879 at the 1971 census and by mid-1974 the Registrar General's estimate of the Harris population was 2,696.

The 1966 Harris study drew attention to structural changes in the population in terms of age and sex ratios during this period.(1) At maximum population an imbalance between the younger males and females was attributed to poor social and economic opportunities for younger women. The sex ratio of 114 females to 100 males in 1911 has reduced to 102 females per 100 males at the 1961 census. Decline in population has tended to become more pronounced over this period. A decennial decline of 3.2 per cent was experienced betweel 1911-21, this rate increasing to 19.1 per cent between 1951-61. In 1911 some 39 per cent of the population was aged 15-45 years and 12 per cent over 60. By 1961 these percentages were 34 per cent and 20 per cent respectively.

By 1971 the decennial decline in population had slackened again to 13.7 per cent, indicating that some degree of socio-economic stabilisation was occurring. The 1971 census indicated that the ratio of females to males had remained virtually constant at 103 females to 100 males. In computing these figures from the 1971 census returns, it has been borne in mind that a military establishment on St Kilda, part of Harris parish which had previously been uninhabited, by then carried a population of 65 able-bodied males and one female, who it may be assumed can be allocated to the 15-45 age category. Thus in 1971 the proportion of the Harris population within this age category comprised some 27 per cent of the total and the proportion aged 60 years and over comprised 32 per cent. It can clearly be seen that although some stabilisation was occurring, the population was still progressively ageing. This phenomenon has important implications for community social structure, especially in the fields of conservation of the value-system, community decision-making, the exercise of initiative and innovation.

At its maximum, at the turn of the century, the population bore heavily upon the island resources — especially food production in what was still chiefly a subsistence economy. The signs of cultivation in terms of abandoned 'lazy-beds' (*feannagan*) are still a dramatic feature in the Harris scenery, extending well up the lower slopes of bogland on most of the more accessible hills, up to and beyond the feasible climatic limits of potato and oat cultivation. Some relocation of population in this period by internal migration eased the situation. After the First World War some internal migration occurred from the 'congested' area of the bays to the more fertile *machair* land of the west coast and the Isle of Scalpay. Some of this movement was of squatters settling upon better land after their return from the 1914-18 war. As men had left in the summer of 1914, volunteering for the armed services, fishing vessels had been left at anchor in the mistaken belief that the war would be swiftly terminated. Traditions may have exaggerated the number of boats ruined as a result of protracted abandonment, but privation and land-hunger were real enough in the years after the war. Land-raids were made by bays men on fertile west-coast *machair* land, as at Seilebost. The last of these occurred in 1934. There are survivors in their seventies still settled there.

Decline in population has continued in the 1960s and 1970s. The off-island of Scarp, still with its own school in the mid-1960s, was abruptly evacuated in 1968. The crucial point was reached when insufficient able-bodied men were left effectively able to beach the fishing vessels. In the absence of assistance — for example to purchase a mechanical winch — economic activity based on fishing was no longer viable. Shortly afterwards, the only tweed mill on Harris ceased production. Although neither activity employed large numbers, in such small communities the loss of a 'key' economic activity is marked. The percentage unemployment in this period of the late 1960s and early 1970s stood at around 27 per cent in Lewis and Harris: Britain's highest.

With respect to the age structure of the community the most marked diminutions in the 'pyramid' occur in the late teens, twenties and thirties. In these age groups substantial loss of population from emigration is noticeable: a feature which was of increasing significance during the 1960s. Some improvements in local opportunities in the late 1960s and early 1970s were followed in 1973 by an exodus estimated at around some 200 able-bodied young men from Lewis and Harris to work on the oil-related developments at Invergordon and Nigg on the east coast.

Marriage is typically postponed until the thirties and forties amongst the residual population. Families are started late. Average family size tends to be small — but in recent years there is a noticeable increase in family size (as shown in Table 3.1). A definite upswing in numbers of the live births is also noticeable (as shown in Table 3.2).

TABLE 3.1 Family size, Harris 1961-71

	1961	1966	1971
Total unmarried children under 20	1,040	900	730
Total households	1,061	1,059	955
Single children 20 years or under per household	1.02	1.18	1.31

Source: 1966 Census (Scotland).

TABLE 3.2 Live births, Harris 1964-72

Year	Live births	
1972	40	Largest total enumerated since 1953
71	24	
70	14	
69	35	
68	22	
67	30	
66	22	
65	7	
64	6	Lowest ever recorded number of live births

Source: Local register of Births, Marriages and Deaths.

These factors may be associated with age at which a croft may be inherited or a steady job secured. Fishing developments in Scalpay and to a lesser extent in the bays area and the reopening of the Geocrab tweed mill in 1972 may be in part contributory to these trends.

The bias towards older age groups in the demographic structure of Harris has the effect of conserving societal values, social customs and language-use. (Harris is not necessarily politically conservative: it is part of a traditionally Labour constituency which was the first in Scotland (and Great Britain) to elect a nationalist MP at a general election. It was also the only UK region completely to reverse the national voting pattern at the 1975 EEC Referendum: 70.5 per cent against entry, 29.5 per cent for.) From the point of view of religious life, the older age groups are insistent upon adherence within the family to church attendance, Sabbath observance, family worship in the home and observance of the island's religious mores generally. In terms of the informal self-government of the community Harris is a geronto-cracy in which church elders (without exception older males) take a prominent part in decision making. The effects of this upon language-use is to conserve Gaelic (for it has an important religious

function). The possibility is of course that Gaelic might tend to
be associated with a conservative way of life by younger and more
progressive elements. There is not a great deal of evidence for
this, except that younger people will tend to a more general use of
English and a number of people in certain public callings (certain
teachers and shopkeepers) although they undoubtedly know Gaelic never
seem actually to use it in public.

Although the skewed age-distribution of the population is a contributory factor to caution regarding innovation, the Harris people
are certainly not without initiative regarding economic developments. The development of fishing in Scalpay is a notable example
of local initiative, once a reasonably stable prospect of employment and economic return is perceived. Recent years have seen the
development of shell fishery from the bays area (initiated by an
incomer, but taken up locally), the establishment of a craft guild
in Harris (utilising, inter alia, pelts from the seal cull), and
a home knitwear industry of Scalpay. Generally there has been a
steady response to the development of tourism and these developments
are still almost wholly undertaken by local people (albeit on a
small scale). Uncertainties regarding tourism in the mid-1960s (a
seamens' strike rendered a new ferry out of action during its first
summer season) brought about a reduction of bed-and-breakfast accommodation from 218 to 155 beds between 1964 and 1966.(2) By the 1974
season this had increased to 209 inclusive of 16 static caravans and
5 cottages being let by local people.(3)

Community social structure is, however, principally based upon
crofting as a way of life and as a form of occupance of the land.
In its present form it is a form of land-use protected by acts of
parliament (1886-1961) and supervised by a permanent commission
whose headquarters are in Inverness.(4) The crofts legally are under
75 acres, and as first-class agricultural land is rare in the Highlands (and especially so for Harris), a croft is incapable of development for commercial farming and typically provides subsistence for
a single small family. As the croft cannot be sub-divided it is
passed intact to a single heir. The crofter's children leaving
school will have to find economic support elsewhere. Typically only
the eldest male is likely to remain or to return to run the family
croft. Even so, a croft cannot in general provide a complete
living: it must be supplemented by part-time or full-time work
elsewhere. In Lewis this is typically by combining crofting with
hand-loom weaving for the Harris tweed industry. With the closure
of the Tarbert Mill, the Harris tweed industry is of very small
account in Harris today (there being only a literal handful of
families involved in domestic weaving). The age-structure of Harris
being what it is, crofting provides a form of 'semi-retirement' in
very many cases. On Scalpay fishing prospects and demands upon time
have reputedly resulted in neglect of croft-land, but this is not
very obvious.

Crofting carries rights to common grazing. A few cattle are kept
(principally milch cows) but overwhelmingly the grazings are under
sheep. Harvesting on the croft is generally within the capability
of the family. The arrangement of grazings requires communal work
and co-operation between the families of the crofting township. The
townships and their common grazings provide the meaningful divisions

of the landscape from the point of view of the Harris people. Outsiders may not appreciate that what could appear as a continuous
settlement (with an incongruous cattle-grid in the road), might in
fact be organised as two separate crofting townships, one of which
may have houses some distance away at the other end of the common
grazing. A 'souming' states the notional maxima of animals (sheep,
cattle and horses) that the grazing can support. In winter, after
harvest, these animals may pasture at will over the croft land. In
summer they are excluded and pasture 'on the hill'. On the common
grazings of the fertile *machair* land of the west coast, crops of oats
or potatoes may be rotated — hence the adjacent lush pasture is
excluded for grazing. Apart from a handful of ponies (and an odd
goat) the crofters' animals are predominantly sheep. The soumings
tend to be exceeded — and the overgrazing by sheep results in poor
quality animals and noticeable mortality.

The decisions regarding grazing are taken by a township grazing
committee. The crofters of each township elect a clerk who is
responsible for convening meetings and settling dates of crofting
events. Fank-days for dipping, shearing and ear-marking are decided during the year and these provide focal points in time when
the majority of the township, men, women, children, the retired, the
visitors and friends turn out to assist in proceedings. These are
in general communal gatherings of a solidary character and high
social morale. There is a lot of hard work, a lot of communication
and shared observations and humour. The situation is very strongly
Gaelic. The ear-marking of sheep is undertaken in accordance with
an entirely Gaelic system.(5) This is the only true instance of
Gaelic entering the commercial advertising domain: notices and
small advertisements for lost and found sheep are of necessity in
Gaelic.

In autumn 'ramming' provides a further event in the crofting
calendar which engenders contacts within the community. The men
take rams around the crofts to serve the ewes. It is an occasion
for contacts, banter and solidarity amongst the men.

The winning of peat is likewise undertaken by communal labour
but on a smaller scale: typically by a number of families working
together. Here likewise is an important series of events — peat-
cutting, transportation and stacking — all of which are strongly
supportive of the use of Gaelic.

The supplementation of croft work is generally small-scale and
includes such occupations as tourist accommodation, inshore fishing,
motor and lorry hire, knitting, weaving, craftwork, kitchen garden-
ing, shopkeeping. In the Bays area of Harris, five crofting townships totalling 68 households mustered between them 6 bed-and-
breakfast establishments, 1 caravan to let, 15 vans, 1 lorry, 46
households knitting for sale, 5 weavers, 31 kitchen gardens, 16
boats, 3 shops and post offices. This area also contained the re-
opened mill employing about twenty local women. Few of the 'weavers'
were producing regularly and in the vast majority of cases boats and
kitchen gardens were producing food primarily for home consumption
and gifts — much the same could be said for knitwear production.

However, these types of small-scale opportunity are of great
importance for the stabilisation of the local community. In general
people are making a living but not producing any great surplus which

can provide capital for truly remunerative subsidiary occupations. Where this has occurred — as on Scalpay — societal stabilisation has been associated with the higher levels of language-maintenance for Gaelic. Scalpay and the Bays area of Harris provide the best examples of language-maintenance on the island — exceeded elsewhere only in the Lochs and west-coast areas of Lewis. At the 1961 census the highest rates of Gaelic language-maintenance amongst the enumerated population aged three years and over were: the Park section of Lochs (99.2 per cent), Barvas (S)(98.8 per cent), Barvas (N) (98.7 per cent), and Harris (Middle) comprising Scalpay and the Bays area (98.2 per cent).

Economic development as related to community social structure and societal values, does however seem to have been influenced very much by the tradition of communal work and joint decision taking. Croft-work, as we have seen, depends on mutual co-operation, and major decisions are taken by a township committee. This tradition, according to Caird and Moisley(6) seems to have inhibited individual initiative and caused the local communities to be reluctant to innovate. Both leadership and innovation from within the community appear to have been held back by the operation of this system. However, although most of the economic developments started up in the Outer Hebrides have been as the result of entrepreneurial initiative on the part of the outsiders, Caird and Moisley do note the response of crofters to the Harris tweed industry. In Harris, of course, since 1961 this has declined substantially but developments in fisheries have had a noticeably stimulating effect — especially in Scalpay. Caird and Moisley's conclusion of 'leadership and innovation from within' has been borne out here. It is noticeable that this form of venture involves co-operation at the 'grass-roots' level. Joint skipperage and crew recruitment is along lines of neighbourhood, kin and community.

The Gaelic word 'cuideachd' has the significance of 'helpers', 'sharing', 'commercial company', 'kith-and-kin' and 'assistance', in English. Success in small-scale economic development and innovation in community leadership for a Gaelic community such as Harris seemingly awaits forms and patterns which recognise these continued social realities.

COMMUNICATIONS

The introduction of the Hebridean Ferry linking Tarbert with Uig in Skye in 1964 was the first of a number of changes fundamentally altering the pattern of the communication network of the 'Gaelic West' in general. Up until that time a steamer circular route linked Mallaig and Kyle, the mainland railheads, with ports in Skye, Lewis, Scalpay, Harris, the Uists, the Small Isles. Another circuit, connecting at Lochboisdale (South Uist) linked Barra, the Southern Hebrides and the railhead at Oban. Although not a modern roll-on, roll-off service, these steamer routes effectively linked island to island and isolated mainland community to community, providing an internal communications network within the northwest and Hebridean area.

Today with the new ramp-loading and roll-on, roll-off facilities, the pattern in the Hebridean area has changed from an interconnecting figure-of-eight pattern to a pattern of strong east-west lines linking each island direct to a coastal railhead or port to the east and by means of an improved east-west (or retained rail) link to an eastern 'metropolis', e.g. Inverness in the case of Harris and North Uist, Dingwall in the case of Lewis, Oban in the case of South Uist and Barra. There is likewise no air service connecting all the outer islands to one another. The routes now run east.(7)

The implications of these changes for the Gaelic-speaking area and its communities is to separate the culture-province into isolated islands and coastal enclaves, well-connected with the anglicised administrative and economic centres in the east. Tourism has been developed along these routes. In some cases centuries-old community connections between islands have been broken (e.g. Canna-South Uist). Tourists come in along these new routes and schoolchildren depart in order to board away from home and migrants in search of work elsewhere use them to leave home.

The cultural integrity of the *Gàidhealtachd* — the Gaelic-speaking area and its community — is affected by these changes. Islanders are less in contact with one another, more dependent upon agencies 'outside'. Each island forms part of the 'periphery' of the economic sphere of influence of a different 'metropolis' to the east. A graphic illustration of this occurred in Harris in 1973 when new routes and schedules introduced by MacBrayne's, the shipping company, caused the regular laundry consignments from Tarbert, Harris to Stornoway, Lewis (on the same island land mass, 36 miles apart) to be sent by sea to Uig in Skye, by road to Kyle on the mainland, by rail to Inverness, by bus to Ullapool and by sea again to Stornoway: a round trip of 200 miles. The Gaelic-speaking areas, although continuous and contiguous throughout northwest Scotland, are thus effectively isolated from one another.

The fragmented character of Gaelic Scotland has been persistent throughout historic times. On the mainland deep glens separated by high mountains and off-shore the islands separated by sea passages make up a region of difficulty into which innovation has been slow to penetrate. The region conserved ancient forms of social organisation into modern times. It has conserved its own distinctive language and way of life. Ostensibly, Gaelic Scotland has survived as such as the result of 'cultural lag' in a region of geographic, climatic and economic difficulty. Such an explanation, although plausible, fails to account for the fact that islanders particularly are typically widely travelled, the menfolk at any rate, through service in the merchant navy and armed forces. The sea has been a connecting factor as much as an isolating one. The Gaelic dialect of Harris for example, has a great deal in common with the dialect of the Uists. Harris Gaelic is readily distinguishable from the dialect of Lewis. The mountain range of North Harris has been a more formidable isolating factor than the sea-passages to the south.(8)

Although dialects within Scottish Gaelic are very marked and although social intercourse within the *Gàidhealtachd* is very difficult, there is nevertheless a local patriotism to the Gaelic character of the community. The terms Gael, Gaelic and *Gàidhealtachd* are the foci of a definite communal feeling. There is, however, no

standard Gaelic dialect or norm of speech universally accepted as
'proper'. In speaking to Gaels from different islands and districts I have found that it is common for them to volunteer such
observations as, 'of course, we do not speak the proper Gaelic in
our part'. This may often be an excuse to save the speaker from
accepting an invitation to speak in public or to use his Gaelic
when strangers are present. One Harris girl, however, felt that
the Gaelic dialects really 'made' the Gaelic language. English may
be strongly preferred in such circumstances even when clearly the
speaker is more at home in Gaelic. This may be again a further
effect of the cultural domination by the *Galldachd* or English-
speaking community running now through all domains of social interaction except the most intimate and familial. A standardised written language does exist. It is, of course, based upon the eight-
eenth and nineteenth-century translation of the Bible (made after
the common literary Gaelic of the bardic schools had lapsed for some
two centuries or more), but there is evidence of linguistic updating
in contemporary written standard Gaelic. What is very much unstan-
dardised is its pronunciation. As vocabulary has become 'impover-
ished' by diminution in recent times and as distinctive dialect
words — and many other specialist terms — have tended to drop out
of the common everyday vocabulary, lexical differences between the
dialects is not so much a barrier to mutual appreciation as accent
and idiom. Recent correspondence conducted in English in a local
newspaper(9) focussed upon the cultural domination of Lewismen in
broadcast BBC programmes, resented by Skyemen on grounds of language.
A common standardised 'BBC' Gaelic has not developed. The church
failed to standardise the pronunciation owing to isolation of
congregations. The BBC has failed to standardise Gaelic in like
manner as it has helped to standardise English, perhaps chiefly
owing to the fact that so little Gaelic is broadcast by radio or
television.(10)
    The role of the broadcasting media in Gaelic cultural life merits
attention because what little there is of broadcast Gaelic has had
considerable effect in diffusing modern popular culture. Until
spring 1974, the BBC put out a lunch-time programme of Gaelic
records and news every weekday from 1.30-1.45 p.m. It was popular
and its loss is felt. When a Gaelic folk group perform locally
their repertoire is immediately recognised and when a Gaelic news-
reader or comedian is 'sent-up' the inferences are immediately
appreciated by the audience. This is surprising in view of the
paucity of time for Gaelic on the media. With the exception of a
half-hour religious service, Gaelic programmes were transferred
entirely to VHF in April 1974. Although an extra half-hour's
broadcasting time has been made available, few households in the
Gaelic area have VHF receivers — and there are areas in which
reception is poor anyway. A common reaction has been '*Nach d'*
thug iad a'Gaidhlig bhuain-ne!' ('They have removed the Gaelic
from us!'). In the time made available for Gaelic the BBC has been
unable to provide a full range of programme types in Gaelic and the
Gaelic service has tended to cater principally in terms of religious services, talks, record programmes, ceilidhs and news. There
have been relatively few plays — although quizzes and brains trust
types of programme have been undertaken from time to time.

The impression comes over that Gaelic does not or cannot handle the variety of programme types broadcast in English. Inevitably the Gaelic service caters for its majority audience: the older age groups. English-language broadcasting caters in much fuller measure for younger age groups. The Gaelic broadcasting service is provided anyway by an agency outside the *Gàidhealtachd*. The policies, as with transport, are determined by 'national' criteria and the overall planning is undertaken by an authority where priorities and pre-occupations are far removed from Gaelic Scotland. The daily five-minute news programme has been widely criticised for being too short, too hurried and incomprehensible to ordinary people. It does tend to adopt a literally translated style of English language news broadcasts. Typically it comprised translations of the two minutes of 'national' news headlines from London and the three minutes of daily 'Scottish' (which is meant to count as local) news. Very rarely did any of this material relate to the Highlands and Islands or the Gaelic areas especially. Critics seek a content more relevant to local interests and a more natural and relaxed style more familiar to the average Gaelic listener. In spring 1974 the Gaelic department of the BBC in Glasgow attempted to collect news from inside the area daily. As with the provision and planning of transport, broadcasting for the Gaelic community is another example of the cultural dependence of Gaeldom upon the 'core-' or 'mass-society' of modern Britain.

Yet the BBC did float the idea of a Gaelic or a Highland local radio in 1972. This was to be centred in Stornoway, and was to be subsidised by the local authorities of Ross-shire and Inverness-shire. There was precedent here as these authorities were already underwriting from local rates the costs of production by the BBC of schools' radio programmes in Gaelic. Ross-shire was prepared to entertain the idea but Inverness-shire was reluctant. When the finances became publicly apparent, and when it was realised that only twenty hours per week would be locally produced of which only thirteen hours would be in Gaelic, Stornoway Town Council led public opinion in declaring the scheme a bad bargain and the idea was subsequently dropped. Hence there is little prospect of Gaelic Scotland receiving anything approaching local cultural autonomy in the broadcasting media. The suppression of the bardic schools by the Statutes of Iona after 1616 left Gaelic Scotland with a folk-culture only. There is little awareness on the part of the broadcasting authorities of the cultural needs of the Gaelic speech-community in its own language. As the result of public policy — or the lack of it — the aspects of popular culture mediated by broadcasting are supplied to Gaelic Scotland almost entirely through English and the means of developing a cultural autonomy are in large measure absent.

There are, however, a number of institutions which are to some extent supplying this need. Community drama in Gaelic has developed since the last war. There are amateur companies in Lewis and elsewhere but Harris has found it difficult to organise anything on these lines, whether in Gaelic or English. An attempt was made between 1970 and 1972 but it made little headway. From time to time travelling groups visit the island 'on tour'. In March 1973 and 1974 the Glasgow University Ossianic Society brought an evening

of Gaelic entertainment, *Air Thurus*. It was immensely enjoyed, and
represented one of the very few actual entertainments laid on outside the 'tourist season'. Elsewhere in the Gaelic world there are
sufficient numbers of Gaelic groups for two annual Gaelic drama
festivals, in Glasgow and Skye, annually in early May. During the
winter months the total of 'events' held in Harris comprise a public
dance about once a month, a society dinner or dinner/dances of a
similar frequency, annual secondary school concerts and performances
by the occasional touring company (amateur, such as the Ossianic
Society, or semi-professional, such as '7.84').

Commercial recordings provide another important support for
Gaelic popular culture. Again, this is a service undertaken for
Gaeldom from outside, chiefly from Glasgow. In some cases, such as
the Gaelfonn Company (established in 1955), the enterprise is
directed by 'exiled' Gaels. Hamiltons of Glasgow, the Beltona label
of the Decca Group, Waverley (Edinburgh) and Topic (London), which
issue commercially field recordings and archive material from the
School of Scottish Studies are all-important sources of Gaelic
records. Broadcasting and professional entertainers such as
Na h-Oganaich have in recent years assisted the return of such
archive material, via records, to the popular repertoire. A good
example is the humorous song '*Fiollagan*' formerly known only to a
few villagers in Arnol, Lewis, or the Ossianic chant '*Am Bothan a
bh'aig Fionnaghuala*', known only to a few cognoscenti, returned to
popular awareness throughout Gaeldom in a matter of months during
1972-3. Audiences will vigorously join in singing such songs at
public entertainments.

RELIGIOUS LIFE

Religious observance plays an especially important role in Harris
affairs. The community is almost entirely church-going and universally observant of the Fourth Commandment regarding the keeping
of the Sabbath. The population is almost entirely affiliated to
one of the three denominations represented on the island, the Free
Church, the Free Presbyterian Church and the Church of Scotland.
The churches are all Presbyterian and thus governed on similar
lines: through a presbytery of ministers and elders of a group of
churches.

Doctrinally there is little to distinguish these churches to the
casual outsider. They are all Protestant, Presbyterian and Calvinist. The Church of Scotland has shed the more conservative aspects
of its Calvinism nationally, but this is not too apparent in the
islands. The Free Presbyterian Church is the most retentive of
fundamental Calvinism and is the most demanding in terms of rigid
adherence to uncompromising standards of individual morality and
social life.

The Free Church owes its origin to the 'Disruption' of 1843,
when, particularly in the Highlands, many Church of Scotland congregations and ministers separated themselves from the main body of
the church over the issue of 'patronage': the appointment of
ministers by landowners. Clearly at this time the established
church was being used as the means of quietening the people or

terrifying them into acquiescence at the time of the wholesale
evictions and clearances of the population from their homelands.
Although the theological apologia of the Free Church is in terms
of adherence to the Westminster Confession, the Scottish Reformation, the First Book of Discipline and adherence to biblical
precept, sociologically the origin of the Church is explicable as
the reaction of a physically and politically oppressed people.
The 'free' churchmen were not prepared to remain within an established church which upheld the economic and social interests of a
landowning class.   In the early nineteenth century the established
church alone regulated marriage: a testimony of good behaviour was
required from one's minister before a marriage could be solemnised.
(11)   (An unhallowed union before witnesses was the only alternative
recognised by Scots Law.)   Other aspects of social life were alike
regulated by the minister.   As the minister became too obviously to
be seen as the agent of the local landowner, so the seeds of 'disruption' germinated in the church.
   The Free Presbyterian Church (the 'Wee Free' or 'Seceders')
formed their church in 1893 over the issue of biblical scholarship
and adherence to the confession of faith.   The Free Presbyterians
seceded from the Free Church at a point in time shortly after the
first Crofters Act (1886) and after the success of a Highland political movement which elected 'Crofter Party' MPs to each of the
Highland constituencies.   For the first time the Gael had security
of tenure upon his homeland, reasonable rents regulated by law and
the first experience of political success within the polity of the
British State.   It is tempting to explain the movement for return
to the 'purity' of the 1843 Free Church as an attempt to proceed to
'close ranks' in all respects of cultural integrity.   Just as
material and political objectives had recently been secured by the
Highlanders, in like manner there should be a return to the securi-
ties and stabilities of a 'status quo ante' in the symbolic culture
and the value system.(12)
   Today, in Harris, the allegiance of the majority of the people is
to the Free Church and the Free Presbyterian Church.   For various
reasons it is difficult to estimate the numbers involved.   As an
impression, the three churches take approximately one-third of the
population each with a slight preponderance to the Free Church and
the Church of Scotland possibly in a close third place.   The main
Church of Scotland charge at Tarbert was originally a famous Free
Church charge: one, though, which returned to the established
church with the re-union of the present century.
   In their forms of worship the three churches maintain an austere
pattern of the Metrical Psalms sung to the Gaelic 'long tunes',
Bible reading, extemporary prayer and the sermon.   Services are
between one and two hours duration: a midday service and an evening
service at 6 p.m. being commonly the case.   With afternoon attendance at Sabbath School, and family worship, a Harris child has
little opportunity for any non-religious activity on a Sunday such
as play or reading for pleasure,   although a Sunday walk up the hill
is often now an admissible Sabbath recreation.   The Gaelic Psalms
are sung seated.   The Precentor stands and sings one line at a time.
The congregation repeats the line in a decorated and individual
variation.   This unique form of unaccompanied church music may seem

to comprise a cacophonous and wailing 'oriental-type' cantillation
to the stranger who encounters it for the first time. The Gaelic
Psalms are the one aspect of Gaelic musical culture today which are
universally known and practised by the Gaelic communities of the
Northern Hebridean islands and northwest seaboard.(13) The condem-
nation of the secular culture by the Free Presbyterian church and
the inimical attitudes on the part of full members and office-
bearers in the other churches result in the non-participation by
many — particularly the more religious — in popular entertainments.
The Free Presbyterian church is officially opposed to instrumental
music and hymns other than the Metrical Psalms in church services.
It is therefore through the opportunity for individual extempori-
sation in the psalm-singing that the individual church members —
especially the women — are able to contribute a distinctive individual expression within a highly conformist religious culture.

For prayers the congregation stands, often for up to twenty
minutes. Older persons sit down one by one, often with an audible
sigh. This practice may signal to an over-lengthy minister or
missionary that the time has come for the final petitions and the
'amen'. The announcement of the text and the commencement of the
sermon is frequently attended by the widespread sussurus of cello-
phane wrappings as the congregation fortifies itself — and its
children — with the sustaining compensations of boiled confection-
ary. Missionaries particularly are likely to be lengthy in ser-
monising. An hour or more is not uncommon. On one such occasion
a missionary who had been explaining in Gaelic for over an hour
concerning the different prisoners St John was likely to encounter
on the Isle of Patmos observed that there were some who were just
'bial, bial, bial, canntainn, canntainn, canntainn' — 'mouth,
mouth, mouth, talk, talk, talk'.

Gaelic services are general. Each of the churches holds an
English service. An English service precedes the Gaelic service on
Sunday mornings at Tarbert. Only here are English hymns and a piano
to be heard. The small congregations of outsiders or island visitors
trickles out at the end, encountering the great drove of island
people pouring into the church for the Gaelic service.

Church services and church life generally provide a domain within
which Gaelic is still supreme. Local people preponderantly prefer
to worship in Gaelic. The Church of Scotland, Tarbert, introduced
the practice in 1972 of holding one of its weeknight prayer meetings
in English once a month — and this raised protests from Gaelic
loyalists locally. As the Protestant churches set considerable
store upon the preaching of 'the word' and upon fluency in extemporary prayer, verbal skills in Gaelic are encouraged amongst the
ministry, missionaries, church elders, and church members (the males
at least). Although there is to some extent a predictable language
of prayer (comparable with the 'language of Israel' amongst English
non-conformists) and there is much use of biblical and religious
cliché, this field of spoken Gaelic is one in which elaboration of
code is encouraged and generated by otherwise undistinguished community members.

A traditional rhythmic intonation is still to be heard from
Gaelic preachers. After a while the preacher, for emphasis,
develops a run of exhortation in a repetitive rhythmic chant. This

has similarities with the 'hwyl' of a Welsh preacher and with Old
London 'street cries'. Folklorists attribute the origins of this
style to pre-Reformation, pre-Catholic or even to pre-Christian
religious practice. It can often resemble traditional 'Ossianic'
chant. In its manifestations religion is strongly conservative of
the way of life, symbolic values and the language of the Harris
people. The use of Gaelic in religious life has probably been the
chief factor in the maintenance of Gaelic as a community language.
However, when a stranger appears in the congregation the preacher
will shift into English for a significant proportion of the prayers,
Bible reading and sermon also, and as noted above, English has
recently entered into use at prayer meetings, until recently an all-
Gaelic domain.

Sabbath Schools for the children are now almost always in English
for a variety of reasons. In Scalpay the return of Scalpay people
from Glasgow have brought non-Gaelic-speaking children into the
community. The use of the Free Church youth paper 'The Instructor',
which is entirely in English, has shifted Free Church Sabbath
Schools from the use of Gaelic. In Tarbert and Leverburgh the
Sabbath School teachers are non-Gaelic-speaking incomers. Elsewhere an example of a missionary bringing up his children without
Gaelic means that his conduct of his Sabbath School classes is in
English only, so he does not use Gaelic in the Sabbath School —
only in the church itself.

Communions(14) are celebrated twice a year ('Na h-Orduighean
Móra' and 'Na h-Orduighean Beaga') and they rotate around the island,
from township to township: e.g. Tarbert in early March, Manish in
mid-July, Finsbay in early August, and so on. The 'season' lasts
about a week, the principal services occurring between the Thursday
and Sunday. The communion season will be observed by each church in
a given location at the same time, e.g. at Tarbert where there is a
Church of Scotland and a Free Presbyterian Congregation, both
churches will observe the communion season on the same days. Both
churches claim to be the true church — so the observation of communion is equally theirs although celebrated separately. Ostensible
co-operation is in all probability a mutual attempt at pre-emption
of place in community life. Although all Harris people mingle
together amicably in community life (religion is no divider) ministers do not frequently associate across denominational boundaries
whether for religious or secular reasons. Indeed ministers figure
very little in the secular life of the community and are rarely to
be seen on secular occasions or at secular events.

However, communions are occasions of particularly strong social
solidarity. Sociologically the occasion is symbolic as much of
community as religious observation and identification. It is all
still strongly Gaelic. During communion family members, relations
and friends are likely to return home. Houses may be full and the
womenfolk extremely busy catering for guests and observing the
religious duties of home worship and church attendance. This practice provides for regular occasions — apart from weddings and
funerals — when scattered families may re-unite and the village
community encompass again its former members.

Daytime preparatory services bring people into Tarbert when communions are held there. The opportunity may be taken to talk to

friends and relations from other parts of the island and from elsewhere. Religious observation may be combined with business — the
banks and shops are very busy on such occasions — and the conversation everywhere is likely to be in Gaelic, even in the bank where
otherwise this is comparatively rare. Before and after the services
the streets are thronged — especially if it is a fine day — and
the atmosphere is very strongly and publicly Gaelic. The use of the
language is neither sporadic nor 'underground' but *the* language of
the people and the place.

The Friday of Communion Week is observed as '*Là na Cèisd*' ('The
Day of the Question'). The service takes the form of public discussion of a text or a religious problem. It is extemporary and un-
rehearsed — even if an elder or a senior member may have a question
in reserve in case no other is forthcoming. Almost invariably there
is. When the officiating minister invites a member with a religious
problem to declare, at least two or three rise and the first to
declare his 'question' is invited to propose it. The minister con-
siders the problem and declares it a fit question to be raised. He
invites one of his fellow ministers together with him in the pulpit
to give the first exegesis. This may be a new minister, or one who
is not otherwise often heard in the particular church. The minister
then asks congregational elders, missionaries and in particular
visiting church members to speak. As may be appreciated, this is
above all an occasion for new and unaccustomed voices to join those
who are otherwise frequently to be heard. New perspectives can be
admitted. Thus both in secular and spiritual spheres, outside
contacts are brought into the centre of local life. Fresh ideas may,
albeit under social control, prevent local practice from atrophy.
'*Là na Cèisd*' is an all-Gaelic occasion which places great premium
on 'the word' and in which great store is laid upon succinct and
expressive speech. The idea is to be pithy and brief, giving time
for as wide a variety of contributions to be made as possible. A
missionary noted for his long-winded sermons may have his say in
three minutes flat — and may be thought to have said more in the
three minutes than his accustomed hour. However, Harris is one of
the last places to retain the '*cèisd*' service (in the Church of
Scotland at least). It is passing as a central feature of communions as modern patterns of transport, holidays and employment
reduce attendance.

Communion itself is taken by church members only. Full members
may comprise a minority of those present in the congregation — this
is especially true of the Free Church and more particularly of the
Free Presbyterian Church. In one Free Presbyterian church the
minister reckoned on there being about a dozen communicants in addition to officiating clergy and elders from amongst a church filled
with 'adherents' of the church. Communion is served to those sitting
in the central or the front pews. The congregation will thus order
itself as it enters and occupies the church. The adherents will go
to the peripheries of the seating plan. They will not be served
communion.

Typically church membership is entered into in the mid-forties,
as the desires of the flesh weaken and middle-aged folk settle for
a sedate and respectable second half of life. There should be a
converting experience before the individual is admitted to church

membership. Conversion may often be associated with depressive
signs and symptoms. Perhaps an individual, as the years take their
toll, realises that life is passing him by and the younger set he
knew is now no longer around as it once was. Ferocious weather in
winter, lack of entertainments and the dwindling numbers of family
and family friends in a dying community are contributing factors to
a very high incidence of depression in the community. Lewis and
Harris have the highest recorded incidence of hospital admissions for
involutional melancholia in the United Kingdom.(15) The peak age
group for mental hospital admissions is 40-60. Similar incidence is
reported of alcoholism, manic depression and neurotic depressive
reaction. These rates of incidence may approach six times the
Scottish national average for involutional melancholia and three
times the rate for Scotland as a whole for alcoholism.(16) Conversion and admission to full church membership may be a relieving
factor in certain cases.

Certainly the Catholic islands further south do not seem to share
these problems to anything like the same extent and it is tempting
to put forward a hypothesis that the differences result from the
religious culture. It is tempting to contrast the age of admission
to full church membership: ideally in the early teens for the
Catholic, in late middle age for the Calvinist. A certain element
of backsliding is expected during youth, and for the Catholic this
may be absolved weekly on Friday evening. Rectitude is expected
between Friday evening and Sunday morning mass. There is no embargo
on the general run of worldly pleasures for the communicating
Catholic. The full Calvinist member is not expected to involve himself in worldly pleasures at all. There is a seven-day cycle of
religious experience and renewal for the Catholic: the corresponding cycle for the Calvinist extends over as many decades. Expiation
comes in later middle age, for good, to the Calvinist rather than
weekly on Fridays as for the Catholic. Friday night is above all the
night for pleasure-seeking in Harris. Following conversion, the
Calvinist is expected to lead a blameless life: virtual Lenten
abstinence from pleasures for the rest of his life. There is a
Gaelic expression which describes this state, the 'cùram' or to
have the 'cùram' on him.

In any event conversion and church membership represents a status
passage in terms of community life. Before conversion an adherent
may engage in frivolous behaviour. Harris life is not without its
gaieties. There are village dances, typically late on Friday nights
(to avoid breaking the Sabbath after Saturday midnight). These
start after licensing hours and continue into the early hours of
Saturday morning. A certain amount of drink may be smuggled into
the dance hall or available in cars parked nearby. After the dance
an informal ceilidh for drinking and merry-making may continue in
someone's house nearby. The middle-aged are rarely to be seen, and
the converted are never to be seen at these affairs. After conversion complete social and sexual rectitude is expected. The church
member may sometimes be seen at the more sedate type of entertainment such as an annual dinner of a club or society, but almost never
at the normal type of village dance, ceilidh or public entertainment.
In contrast of course to the Calvinistic Presbyterian frowning upon
this secular pleasure-seeking popular culture there has, by reaction,

come into existence an 'underground' fun-culture of the younger
people. There are of course pressures against the children of church
officers — particularly ministers — participating in this. The
younger set gather at the few places of public resort: hotel bars,
cafes, village halls. Of course younger people may go to one of
the two youth clubs and when they are older they may be seen asso-
ciating with the 'underground' and there are some who see the youth
clubs as being at fault in leading young people on to worse things.
On occasions young people can be seen to be taking even their pleasures seriously; there will be the odd case of intemperance —
someone who has worked hard to get himself inebriated within the
hour at some public event.

The youth culture is pragmatic in its use of language. Gaelic
and English are frequently in use — often very much mixed. The two
languages may be used macaronically for humorous effect. The older,
more settled age groups show a more patterned and societally allocated use of language between the various domains: Gaelic for
example, being particularly well-conserved in the religious domain.

The converted enter a new life with new responsibilities. They
have the 'cùram' and in time they may rise to have a prestigeful
position as a community figure or decision-maker within the geronto-
cracy which dominates Harris community life. This is turn may be
marked as 'eldership' in the church.

This decision-making élite comprises about a dozen ministers and
missionaries and about thirty to forty elders and leading church
members. They can be very effective in influencing certain public
issues — especially anything pertaining to Sabbath observance. In
1967-8 the MacBrayne's island tours stopped over at Tarbert for the
weekends, and to fill in the free Sunday ran the tourists over to
Rodel on Sunday afternoons to see the ancient church of St Clements
restored in 1873 'for the worship of God' but not in fact so used
by any of the island's religious denominations. This activity was
vigorously condemned through public opinion and the local papers by
the island's religious decision-makers as 'Sabbath breaking'. Nowhere in the records of this controversy was the point raised that
the object of the visit was to see a church whose restoration had
been undertaken to provide a place for worship. Services could have
been held at times when these tourists visited the church. Island
bus operators were in fact providing bus services taking local people
to church on Sundays. In 1973 the commencement of a public works
scheme brought plant and transport to the quay at Tarbert on a
Saturday. The contractor intimated that he would move this to his
campsite on the Sunday as an indication of his commencing work, and
that there would be no employment for anyone who might refuse Sunday
work. Mobilisation of public opinion was swift. The mainland contractor in fact undertook no work on Sundays. Generally though this
control network operates only in the case of public issues with a
specific and obvious religious connection. It does not seem to be
brought into play in the general run of events which have no specific religious significance. Undoubtedly there is a current of quiet
moral suasion over individual and social matters, but the overt
mobilisation of public opinion is not undertaken over public issues
unless these have some fairly obvious religious significance. In
this connection Sabbath observance is one of the principal marks of

the symbolisation of 'groupness' for the Harris people. Its observation is more rigorous almost than any other symbolic aspect of
the culture.

Vallee has remarked of Catholic Barra, twenty years previously,
that the customs surrounding death and the observance of funerals
provided occasions of community solidarity which were island-wide in
their significance.(17) Much the same can be said for Harris.
Vallee reported that funerals occurring about once a month were
attended by mourners throughout the island — a substantial proportion of the island's population being frequently in attendance. The
funeral procession is functionally ordered in terms of the status,
sex and relationships of the mourners. Males having significant
relationships to the deceased take their turn as coffin-bearers.
Although now mechanised into motor hearses, funeral processions in
Harris may still involve human bearers for significant parts of the
way, for example, through the township. Considerable numbers of
cars may follow the hearse to the cemetery at Luskentyre providing
a similar event of island-wide solidarity as Vallee reported for
Barra. The number of deaths in Harris has risen in recent years.
Between 1962 and 1972 the annual number of deaths rose from 31 to
60 (47 in 1963, 36 in 1964, 32 in 1965, 42 in 1966, 50 in 1967,
39 in 1968, 47 in 1969, 41 in 1970, 38 in 1971), according to the
Harris register of Births, Marriages and Deaths.

There is approximately one funeral a week. Attendances are
likely to be impressive for a young person or a noted community
figure.

Unlike practice in Wales, English and not the local language is
invariably used on gravestones and monuments. However, the services, particularly those in the home, are of all social events the
most notable occasions in which Gaelic really comes into its own.
On the evenings following the death, the minister will call at the
home and hold a service. Relatives, neighbours and friends will
attend and considerable numbers of people will fill the house. A
great feeling of mutual support and release is engendered as the
Scriptures are read in Gaelic, or the minister prays, and above all
as everyone joins together in a Gaelic Psalm. Relatives, neighbours
and friends will form a rota to sit with and to watch over the dead
each night until the funeral. Conversation which is likely to occur
will inevitably be in Gaelic: the language becomes closely associated with such solemn events in community life and thus closely bound
up with social solidarity and individual affection.

THE PATTERN OF AN ISLAND YEAR

Relative to its population the Isle of Harris receives a comparatively large influx of visitors during its short summer season.
Summer in the northwest if brief: mid-May to mid-August. Towards
the end of June numbers of summer visitors start to build up. Book-
ing in advance becomes essential on the island ferries. At times
local life may appear to be 'swamped out' by the tourists, but it
must be remembered that many of these are actually island people now
resident elsewhere returning with their families to stay with relations. Not surprisingly, social life builds up to a peak during

July and August. Numbers of annual events occur at this time of
maximum benefit to island resident, summer visitor and returning
'exile' alike. In recent years a 'Gala' week has been organised
late in July, including dances, barbecues, ceilidhs, a regatta, car
rallies, fishing competitions, charity walks and a 'Highland Games'.
A traditional open-air dance, *danns an rathaid*', is held on the
quay and approach road in Tarbert. In early August the annual
sheepdog trials are generally held on *machair* land on the west
coast and later in August the annual agricultural show, *'sealladh
stoc'*, and handicrafts display is held in alternate years at the
Leverburgh and Tarbert schools. In the summer season dances may
occur weekly or more frequently at the village hall in Tarbert
(and at Leverburgh). Ceilidhs also may be organised on a monthly
or fortnightly frequency.

Campbell and MacLean have pointed out how the principal annual
events supportive of the ethnic culture of the Nova Scotia Gaels
are similarly celebrated during the summer tourist season for the
benefit of tourists and for visiting 'exiles' desirous of a reminder
of local culture during their holidays back home. Campbell and
MacLean allude to this as a 'summer leisure culture',(18) explaining that

Participation in such activities has become almost a full-time
occupation for some during the summer months in eastern Nova
Scotia. During that time thousands of the 'diaspora' return
home to participate in the leisure culture on an ethnic or
regional basis. . . . Urban Canadians and others find this
summer leisure culture a welcome antidote to their own frenzied
pace of pursuit towards the elusive god of progress.(19)

In its own more modest way something of the same may be noted in
Harris.

The summer months in many respects represent the 'peak period'
of the working year for the crofting community. As the days lengthen
in late spring and early summer the peat banks dry out and families
and neighbours assist one another for a day's work 'out at the
peats'. These days are long and hard-working but everyone participates, young and old. Even with visitors present these occasions
will be very Gaelic, cheerful and solidary. After the peats have
been set on end to dry out some weeks will elapse before households
and neighbourhoods will turn out again to bring the dried *caorans*
down to the road, load them, transport them home and stack them near
the house. Any visitors present will be welcome helpers. The returning exile will find himself involved in croft-work as much as in
'leisure culture'. He will be home for the peats if not 'home for
the hay'.(20) With work on the peats, haymaking, work on the crops,
fank days for sheep-shearing and, at summer's end, harvesting, the
summer months provide a greatly increased tempo of life, many
opportunities for human contact, co-operation over group work and
social events. In great contrast are winter conditions when outside
work greatly reduces and opportunities for social contacts are few.

Obviously when visitors are numerous English is conspicuously in
use everywhere. A casual visitor might fail to hear any spoken
Gaelic around him as visitors thronging the shops, the bank and the
tourist office will be engendering the switch to English for all
transactional purposes. In the hotel English reigns supreme where-

ever there is carpet on the floor. For example, the coffee lounge and the cocktail bar are very much the preserve of English as compared with the saloon and especially the public bar where Gaelic is the usual medium. Hotel staff serving in the carpeted lounges are unaccustomed to use Gaelic, especially with visitors. Yet the same girls will be laughing and talking amongst themselves in Gaelic in the hotel kitchens. Ordering coffee for friends in the lounge, I once very much embarrassed the waitress by speaking in Gaelic. She was very uncertain whether to reply in Gaelic or not and finally fled to fetch the order with a brief phrase of English. A similar exchange in an island café resulted in my use of Gaelic throughout — and the waitress's persistent use of English in reply. No amount of persuasion or cajolery could prompt her to deal with the bill or count out the change in Gaelic. Such was just not done.

As autumn succeeds summer, days shorten, visitors rapidly thin out, the island ferry returns to its winter schedule. Depending on the weather final harvests are gathered in. Popular camping sites on the west coast are rapidly denuded of tents and caravans. Children have long since been at school: since the third week of August. The tempo of life slows again. Public entertainments are again scarce.

The island community supports a number of voluntary societies of various sorts: Agricultural Societies for North and South Harris, Women's Rural Institutes in both areas, clubs for badminton, football, angling, sea angling, a gun club, a craft guild, a masonic lodge, hall committees in Tarbert and Leverburgh, a community association on Scalpay, the North Harris Mutual Improvement Association, a fishery board, two youth clubs, cadet and observer corps, guides, funeral clubs and a 'welcome home' fund which was originally founded to provide a public welcome for returning servicemen (it was wound up in 1973, its assets being used to purchase a motor hearse). There is a local branch of the teachers' union, the Educational Institute of Scotland and, with Lewis, a local branch of the Lord's Day Observance Society. A Council of Social Service is active and until 1975 a District Council and an Island District Education Sub-committee were extant. Committee meetings and the organisation of society events involves a steady application of sparetime service on the part of office-bearers and committee members. Outsiders who have settled in Harris are drawn into this work. It seems almost as though they are drawn in by locals, sponsored and promoted as though a tradition of 'noblesse oblige' is expected of them. There is no truly resident 'laird'. The superior of the North Harris estate lives throughout most of the year in the East Midlands of England. A small number of retired professionals has settled in Harris. They are chiefly English and they are, together with other 'outsiders' settling on the island, often encountered amongst the leadership and active membership of clubs, societies and official bodies. Thus within the domain of committee work there is an almost instrumental necessity to use English.

Meetings of the district council and education sub-committee (before 1973 when a number of English 'settlers' were elected) were conducted in English although the membership was probably entirely Gaelic-speaking. At times the district clerk might make an aside in Gaelic to a member more expressively to make or further elucidate

a point; the only Gaelic used was by the minister for a prayer or
'*beannachdan*' said in farewell. Within some committees more Gaelic
might in fact be used: between members for sotto voce private discussion or, as at another committee I attended, for the chairman to
persuade members to take on particular jobs at an event. In this
latter case Gaelic entered those exchanges involving mutual assistance, group support and solidary expectancy and switching to
English occurred whenever technicalities (such as purchasing and
storing gallon tins of ice cream) were discussed. On the whole,
though, club and society life is preponderantly anglicising in its
effects. Public meetings, club and society dinners, dances and
the more formal events, and all public speeches, are in English.
Only at less formal dances and amongst the audience (or the 'crowd'
at games, football and sheepdog trial meetings) will a lot of Gaelic
be heard.

The institution of the old-fashioned *céilidh* is rare. But there
are particular houses where neighbours tend to gather — principally
for gossip. In one case the household from choice has no television
set and members of the household and visiting neighbours from time
to time sing, and keep alive a repertoire of traditional songs, many
of which have been locally composed. The recent death of Mrs
MacSween, Scarista, means that there are no local bards actively
composing on Harris today, although the Scalpay bard D.M. Morrison
is active.

During winter protracted periods of bad weather reduce outside
contacts very drastically. Frequent hurricane-force winds, torren-
tial rain and, from time to time, snow keep older folk and children
indoors for days on end. The traditional Gaelic culture with its
institution of the *céilidh*, the popular folk tale and the epic folk-
song or Ossianic ballad, these were all cultural supports to a
people struggling against the elements during long dark winters. In
their absence, as they have lapsed into desuetude, it really seems
as though a psychological and cultural collapse has occurred within
the community. The region suffers the highest rates of depressive
mental illness (and of alcoholism) recorded nationally. The broadcast media are an ineffective substitute for the old community
culture. The rate of admissions to Craig Dunain (the county's
mental hospital outside Inverness) rises as winter progresses.
'White Settlers' take the opportunity to winter elsewhere.

Public entertainments are few, but for those with the ability
and desire to reach them the bars of the two island hotels do good
trade particularly on Friday evenings. Within the more remote of
these at any rate there is an interesting social patterning of the
drinking space: the inner 'long' bar fills with local men, all
standing and the exchanges animated and all in Gaelic. The outer
bar is the only one in which women are really accepted: a few
settles are provided for seating and here are to be found some of
the younger women and their boyfriends. Virtually in the doorway
between them is the 'respectable' drinking area served by a corner
of the long bar. Here are to be found the more locally integrated
of the outside settlers and the island entrepreneurs. Conversation
here is in English. These gradations are not found at the other
hotel which provides a 'long bar' or public-type bar, a saloon or
private bar, and in the hotel proper a cocktail lounge. As may be

expected the long bar is local and Gaelic, the saloon is respectable, mixed in clientele and language, women are welcomed here. The cluster of standing local males around the bar tends towards a more expressive use of Gaelic. The carpeted cocktail lounge is primarily for hotel residents, visitors and the upper social strata. Here English predominates.

Until 10 p.m. the bars provide one of the few available opportunities for social contacts of the winter period (apart from evening classes, badminton clubs and the occasional dance and society meeting). The evening — especially on Fridays — will be bright, lively, convivial and Gaelic. As 10 p.m. approaches 'carry-outs' may be ordered and the conviviality may continue in a private house nearby.

Christmas has only recently become acknowledged in the community. It is not celebrated as a religious observance within the practices of the more conservative island Calvinism. *Oidhche Challuinn* (New Year's Eve) and Hogmanay are still the more important mid-winder festivity. The practice of New Year's visiting is still well kept up, although 'guising' at the New Year amongst the island's children is really now dead. (It is moribund also at Halloween: there are few areas where sufficient numbers of children enable viable peer-groups to perpetuate the rhymes, games and customs.) Neighbour and family visiting may continue for some days into the New Year. 'First-footing' with the customary dram continues. This provides a welcome focus of social intercourse in the darkest phase of the year. Children and students returning home for the midwinter vacation look forward to — and enjoy in retrospect — the contacts with community, family and friends that this custom affords.

The period between New Year and Easter is the dullest and most difficult of the island year. The winter seems scarcely to abate. February is likely to be the coldest month. Bad weather is persistent. For the more religiously inclined, communions in different parts of the island provide foci for renewed social contact. Within this period admissions for the treatment of depression reach their peak.

As days lengthen preparations may get under way for sowing and other croft-work. About Easter time the opportunity is taken with the first of the periods of good weather to commence peat-cutting. Groups of neighbouring families again set out to work together.

CONCLUSION

The 'Highland way of life' and Gaelic culture are from time to time questioned as viably continuing under contemporary conditions. As can be seen above, the island community of Harris evidences many aspects of social life which distinguish it from the 'mainstream' or 'core' society of modern Britain.

There is a general feeling of distinctiveness compounded of awareness of a local language and its attendant linguistic culture, of distinctive religious affiliations and observances, of the continued integrity of the crofting practice in agriculture and of the retention of distinctive customs of social life. As none of these institutions prevents community members from participation or movement within the mass culture, the 'Highland way of life' or Gaelic

culture may be regarded as a local option (like the veto poll):   it
is always there for people to use, to fall back upon and to choose
between.

There is, therefore, a local culture and a local solidary community life. Although particular aspects of local culture have
lapsed into desuetude (e.g. children's games), a generally coherent
and viable local culture is still demonstrable. At the foundation
of this there is a strongly maintained practice of the sharing of
work throughout the community. Traditional values of politeness,
hospitality, welcoming the stranger, and deference to a local un-
official decision-making gerontocracy are all strongly continuing.
Enjoyment of Gaelic village bards, Gaelic songs and oral culture
persist. Worship in Gaelic is general in home and church.

The extent to which an autonomous sub-culture remains a feature
of community life is problematic. The institution of education is
probably the most crucial factor in the processes affecting local
society. External pressures and influences are very strong — yet
local Gaelic culture has in certain instances been able to with-
stand and adapt in the face of them. The school operates within the
dimensions of the local community. The operation of the school will
be examined to illustrate those ways in which it is supportive of
the local culture and has been able to substitute for deficiencies.
It will also be seen to operate as means of shaping local society
physically: selecting, promoting and exporting sections of the
child population and encouraging definite demographic effects within
the population structure of the island community. The following
chapters indicate the importance of the school as an agent of control
operating at symbolic and physical levels within island society.

Chapter 4

ETHNIC LANGUAGE IN EDUCATION

This chapter, and the two following, are concerned with the place of Gaelic in the education system and the operation of the school as an agency of social control within the social structure of communities such as Harris.

An analysis of the function of the school is crucial to an understanding of social processes in bilingual communities. The ways in which the two languages are used in the school curriculum are relevant to the understanding of symbolic aspects of the local culture and its values. The relationships between the two languages within the school symbolise and epitomise — and may be held to affect — power relationships within the local community whereby intrusive institutions import new values upon the local community and local institutions conserve local values. Within the bilingual community such relationships are realised within the socially-sanctioned usages of the two languages.

On another level the school as an institution effects physical control over the dimensions of the local community. Selection at the secondary stage involves a move away from the home community for the academically brighter children. They are socialised into early separation from the home and prepared for eventual migration away from their community. Younger people displaying intelligence, leadership potential and readiness to innovate tend to be removed, and so both social structure and the qualities of social life are affected by the operation of the school as a social institution.

GAELIC IN THE EDUCATION SYSTEM

Until 1975 Harris was administered as part of the Inverness-shire education authority: a sprawling and sparsely populated county extending from the uninhabited Rockall and St Kilda in mid-Atlantic across the southern Outer Hebrides to the isolated peninsulas and glens of the northwest mainland and the North Sea coastlands east of Inverness. Administration was centred at Inverness and advisory staff were based there. Hence there are considerable administrative problems for an area like Harris out on the periphery. Since May 1975 Harris has formed part of the new Western Isles 'Island

Authority':   a 'most-purpose' authority based on Stornoway.
   In a report of 1955 Inverness-shire sought to introduce a new
Gaelic Education Scheme for its bilingual areas based upon the
recognition of Gaelic as the local community language and imple-
menting virtually for the first time the spirit of the 'Gaelic
clause' in the 1918 Education Act.(1)   It was intended that this
scheme should start in the session 1956-7 in order to implement the
revised Schools Code of 1956 regarding Gaelic (para. 21)(3) but it
did not really get under way until 1958 and its first published
scheme of instruction was not available until 1959 and was issued
to the schools of the bilingual areas in 1960.   A revised scheme
was published in 1964.(2)   The Scottish Education Department have
issued policies regarding Gaelic in the Schools in 1955 (Junior
Secondary) and 1965 (Primary).(3)
   The Junior Secondary report was written by HMIs and the Primary
report by practising teachers.   The effectiveness of Scottish educational reports has been criticised as being 'no guarantee of effective change. . . . Teachers vary in their response . . . some reject
them out of hand, some never look at them. . . . It has become clear
in Scotland that advice without follow-up . . . is likely to be
ineffectual.'(4)   Gaelic in education is a case in point.   The
physical isolation of Harris — and staffing difficulties — have
made great difficulties for HMIs and county advisers and has posed
considerable organisational and human relations problems.   Enquiring
about the implementation of these policies in one island school, I
was asked by the head teacher what these policies were, and having
outlined them, I was informed that they just could not be carried
out under the county's present requirements, moreover the documents
referred to were unknown.   Even in the schools where these policies
and reports are known the same practical difficulties apply:
pressures on time, scarcity of resources, isolation from other
teachers with similar problems and attitudes towards the language
inherited from the past.
   The aims and methods urged by these various reports are broadly
similar to comparable material in Wales.   Although undoubtedly great
improvements in the situation regarding Gaelic have occurred compared with the pre-1955 situation, bilingual education in Gaelic
Scotland is of a rather different character from that in Wales.   The
post-war years have witnessed in Wales the development of a Welsh-
language-medium schools system from nursery stages (commencing in
1949) through the primary and secondary stages and now making itself
felt in tertiary education.   Parallel with the 'Ysgolion Cymraeg'
have been the 'bilingual' schools in which both Welsh and English
have been used as teaching media, and since the Gittins Report(5)
the availability throughout the schools system of education in the
'other tongue' for all who want it.   In Mackey's typology(6) of the
bilingual school, Wales provides examples of at least six of his
types, representing the varying extent and purpose of the use of
Welsh either as community or as second language in the school
curriculum.   Harris and Gaelic Scotland display merely the one type
in which the area is bilingual but in which the home language essentially enters into the initial stages of education as a teaching
medium and typically from the later primary stage becomes a 'specific subject' only.   In comparison with Wales, bilingual education as

understood in Scotland is of far less comprehensive range. Nowhere,
for example, is Gaelic used as an 'official' or 'administrative'
language in the school. The use of Gaelic as a medium of instruction
is very rare for subjects other than 'Gaelic' and sometimes religious
education. Gaelic was encouraged by the J.S. report for such subjects as 'local geography and history, music, nature study, rural
subjects, homecraft and games' (p. 275). This does occur within the
Harris schools but typically as an activity within the 'Gaelic'
lesson, rather than in the geography or history lesson as such. The
education authority in its recruitment and staffing policy does not
appear fully to realise the implication of its own bilingual education policies for the Gaelic areas, since in the secondary schools
it has appointed monoglot English-only staff as specialist subject
teachers. The impression is strong that no one has actually gone to
see how these schemes have been developed in practice in Wales in
order to devise practical policies capable of catering for Gaelic
conditions. Research findings in other bilingual countries are not
readily appreciated, neither have facts from Wales (such as the
effective acquisition of English within Welsh-language and bilingual
schools) been generally made available. Hence in attempting to
implement a bilingual policy, residual attitudes to Gaelic on the
part of administration, teachers and parents have often unconsciously
shaped practice.

The use of Gaelic is seen as practical for teaching children to
read and in familiarising them with English as they enter the schools.
In some cases a similar effort is made to familiarise English children with Gaelic. In two or three schools this has been efficiently
achieved with conspicuous success. Otherwise — for example in larger schools — pressures upon the teacher make this difficult. One
primary teacher believed that to use Gaelic to teach reading in the
initial years would be confusing to the child 'because Gaelic was
a difficult language and its spelling was complicated and strange to
the child'. (Its spelling system is, of course, rather more regular
than English.) Time spent on Gaelic may still be seen by some concerned as less time for English and other subjects and therefore
a cause of retardation. The J.S. report denied this and urged
teachers to a more enlightened view (p. 275), and experience in
Wales suggests that time spent on Welsh whether as a first or second
language appears to have considerably improved ability in pupils'
English. Workshops and conferences for Gaelic-speaking teachers
and teachers of Gaelic have been held from time to time and sometimes cancelled. However, Lewis and Harris Gaelic teachers met
together as a body in 1973 for the furtherance of their work. It
was considered newsworthy that they resolved that their deliberative
language in all their proceedings should be Gaelic. Harris teachers
have taken a leading part in devising new material and text books
in Gaelic, in the Leverburgh school conspicuously so (its teachers
have published three books now widely used in Gaelic education).

The emphasis in the J.S. report has been upon the engendering of
confidence in Gaelic — and through Gaelic. It also emphasised
standards of correctness in usage, richness of idiom and vocabulary.
It encouraged the development of a spoken Gaelic understandable
'from Sutherland to Kintyre' (p. 279). It would have been valuable
to know something of the precise characteristics of such a standard

Gaelic. The collection of information regarding folk-life was
urged (p. 278). Harris schools have taken this up with conspicuous success: national prizes have been gained in a number of cases.
Contributions to the linguistic survey of Scotland have been forthcoming as encouraged by the report (p. 278). Altogether the response in Harris to this early report (despite local handicaps, its
small school and staff populations and its isolation) has been
remarkable. It also encouraged the more widespread use of Gaelic
as the teaching medium (p. 275) and the language of worship (p. 276)
and extra-mural activities (p. 276).

     The Inverness-shire report of 1955 focussed attention upon
changing inimical parental attitudes, for 'bilingualism gives increased intellectual power' (p. 2). Lack of prestige was to be
overcome only by 'sound and effective instruction in the schools'.
'The aim must be to make Gaelic-speaking children completely bilingual' and 'the children of Gaelic-speaking parents should be
encouraged by every means possible to learn Gaelic at school' (p. 3).
Teaching methods were to be updated and information sought from
Ireland and Wales. In this connection the BBC was urged to provide
schools broadcasts (p. 4). These were not forthcoming until 1970
and only then as the result of the secondment of an education offi-
cer to produce them with an additional subsidy from the rates to
the BBC to cover production costs. The director of education also
anticipated that Gaelic films would be available.(7) To date, to
my knowledge at least, no Gaelic film as such has ever been made by
anyone. He also anticipated a propaganda campaign amongst parents
using posters and public meetings. This does not seem conspicuously to have occurred. A daily Gaelic period was to be introduced
'as a matter, almost of sacred duty' (p. 6). Systematic instruction
in Gaelic was to commence at age nine and continue throughout the
whole course, primary and secondary. Gaelic was to be used at
school events, committees and by teachers outside the classroom
(p. 5). Two decades later, much of this has still to be implemented
in Inverness-shire schools.

     The 1964 report was still urging schools to make the fullest use
of Gaelic as an educational instrument and to engender confidence
in Gaelic language and culture. Its aims were: (a) the general
educational development of the Gaelic-speaking pupil, and (b) the
perpetuation of Gaelic as a spoken language (p. 3). There should
be a formal Gaelic lesson of at least 30 minutes daily — but there
should be no limit to the use of Gaelic as a teaching medium together with English for 'Scripture, local geography, history,
nature study, games and art' at least (p. 4). As liberal a use of
Gaelic as practicable should be made in all school activities (p. 5).
The report comprises a fairly detailed teaching scheme for Gaelic
year by year throughout the primary stages, with many practical
suggestions for topics, activities, projects and material.

     The 1965 SED report charges the primary school with the duties
to maintain and develop Gaelic as a living means of communication
and expression (p. 199). Gaelic-speaking children have to be
taught English, but it would be absurd that such children should
have their early lessons in reading and number in English. Although
teachers in the Gaelic area were keen to introduce reading in
English early, the report urged mastery of the mechanics of reading

through the medium of Gaelic — and subsequently the two languages could 'support each other' in developing comprehension. Formal translation was to be avoided and encouragement given to use fluent Gaelic-speakers to develop oral confidence. Whilst rigid correctness of spelling was not a prime objective this was to be developed by reading and by a variety of approaches in writing: diaries, magazines, work books and letters. Drama, singing and recitation were to play their part in developing oral Gaelic — but above all the living character of Gaelic was to be developed by its general use as a normal medium of communication and its integration with other aspects of the curriculum. Some subjects were seen as lending themselves to such treatment, 'particularly those which have an obvious connection with the school environment . . . religious education, natural science, local history and local geography' (p. 201).

Altogether the reports provide an official encouragement towards a fully bilingual and bicultural system of education.   It is not, in general, completely realised in practice. This is not to deny the successes of Gaelic education in Harris schools: the acquisition of Gaelic by non-Gaelic children in Harris primary schools, interesting and ambitious projects in Gaelic within and beyond the suggested subject range (one rural primary school undertook a Gaelic project on the moon-shot), impressive local studies undertaken in Gaelic in the island's junior secondary schools, the production of Gaelic teaching material and the group composition by the children of plays in Gaelic, the discussion of current affairs in Gaelic undertaken by some teachers and high standards of Gaelic literacy all round. Were fully bilingual education schemes effectively implemented to subserve the aims of these various reports in causing the schools to perpetuate the Gaelic language in those cases where the home is not doing so, then the situation would have very different results from what it was in 1972. In the 1972-3 session out of 286 children in Harris primary schools only 190 (or 66.4 per cent) were Gaelic-speaking. By contrast in 1957 of 380 primary children 356 (or 93.7 per cent) had been Gaelic-speaking,(8) a decrease in language-maintenance over fifteen years of 28.8 per cent to 71.2 per cent of its former rate.

The responsibilities for development of teaching methods for Gaelic education is unclear and confused. A centre for development of methods of language teaching for all languages taught in Scottish schools has been established at Aberdeen (the Scottish Modern Languages Centre). It has a responsibility for Gaelic but has so far been inconspicuous with regard to the production of teaching materials. There is no comparison, for example, with the Welsh National Language Unit at Treforest. In any case the remit of the Aberdeen Unit is that of treating Gaelic on a par with other modern languages, i.e. as a second or foreign language. It is not intended as producing material in Gaelic for general educational purposes. The equivalent of the Schools Council in Scotland is the Consultative Committee on the Curriculum appointed by the SED and chaired by its permanent secretary. The more centralised arrangements for curricular reform in Scotland, as compared with England, has not meant a more direct implementation of education department policy so far as Gaelic education is concerned. The consultative committee has, as yet, given little concern to Gaelic. This is not surprising

when the cost of effective research and development schemes for
Welsh in education, as financed by the Schools Council, had by
1975 topped £245,000 and was involving the secondment of increasing numbers of serving teachers.

The direct links between the Scottish Education Department and
the colleges of education have not resulted in any explicit quota
scheme for the education of teachers of Gaelic or of teachers
through the medium of Gaelic. A circulation of the Scottish colleges of education produced the distinct impression that the latter
had received little general attention in most colleges: the need
specifically to prepare teachers not 'of Gaelic' but 'of Gaelic-
speaking pupils', to teach not 'Gaelic' but other specific subjects
through the medium of Gaelic in line with official Scottish Education Department policies seemed to be unrealised. One college
stated that some of its Gaelic-speaking students might follow other
specialisations such as art, physical education or music and then
this alone would be sufficient qualification for them to teach in
a Gaelic-speaking area. The point of specifically discovering or
recruiting and then specifically preparing such students did not
appear to be realised by this college. Another college replied
that there was no special provision for Gaelic-speaking students,
'the problem had never arisen *which may not be surprising in view*
of the fact that we train only teachers of Physical Education. We
would make special provision, if there were any need, as we do have
members of staff who speak Gaelic.' Another college commented that
there were 'some few students from Gaelic-speaking areas, who appear
to have returned home to teach, the number has never at any time
been significant enough to warrant special treatment.' Altogether
some three of the ten colleges of education reported that they prepared teachers of Gaelic: Aberdeen, Jordanhill and Notre Dame.

The education authorities complain from time to time of the
difficulties in attracting qualified staff — including teachers of
Gaelic — for the Gaelic areas. These are in general areas which
qualify for the 'remote area' and 'island' allowances in the salary
awards. In 1972 two recently-qualified Gaelic-speaking primary
teachers from the Inverness-shire islands sought employment in the
home area and were unsuccessful in gaining employment. At the same
time two non-Gaelic-speaking English primary teachers were appointed
to one of the Harris schools. The issue developed into a public
scandal in the local newspapers and was featured on the Gaelic
monthly current affairs programme on television, 'Bonn Comhraidh'.
At the same time one of the colleges of education reported 'students
who qualify for Gaelic in the secondary schools are finding it
extremely difficult to get employment teaching Gaelic. Unless they
have at least one other main subject to offer, their chances of
employment are nil . . . and consequently abandon it.' Particular
difficulties have been experienced in Harris in finding a qualified
teacher of music for the island schools and for a few years the
island was without a teacher of physical education. The authority
complains that it is unable to find these specialist teachers — even
following advertisement in the educational press. There is clearly
the need for an active recruitment policy on the part of the authority and some quantified assessment of the educational needs of
the bilingual area. At the present time manpower planning for

staffing as it affects parts of the area such as Harris is on a
rather hit-or-miss basis. If, for example, a music teacher is
recruited for Harris he is not very likely to be Gaelic-speaking or
to have any particular knowledge or awareness of the unique musical
culture of the Gaelic community.

Such practical difficulties of provision of teaching services
are acknowledged in an HMIs report of 1973 (published in 1974).(9)
The report points out that there is no teachers' centre maintained
by the authority in Inverness-shire and if there were it would of
necessity need to be residential. However, residential courses
had been organised at Dingwall, Strathpeffer and Inverness, although
owing to staffing difficulties in the remote areas, the county's
teachers have been under-represented on national in-service
courses.(10)   Groups of teachers of Gaelic in Harris and elsewhere
have been developing teaching material.(11)   The report draws
attention to the development of schools broadcasting in Gaelic
which Inverness-shire and Ross-shire subsidised from the rates.(12)
Teachers of the primary pupils are being 'encouraged to make the
widest possible use of Gaelic in class,(13) whilst through conferences of secondary teachers in Uist and Barra new courses have
been planned for non-certificate pupils in SIII and SIV 'assuming
that many topics, particularly those of a local scientific and geographical nature, should be handled in Gaelic as much as English.
A similar approach is evident in the Harris Secondary Schools.'(14)

The report proceeds to note that
there are indications of a move towards the treatment of Gaelic
in both primary and secondary schools as a living language to be
used for both study and pleasure and not as a separate academic
discipline. The most successful results have been obtained in
primary schools where Gaelic has been used in a natural way
alongside English for a wide range of activities and studies,
and where the skills of speaking, reading and writing have been
exercised and improved, usually in a local context.(15)

Bernstein has drawn attention to the way in which weak classification and framing of educational knowledge and their embodiment
in 'integrated' types of educational knowledge code may typically
be exemplified in low-status areas of the educational system.(16)
Moreover, the contrasted 'collection' type of educational knowledge
code in which classification, the separation of subject areas by
more rigid demarcations, has the property that as the children
progress through the school system they 'become increasingly different from others . . . specialisation very soon reveals *difference
from* rather than communality with'.(17)   Gaelic in these cases
tends to be a low-status educational area.

It is clear that for the 'non-certificate' course pupil there is
no pressing social necessity for him to be rendered particularly
'different from' his fellows. Indeed if he is to remain to live
and work within the Gaelic home area, it may be argued that socially
it is more functional for him to maintain 'communality with' his
peers. In this regard it may be that the schools system is moving
towards a position more supportive of the local culture than here-
tofore.

The report concludes by noting that, 'The wishes of parents have
been sympathetically considered in the provision of education as

near home as possible, and in the maintenance of Gaelic teaching to
native speakers and its promotion in other areas.'(18)   Earlier,
attention had been drawn to the fact that small primary schools
such as Northton in Harris had been retained as the result of
parents' express wishes.(19)   In general the tone of the report is
sympathetic to the maintenance of Gaelic language and culture, as,
for example, in its observation that, 'A heritage of music and literature maintains itself now with difficulty in the face of the mass
media, the attractions of urban careers and amenities and the influx
of tourists, soldiers and construction workers'.(20)   Such sympathetic tone is scarcely surprising as the anonymous author is
undoubtedly Murdo Macleod, Senior HMI in the area, himself a Gaelic-
speaker and an important contributor to the literature of Gaelic in
education.
     Reference has already been made to the study 'Gaelic-speaking
Children in Highland Schools'.(21)   The following studies of the
primary and secondary stages of education in Harris utilise data
derived from that report, and data derived from my own re-issue of
its questionnaires as a part of the present study, some fifteen
years later.   The original report urged that its surveys should be
utilised as a starting-point or base-line for further studies.(22)
The report acknowledged that its 'surveys have simply been surveys'
and did not claim that beyond providing a factual and up-to-date
description of the contemporary bilingual situation the investigation represented any study in depth of the bilingual problem in
Gaelic-speaking Scotland.(23)   The authors of the report felt it
would be a misfortune if the opportunity were not taken more adequately to explore the situation whilst it still remained.   There
have not been a large number of studies of Gaelic in education
following this report but those few have been noteworthy: Finlay
Macleod's study of cognitive performance of bilingual children in
Lewis,(24)   Vernon's studies of intelligence amongst children in
Lewis,(25)   and Morrison's application of a Gaelic translation of
the WISC test,(26)   a reminder of the truth that such material
'cannot simply be borrowed from other situations.   They have to
be specially made and refined for use in this particular area.'(27)
     The focus of interest upon these problems in Scotland has been
chiefly psychological until recently.   The area and the field of
enquiry have not attracted much sociological or sociolinguistic
attention.   The 1961 SCRE report probably conceived the dimensions
of the problem more at a psychologistic level than at any other.
It called for the development of suitable Gaelic linguistic scales,
word recognition and vocabulary tests, verbal and non-verbal intelligence tests and standardised attainment tests: the recognised
battery of devices for psychological measurement.   The report had
claimed to have recognised the realities of rapid language-shift
('As the figures for Sutherland show . . . a language can virtually
disappear in a community between one generation and the next but
one').(28)   The report recognised the fact that 'although a language
may continue to be spoken by the older people among themselves, their
children may find no cause to use it.'(29)   It also alluded to such
factors underlying the decline of Gaelic as a spoken language as
'the position of Gaelic in the home, the position of Gaelic in the
community, and the influence of socio-economic factors'.(30)   A

relationship between socio-economic or 'occupational' class of
parent and incidence of ability in Gaelic if the children within the
bilingual area was suggested but not particularised: 'the figures
. . . reveal a relation between occupation and first language in
this area which is greater than might be due to chance. Beyond that
it is unsafe to draw conclusions. It is not possible to say what
socio-economic factors are at work and what effect these are having
but that they are affecting the bilingual situation is undoubted.'
(31) The report saw the process of language-shift in terms of a
'pale' spreading out from ports and urban centres on the islands
from whence the influence of the English language inexorably
spreads.(32) 'The community, the playground and school, and finally
the home represent the successive stages in this development.'(33)
The report saw the implementation of provision for Gaelic in the
schools after the 1918 Education Act as seemingly sufficient.
'Nevertheless, the hopes which were raised by the introduction of
the 1918 clause have not been realised. It is a fact that the
present educational provision for the teaching of Gaelic has failed
to increase the number of Gaelic speakers. It is apparently power-
less, at least in the present form, to prevent the continued fall
in number.'(34)
    In all of these points the report shows some sensitivity towards
and awareness of sociological issues and approaches to the problem.
But it does not show any ability to gear itself to the problem beyond that of urging greater attention 'in depth' by 'more specialised
studies'.(35) The report is perhaps over-cautious in eschewing the
temptation to discuss on the strength of the evidence presented any
societal model or typification of social process by means of which
the relationships of language-shift may be causally associated with
socio-economic phenomena, except for the descriptive model of the
'pale' (or 'bridge-head') process referred to above. The essentially
descriptive model is very weak as an explicative tool. It does
not say why or how English should spread at the expense of Gaelic,
neither does it explain why the tempo should increase over time but
reach particular stages at different times in ostensibly similar
areas. The approach to the problem by a very pessimistic view of
the efficacy of Gaelic in the schools either in increasing the number of speakers or halting their decline(36) is disconcertingly
naive, from a demographic perspective. For all we know, one way or
the other, the use of educational policy 'as a *conscious* instrument'
for the purpose of preserving or restoring a minority language in
the face of the cultural pressure of mass-society may not have been
without effect.(37) The report states that 'however sufficient the
present educational provision may be it is having little effect on
the decline of Gaelic'.(38) That having been said, 'educational
provision' may hardly be regarded in any sense 'sufficient' for the
purpose. Moreover, the figures could conceal the existence of a
very real cultural support of Gaelic in the schools (and as the
present study suggests, some small but nevertheless real success in
promoting effective bilinguality amongst English monoglot children).
For the report ignores two very obvious factors having considerable
bearing on the problem: fertility and migration. Decline in birth
rates and declining child populations of the Gaelic areas will
inexorably reduce the size of the Gaelic-speaking population

whatever the language ability of successive age-cohorts. If their
numbers decrease, so must the size of the speech-community. Rates
of outward migration from the remote areas are very high. If
families leave Scotland altogether for any other part of the United
Kingdom, they cease to be enumerated on a census as 'Gaelic-speaking'. If Gaelic-speaking children proceed into the armed forces
abroad, or into the merchant navy serving outwith Scotland, they
cease similarly to be enumerated. For all we know, the school in
Gaelic Scotland might well be maintaining a viable level of ability
in Gaelic — might even in fact be causing effective ability in
Gaelic to increase in real terms. Its efforts, however, may be
reversed by an entirely extraneous factor of high net outward migration. A secondary consideration within this problem area is the
'intensity-factor'. Decline in the native population may be associated with high rates of language-maintenance. However, even if
the rate of inward migration of non-Gaelic-speakers is small or
static, there will register in the census statistics a decline in
the percentage of the Gaelic-speaking population locally.

  The questionnaires(39) devised for the surveys of 1957-8 and
1959 had obviously to be simple, manageable, capable of ready comprehension and completion by primary school teachers, first-year
secondary pupils and head teachers. The questions can, of course,
be criticised on the level of their meaning for different respondents. It would be difficult to imagine any child in an effectively
bilingual area literally having 'no knowledge' of the second language — unless it were a very recent incomer. What, however, con-
stitutes 'understanding the language', 'elementary conversation',
'simple lessons' and 'fair fluency' as used in the questions? More
important perhaps is the unproblematic and supposed homogeneity of
behaviour in a particular domain, as, for example, in the questions
relating to which language is spoken in the home to parents or
guardians, to sisters and brothers, to the teacher, to other children
and in the playground. In the complex situation of the bilingual
community the child may well be using its two languages with some
discrimination and sophistication. It is possible that English
might predominate in the home — and yet even there for Gaelic to be
used in specific circumstances (e.g. in religious worship, family
prayers and for handling moral aspects of everyday life and ethical
teaching). Different languages may even be used between different
pairs of brothers and sisters. Observation of playgrounds has
tempted me to the view that this domain elicits the production of
sounds rather than language. In any case, today it is unrealistic
to talk about 'the' language of a playground as a whole. What might
be interesting — and quite realistically possible for a teacher to
report upon — might be not what is the predominating language used
by a pupil to the teacher but in what circumstances, for what purposes and to what extent the two languages are used. Questions
were asked in the Secondary Survey concerning whether parents *can*
speak Gaelic. More to the point would have been the question, *do*
they? As between the Primary and the Secondary Surveys the definition of 'first language' varies: 'The *first* language is to be taken
as meaning the language in which the child is more at ease and the
one which he or she tends to use first in conversation' (Primary
Survey, Question 7); 'Your *first* language is to be taken as meaning

the language which you usually speak in your home' (Secondary Survey, Question 7). Really it is a misnomer to speak of a 'first' language here. Although in most cases there will be a correspondence of 'mother tongue', 'first language', 'language of conversational ease', 'language of immediate conversational response', and 'familial language', there will be cases where this equivalence is not in fact empirically the case. These children might be amongst the more interesting to study in the elucidation of the processes of language-shift. The surveys did not raise the question of attitudes to language or language-variety.

As these questionnaires — whatever their interpretation had been fifteen years earlier — had been the actual measuring device for assessing the place of Gaelic in the schools and amongst the children in Harris, I decided to reproduce them and to re-issue them as originally used. The results of the 'second-run' of these questionnaires are given in the chapters on the primary and secondary schools as a simple updating of these issues after fifteen years.

It was decided to explore the phenomena ignored or taken for granted in these surveys by other means: by questionnaires separately and somewhat later administered by an experiment using speech samples, by discussion and interviews with older secondary students. The ensuing chapters discuss the results.

In comparison with these surveys of Gaelic-speaking children in the schools of the Highlands, and more particularly of Harris, it may be apposite to review in contrast with them a recent study of the Welsh language in the schools of Wales.(40) In terms of resources the Welsh study was more comprehensive and at greater depth. It was similarly able to investigate the problem by means of a more sophisticated methodology. It represents the kind of results which might be forthcoming from the 'more specialised studies' conducted 'in depth' as called for by the Gaelic study.(41)

ATTITUDES TO WELSH AND ENGLISH IN THE SCHOOLS OF WALES(42)

This study represents the results of a research project financed by the Schools Council and carried out between 1967-71 within an overall sample of 12,000 children and a pool of 1,549 schools. The aims of the study were:

1 To establish patterns of attitude to Welsh and English in three age groups in schools throughout Wales (fourth year Juniors, second and fourth year Secondaries);
2 To determine whether there is a significant relationship between attitude to each language and attainment in it;
3 To examine some of the other factors in the language-learning situation in Wales;
4 To consider methods and materials used in the teaching of the two languages.(43)

The study comprises a workmanlike survey utilising large samples, rigorously defined in statistical terms, and applying a research methodology, involving the construction and application of Thurstone and Likert-type attitude inventories, a semantic differential test and standardised Welsh and English attainment tests. A multivariate analysis is used to assess the relationship between language attainment (principally English and second-language Welsh), sex of respondent, general ability, linguistic background, socio-economic background and attitude. The report also contains a useful study of the use of Welsh in school activities.

In comparison with the SCRE study of Gaelic-speaking children in Highland schools (which is a mere sketch in comparison and more limited methodologically), the Welsh study emphasises the very areas that the Gaelic study ignored or was so cautious in handling: attitudes of the pupils towards language, relationship between language and socio-economic factors, more detailed study of the use of ethnic language within the domain of the school.

The Welsh report rightly states that 'The task of preparing a bilingual test thus became one of equating pairs from material submitted rather than one of preparing the test in one language and translating it into the other.'(44) In this the Welsh report echoes the earlier Gaelic study, although the latter may not have nearly so clearly in mind an image of differentials in linguistic culture. The study is similarly sensitive to other cultural factors such as the difficulty in equating the concept 'upper class/lower class' readily in Welsh. (The Welsh adjective '*gwerinol*' does not convey the idea of lower or of class as it derives from '*gwerin*', the folk, the people). Again the Welsh '*cartrefol*' might yield a literal translation of 'homely' in English but the connotations of the Welsh '*cartref*', home, extend beyond those of the English concept. (45) The relationship of attitudes to language and attitudes to the speakers of the language is seen in the study as problematic. An anglicised Welsh community is reported as having a favourable attitude to the Welsh people and to the English language. 'But their attitude towards the English people, though tinged with a corresponding admiration, was also heavily weighted with dislike, resentment and fear. So that it may well be the case that, in the Welsh context, the correlation . . . between attitude towards a language and attitude towards speakers of that language does not exist.'(46) That is to say, does not *necessarily* exist, for the existence or otherwise of such a correlation must surely depend on the nature of the local linguistic culture: the nature of the ethnic consciousness of the community and the way in which language enters into social processes. Unfortunately, the report continues, 'Although it would have been of academic interest to have pursued this enquiry, it was decided not to do so for the purposes of this project.'(47) The results of the project provide such a usefully explored basis of study of the articulation of language as an institution with the value-system that it is a pity not to have extended the study into a consideration of the societal processes linking this level of explication with macro-societal processes. The study, however, might well provide a sound conceptual base for such a task to be attempted.

Likert scales were found to be unsuitable for the purposes of the study: 'The Likert scale of attitude towards English played off one language against the other, and did not present attitude towards English independently of attitude towards Welsh.'(48) The results for English and Welsh tended to come out as reciprocals or mirror-images of one another: 'A careful scrutiny of the Likert test of attitude towards English seemed to point to the possibility that

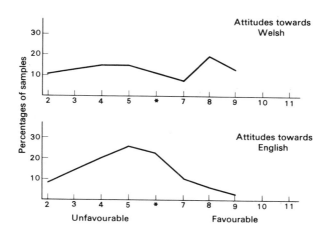

FIGURE 4.1 Frequency-distributions of attitude-scores: Thurstone
Scales, Welsh children 1969-70 (after Sharp, D. et al. (1973)
'Attitudes to Welsh and English in the Schools of Wales', London:
Macmillan, p. 54).

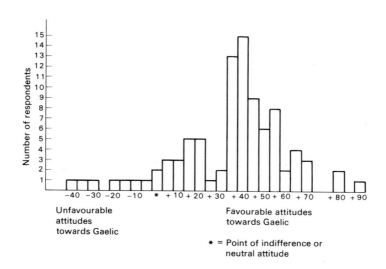

FIGURE 4.2 Frequency-distributions of attitude-scores: Likert
Scale, Harris adults, 1973, from present survey, ch. 7.

this was really a test of attitude towards Welsh in reverse.'(49)
Although the Likert test was abandoned 'as it could not test the
whole of attitude towards English as well as the Thurstone scale
could'.(50)   Nevertheless, it was felt that the Likert scale was
probably a very good measuring device for the phenomenon of language-
loyalty per se.(51)

The results of the investigation of attitudes to Welsh and
English using the Thurstone scales indicated a bimodality of atti-
tides towards Welsh in 11 of the 24 categories of types of school
by linguistic background. 'This fact, together with the relatively
low percentage figures appearing in the neutral category, is indicative of a polarisation of attitudes where Welsh is concerned.
There is a tendency to be for or against — rather than simply
indifferent, and this naturally produces a tension between groups.'
(52)   Only 2 of 24 categories showed similar bimodality with regard
to attitude to English.

Histograms illustrating the distributions of attitude-scores as
exemplified in the case of 12-year-olds in grammar schools in semi-
Welsh-speaking areas (containing 48-55 per cent Welsh-speakers) is
taken as an illustrative case.(53)   Concerning attitude to Welsh
there is a low response (around 7 per cent) at the point of indifference, a marked 'peak' at about 20 per cent at a moderately
favourable point and a well-pronounced 'hump' across several moderately unfavourable points on the scale. Attitudes towards English
are reasonably normally distributed, slightly skewed, however,
towards a slightly unfavourable point on the scale.(54)   It is
interesting to add that in the case of the investigation of attitudes to Gaelic in the present study, no such bimodal distribution
was found. It must be pointed out, though, that the present study
utilised a Likert-type scale and that this was used with a very much
smaller sample and one drawn from an adult population. Methodologically we should regard the Likert scale as almost entirely a
measuring device of language-loyalty towards the local or ethnic
language amongst native-speakers. The Gaelic distribution indicates
a preponderant 'peak' at the point of moderately favourable attitudes towards Gaelic and subsidiary 'peaks' at points of slightly
and strongly favourable attitudes. In terms of the discussion of the
Welsh results this may be indicative of lack of any pronounced
polarisation, the lack of any over-riding sense of tensions between
groups and a supportive attitude towards the local language in the
nature of a taken-for-granted type of language-maintenance rather
than a conscious, activist, overt language-loyalty.(55)

The results then, indicated to the authors of the report that a
number of factors might be operating together within the overall
attitudes towards Welsh and English. Attitude to Welsh might form
a fairly uni-dimensional phenomenon — although the report does note
that there was ready discrimination between favourable attitudes to
Welsh even amongst those unable to speak it and a reluctance to have
it forced upon anyone unwilling to acquire or use it.(56)   Whereas
attitudes towards Welsh might comprise principally a language-
loyalty factor, attitudes toward English are seen as comprising two
chief components 'one of which remains fairly constant from area to
area and age to age', namely 'objective assessment of the position
and status of the English language and its value to the . . .

speaker'.(57)   The other component appears to be the reciprocating
value placed upon English as opposed to Welsh.(58)   This latter
concept is not too well articulated by the report but it seems to
indicate the function of language as a symbol of 'groupness',
'nationism' or even nationalism in Fishman's terminology, the function termed the symbolic function of language in this study.(59)
The former component of attitudes to English cited above in the
Welsh report would seem to comprise an instrumental image of language: language seen as an instrument of wider communication, rather
then as a symbol of group loyalty and solidarity;   language principally used to transmit or to communicate information — in this
case across a wider context than the local or national community.
The Welsh report thus sees in its results not only a tension between
groups illustrated in the polarisation of attitudes towards language,
but also specifically notes a 'tension *within* individuals'(60) resulting from, as we might say, their having to handle and conceptualise varying images of and funtions of language as epitomised in
the social institutionalisation of the two languages in the bilingual community.

   From a sociolinguistic or sociological point of view, Chapter 3,
Background Information, is one of the most interesting and is tanta-
lisingly short.   The chapter provides a sketch of some aspects of
societal bilingualism within the world of the pupils;   school   subjects and specific activities within the school, extra-mural activities, parents' associations, home and community.   It is a great pity
that in these respects the report does not provide a full account of
the results that it did in fact collect.   The report provides information in some detail on attitudes and attainments in Welsh and
English for type of school, type of area (linguistically), sex of
pupil, general ability, socio-economic class, length of residence in
Wales and linguistic background of the pupil.   In this last respect
a five point scale ('English always', 'In English more often than
Welsh', 'In English and Welsh equally', 'In Welsh more often than
English', 'Welsh always') is utilised to assess the extent to which
each of the two languages was used 'in school, at play, in the home,
etc'(61)   Later discussion reveals that this 'etc.' comprises eight
'fields of usage': 'church and chapel', 'talking to teachers in
school', 'running errands', 'talking to people outside school'
(adults are intended), 'playing with friends', 'writing to friends',
'listening to radio or television', and 'private reading'.

   The results of the survey of 'fields of usage' merit similar comprehensive tabular form of publication vis-à-vis the results of the
Thurstone and Semantic Differential tests.   The report hints at an
awareness of the importance of a model of the articulation of 'the
fields of usage linking the child with the adult community . . .
and usage linking him to the rest of the child community'.(62)   The
report raises awareness of this issue, briefly alludes to it, and
drops it without providing the data it has collected to enable the
reader to hypothesise for himself.   This is unfortunate for the
sociologist of language or of education.

   The details which are given, however, indicate a decrease in use
of Welsh as children progress through the school.   They also indicate
a greater intrusion of English into domains of the pupils' extra-
mural activities in the more anglicised areas.   This is hardly

surprising but the report notes two interesting exceptions to these
principles. In the most strongly Welsh areas, Welsh-speaking pupils
at twelve-plus, in the early stages of secondary education, showed
a definite shift towards English in talking to teachers, but there
was a shift towards Welsh outside the school, and the pupils in
comprehensive schools showed a stronger 'come-back' for Welsh than
pupils in grammar or modern schools in these respects. In the
moderately Welsh or mixed areas, Welsh-speaking pupils used slightly
more Welsh in speaking to teachers at ten-plus than did Welsh-speaking pupils in the more strongly Welsh areas. In commenting upon the
findings of the report, it may seem suggestive that these two exceptions may represent the functioning of Welsh as a 'cultural prop' or
'support'. As Welsh-speaking pupils transfer into a large comprehensive in a linguistically mixed area they may more readily retain
and strengthen their relationships with Welsh-speaking friends —
and resort to Welsh to a greater extent in home life by way of com-
pensation for increasing anglicisation accompanied by the dislocation or 'culture-shock' of a new and larger school. Something of a
similar phenomenon was found in the present study with regard to
Gaelic-speaking children leaving home to reside in a hostel for the
duration of their secondary schooling.
     The Welsh study also interestingly indicates a much commoner use
of Welsh in speaking to teachers than would likely be the case with
Gaelic-speaking children at any of these ages. By the later primary
stages, Gaelic-speaking children are accustomed to using English to
teachers almost exclusively, except to answer a question specifically put in Gaelic in a Gaelic lesson. The 'Welsh' or 'bilingual'
schools represent a linguistic situation — even in the more substantially anglicised parts of Wales — where Welsh is used as an
official or administrative medium in the school and as the teaching
medium for the greater part of the curriculum. In the home and the
school there is substantial reinforcement of use of the Welsh
language — even where the community language is English. In both
of these respects, the school in Wales may be seen as very consciously providing a 'domain' within which the Welsh language may
be retained and even promoted. Schools of this type have not been
established for Gaelic-speaking areas and teachers encouraging or
prompting general use of Gaelic within the school are very rare in
Scottish bilingual situations.
     The Welsh report felt that the numbers involved and pattern of
provision of education was such that it was not possible specifically to elicit the effect of the factor of urban v. rural settings
for the school. This was so owing to the fact that centralising
policies for secondary education result in the post-junior stage
almost invariably being located in *town* rather then *countryside*
in all parts of Wales. It would be interesting, however, to examine
the data of the Welsh study for the ten-plus age-group in order to
ascertain how far across the range of domains the two languages
extend in the three linguistic divisions in urban and rural milieux.
One might hypothesise that use of Welsh would be stronger and extend
further across everyday life in rural rather than more urbanised
settings. It might be possible to utilise the results of the 'running errands' question to gauge whether Welsh was used transaction-
ally in a given community and thus to function as a sufficient

medium for the whole range of exchanges of everyday life. In this way a linkage could be made with patterns of language-use at the personal interactional level with wider societal institutions and processes.

The report concludes that 'socio-economic status of parent is highly significant at the J4 level'(i.e. at 10+), 'but tends to decrease in importance progressively in the secondary school.' (63) This may provide bases for an argument that a causal correlation may exist between favourable attitudes to Welsh, lower-status occupations and membership of the Welsh-language community within the world of the primary-aged child. As wider social pressures may be felt as the child progresses through the secondary stage, the report notes that use of Welsh tends to decrease, favourable attitudes towards English develop independently of attitudes to Welsh, but that educational experiences do provide for the child an image of Welsh language and ethnicity which are not necessarily dependent upon nor to be significantly causally correlated with the child's initial socialisation either with regard to occupational class of parent or original milieu. However, linguistic background was found to be 'the most highly significant source of variation of attitude towards both languages'.(64) This was especially so in the Welsh schools in anglicised areas, as here the choice of school was linked with deliberate choice of a family to retain familial use of the Welsh language.

The results of the survey do not enable a hypothesis to be suggested, spanning and conceptually linking microsociolinguistic phenomena and wider societal features, but it seems likely that the data provided by this survey could in fact form the basis of such an exploration.

The survey found that girls tended to a more favourable attitude to Welsh and a less favourable attitude towards English than did boys.(65) This may be a similar phenomenon to the way in which girls retain a greater commitment to Gaelic than do the boys when they are boarded away in hostels for secondary education. This may in Scotland be linked with social processes which cause young people in general to leave home for education and work elsewhere but bear more heavily upon the girls. If girls are extruded from their home situations to a greater extent than boys, there may develop a stronger compensating symbolic identification with the home language and culture as a 'prop' or 'support' in the new circumstances where they will have physically to be separated from them.

Unfortunately, with the data provided, attempts to link linguistic and social phenomena in this way can only be speculative — and the Welsh report itself rigorously avoids open speculation of this character. The following chapters of the present study focus upon the ways in which the ethnic language in Harris enters into the social world of the schoolchild at primary and secondary stages. It is hoped to indicate something of the linkages and dicontinuities of the social use of language in the school and in the wider community.

Chapter 5

GAELIC IN HARRIS PRIMARY SCHOOLS

Although educational reports have called upon the school to become the principal means of language-conservation in the Gaelic community, the school has in this situation to cope with the fact of the full range of mass-media operating almost entirely through the medium of English. This represents a very 'tall order' for the school; but recent experience in Wales indicates that it is possible to achieve success. Local teachers attribute the decline of Gaelic amongst primary-aged children to the coming of the television service, which reached the island in 1965. It was at about this time also that the introduction of the MV 'Hebrides' car-ferry started to bring substantial numbers of tourists to the area.

The decline in Gaelic language-maintenance may in part be attributable to the strengthened 'presence' of English in community life which improved communications have brought. The shift to English as a mother tongue amongst primary-aged children may, however, have commenced as early as 1952, as may be evidenced in the drop from 96.2 per cent to 88.1 per cent of the age-cohort speaking Gaelic as a mother tongue between the first two primary years in 1957-8 (Table 5.1). The 1972-3 results clearly indicate a further decline over the fifteen intervening years. If the changes in the provision of communications did initiate this shift, then their effects in bringing an audio-visual English-language 'presence' into almost every home and considerably multiplying the presence of English-speaking visitors in the summer months have clearly reinforced an already existing trend.

Table 5.1 illustrates the decline in incidence of Gaelic as a mother tongue amongst primary-school children at school in the academic year 1957-8 compared with the situation in 1972-3. The original results are as published in the Scottish Council for Research in Education (Committee for Bilingualism) report of 1961(1) and the findings are based upon questionnaires issued to primary-school teachers (and reproduced in the report). The results for 1972-3 represent the reissue of these questionnaires in as exactly comparable a manner as possible. It must be remembered that with regard to this and to subsequent findings and comparisons that the completion of the questionnaires by teachers indicates teachers' observations, views or beliefs concerning the language-situation of the

individual children in their care. However, in a community such as
Harris where class sizes are small and the teacher knows the parents
and families of her children personally, and indeed resides within
the community as a neighbour, we may be justified in ascribing
reliability to the teacher's knowledge of the home and family circumstances of the child — even within such intimate aspects of
behaviour as the use of the particular language in specific situations.

TABLE 5.1 First- or mother-tongue language-maintenance amongst
primary-aged children in Harris, 1957-73

Class	1957-8			1972-3		
	No. of children speaking Gaelic as a first language	Total	% of total speaking Gaelic as a first language	No. of children speaking Gaelic as a first language	Total	% of total speaking Gaelic as a first language
PI	52	59	88.1	29	39*	74.4
PII	50	52	96.2	29	47	61.7
PIII	48	51	94.1	28	49	51.7
PIV	53	56	94.6	24	40	60.0
PV	52	56	92.9	23	34	67.6
PVI	53	56	94.6	26	37	70.3
PVII	48	50	96.0	31	39	79.5
Total	356	380	93.7	190	285*	66.7

Source: SCRE (1961), 'Gaelic
Speaking Children in Highland
Schools', pp. 44-5

Source: returns of ques-
tionnaires to primary
teachers for surveys of
the present study

* Excludes one immigrant Urdu-speaker in Primary I at Tarbert.

Table 5.1 illustrates both the decline of the primary-aged child
population in numbers of the fifteen-year period and in particular
in the decline in the proportions which are Gaelic speaking as a
first language. (In this and in subsequent tables Scottish Education Department and the general Scottish local education authority
nomenclature is used: PI and PII correspond to the infant stage of
primary education in England and Wales; PIII-PVI to the junior
stage, PVII represents the age-group having proceeded to the first
year of secondary education in England and Wales.)
    As can be seen from Table 5.1 the situation is a general, but not
consistently even, decline year-by-year for Gaelic as a mother tongue
amongst Harris children. The drop in numbers of primary-aged children across the fifteen years is a reduction to 75 per cent of the

original figure. Even more dramatic is the drop in the proportion
who are Gaelic-speaking from 93.7 per cent (closely comparable with
the incidence of Gaelic in the population as a whole at that time)
to 66.7 per cent (strictly speaking 66.4 per cent): a decline to
71.1 per cent of the proportion who could speak Gaelic fifteen years
previously). As may be expected, the rural population outside the
island capital shows the greater decline in primary-school population over this period, and school closures have concentrated the
primary-aged children to a lesser extent at Leverburgh but to a much
more marked extent at Tarbert. Within the more rural areas Gaelic
has been maintained to a much greater extent as the mother tongue
amongst primary-aged children. If the returns for the rural schools
are separated from the returns for Tarbert a significant difference
emerges which can be clearly seen in Table 5.2.

TABLE 5.2 First- or mother-tongue language amongst primary-aged
children at Tarbert and in rural areas, 1972-3

School attended	No. of children speaking Gaelic as a first language	No. of children speaking English as a first language	Total	% of total speaking Gaelic as a first language
Tarbert	38	73	111	52.1
Rural areas schools combined	152	23	175	86.9
Totals	190	96	286	66.43

χ^2 = 84.3436 Significant below 0.001 level at 1 degree of freedom.

As there has been a policy of closing smaller rural primary-only
schools in recent years primary-aged children from outlying areas
have been brought to more 'centrally' located schools by bus.
Between 1965-72 the total Harris school roll as notified by head
teachers annually to the local education authority rose from 480 to
488 children. The roll increased from 288 to 344 at Tarbert and
Leverburgh combined and decreased from the 192 in ten other schools
in 1965 to 144 in the remaining six schools in 1972. Fourteen out of
the thirty-three children in classes Primary I and II at Tarbert
travelled in from outlying villages in 1972-3. These children are
noticeably more strongly Gaelic-speaking than the Tarbert resident
children, as may be seen from Table 5.3 in which the rural children
in Primary classes I and II resident outside Tarbert have been
separated from those living within Tarbert. The association of
mother tongue with area of residence is still very significant in
this case (Table 5.3).
However, as returns were only available for the Primary I and II
groups, it is not possible to separate the rural children coming in
to school at Tarbert from the children resident in Tarbert for each
of the other age-groups. However, it is suggested, although the

numbers are small, that these children form something of an intermediate group between the rural children attending a rural school
amongst whom incidence of Gaelic as a mother tongue is high and the
Tarbert-resident children amongst whom Gaelic language-maintenance
is low.

TABLE 5.3 First- or mother-tongue language-maintenance amongst
Primary I and II attending school at Tarbert, 1972-3

	Gaelic as first language	English as first language	Total	% Gaelic-speaking
Resident in Tarbert	5	14	19	26.3
Resident outside	9	5	14	64.3
Totals	14	19	33	42.4

χ^2 = 4.7576 Significant below 0.05 level at 1 degree of freedom.

Having considered how Gaelic language-maintenance amongst
primary-aged children is distributed geographically or spatially
within the island community, we may attempt to depict in greater
detail how language-maintenance has featured amongst the younger
school-aged children over time. Table 5.4 attempts to collate all
the available data illustrating the changing incidence of Gaelic
amongst the younger school-aged population, in comparison with the
population as a whole. The sequence of results is set out in Table
5.4 so that the successive age-cohorts follow one another down the
table and the census findings are interpolated as closely as possible
to the year of birth of the corresponding age-group, for purposes of
easy comparison. Thus we are able to gain a clear impression of the
general decline in incidence of Gaelic amongst school-aged children
in Harris over a period of some twenty years.

Although there is some variation from the overall trend in
Table 5.4, the results clearly indicate that there is a more pronounced downward trend amongst children and the school-aged population than there is amongst the population as a whole. Societal
language-shift appears to have commenced during the period since
1951 as an increasing number of families ceased to pass Gaelic to
the ensuing generation in the process of socialisation. Alternatively, it might be argued that the school is itself an anglicising
agency. However, in the earlier period, at least, the school was
passive in its stance regarding language. Children arrived at
school Gaelic-speaking in the main or English-speaking. Today increasing numbers of children are entering school already bilingual
and it is only in recent years that any number of children may be
said to have shifted from Gaelic to English *as a first language*
during the course of their school career. The school is today more
officially supportive of Gaelic and has had some success in promoting
ability in Gaelic amongst English mother-tongue pupils. On the other
hand, there are definite, though few, instances of children shifting
from Gaelic as a first language in circumstances where doubtless a

TABLE 5.4 Language-maintenance amongst schoolchildren and the general population: Harris, 1951-74

Source		Gaelic-speakers amongst school-age children in forms				Gaelic-speakers amongst total population		Gaelic-speakers amongst population aged 3 years and over	
		All Gaelic-speakers		Native Gaelic-speakers only					
		Number	%	Number	%	Number	%	Number	%
1958-9 Survey	SI	53	96.4	49	89.1				
1957-8 Survey	PVII			48	96.0				
	PVI			53	94.6				
	PV			52	92.9				
	PIV			53	94.6				
	PIII			48	94.1				
1951 Census						3,668	91.9	3,668	96.5 (estimated)
1957-8 Survey	PII ⎫ PI ⎬	105	95.5	50 / 52	96.2 / 88.1				
1972-3 Survey	SIV			27	85.2				
	SIII			26	80.0				
	SII			36	72.2				
	SI	41	95.3	35	81.4				(includes one non-Gaelic-speaking girl away at Stornoway)
			(97.6)		(83.3)				(excludes one non-Gaelic-speaking girl away at Stornoway)

1973-4 Survey	SI	35	85.4	28	68.3
1961 Census		2,940	89.5	2,940	93.6
1972-3 Survey	PVII			31	79.5
	PVI			26	70.3
	PV			23	67.6
	PIV			24	60.0
	PIII			28	51.7
	PII	70	81.4	29	61.7
	PI			29	74.4
1971 Census		2,498	87.4	2,498	92.3
				(estimate for Harris less St Kilda)	

Sources: Census volumes for Gaelic; 1957-8 and 1958-9 Surveys from SCRE Report, (1961), 'Gaelic-speaking Children in Highland Schools', Table III, p. 29, The Bilingual Area in Greater Detail and Table XII, p. 52.
1972-3 and 1973-4 Surveys: own Surveys (results of questionnaires to primary and secondary school teachers and first-year secondary pupils).

combination of family, scholastic and communal pressures irresistably acted together in favour of English.

Having noted locational and chronological factors in operation, it will be valuable next to consider such social factors as occupational class of parent. In terms of 'class structure', Harris is not greatly differentiated. The community is face-to-face and relatively homogenous. There are no great discontinuities in social composition of the population except that some formal differentiation in occupational status or prestige may be attributed to various occupational levels or gradings. The present study has utilised the same gradings which were used by the 1957-8 survey, as this will enable comparisons to be readily effected. Harris has no true 'middle class'. There are a small number of professionals (and others, chiefly retired, who may be said to be of mainland and middle-class origins) who comprise a small middle-class element in the population. There may also be said to be a lower-working-class level comprising the non-crofter casual manual labourer or 'unemployed' categories. We shall now turn to a consideration of this factor, as illustrated in Table 5.5, where the association between mother tongue of the younger primary school-aged children and the occupational categories of their parents is detailed.

The incidence of Gaelic as a mother tongue amongst schoolchildren clearly and significantly differs with regard to occupational class of parent. That there is a relationship between occupational class on the one hand and the incidence of Gaelic as a mother tongue amongst Harris children is undoubtedly clear. However, this relationship is probably far from simple. Her Majesty's Inspector of Schools for Gaelic in the northern area has the common-sense hypothesis that if Gaelic-speakers are moved into a street of houses, this in itself will be sufficient to induce language-shift to English. That there is some truth here is borne out by the results in Tarbert where the majority of the English mother-tongue group reside in areas of local authority housing (but not in similar areas of West Tarbert). What may in fact be operating here are deliberate choices amongst bilingual parents of the lower socio-economic levels to bring up children solely through the medium of English. There are still residual beliefs that Gaelic 'holds children back'. As parents desire improved life-chances for their children so they may seek to assist this by withholding their children from exposure to Gaelic. Gaelic language-maintenance is stronger amongst categories D, E, F, G, representing the 'lower' occupational categories. The 1957-8 SCRE survey of the bilingual area as a whole had overlooked the fact that its results showed a weaker incidence of Gaelic within the lowest category G (parent unemployed) than for the two 'higher' categories immediately 'above' it: F (manual workers) and E (agriculture and forestry). Category C (commercial, including shopkeepers) had also been irregular, evidencing the weakest incidence of Gaelic of all.(2)   The present results from a much smaller sample are probably too inconclusive for precise conclusions but certainly show a similar general tendency. In the present sample Gaelic is weakest in the professional category A.

TABLE 5.5 Association between mother tongue and occupational class: Harris schoolchildren, 1972-3 and 1973-4

Occupational class	PI and PII 1972-3**			SI 1972-3			SI 1973-4		
	Gaelic	English	Total	Gaelic	English	Total	Gaelic	English	Total
A (Professional)	1	6	7	0	1	1	0	2	2
B (Public service)	3	3	6	2	1*	3	1	3	4
C (Commercial)	4	5	9	0	0	0	0	1	1
D (Technical)	9	5	14	2	2	4	6	4	10
E (Agricultural)	18	3	21	13	2	15	6	1	7
F (Manual)	22	4	26	16	1	17	14	2	16
G (Unemployed)	2	1	3	3	0	3	1	0	1
Totals	59	27	86	36	6	43	28	13	43

$*\chi^2 = 19.148$
Significant below
0.005 level at 6
degrees of freedom

$\chi^2 = 11.1475$
Significant below
0.05 level at 5
degrees of freedom

$\chi^2 = 14.4128$
Significant below
0.05 level at 6
degrees of freedom

*   includes one girl attending at Stornoway (E)

** excludes three absentees at Tarbert

Note 1: A non-Gaelic-speaking child whose first language was Urdu is included as an English-speaker in the figures for Category C in the PI and PII 1972-3 sample.

Note 2: A Professional - doctors, trained nurses, ministers of religion, teachers, lawyers, bankers;
B Civil and public servants - Post Office officials, police, harbourmasters, county officials, missionaries;
C Commercial - shopkeepers;
D Technical (demanding apprenticeship) - garage workers, plumbers, joiners, electricians, seaweed factory technicians, hydro-electric technicians, weavers, seamen;
E Agriculture and forestry - large farms, small farms and crofts;
F Manual workers - hydro-electric labourers, fishermen, drivers, ferrymen;
G Unemployed.

   The strongest categories for Gaelic comprise E (agricultural —
including the most typical occupational category, 'crofter') and F
(manual, including the second most typical occupational category,
'fisherman'). These categories contain 102 of the instances, or
almost two-thirds of the sample, representing the children of the
preponderant social 'core' of the island's community. Here, as
expected, maintenance of Gaelic as a community language is best
evidenced.
   Concerning the relationship between occupational class and first
language, the SCRE report 'Gaelic-speaking Children in Highland
Schools' commented,

   That there is some connection is definitely shown. . . . It is
   apparent . . . that category E, which includes crofting . . .
   accounts for proportionately more of the Gaelic group than it
   does of the English group. . . . There are also proportionately
   more of classes A (professional), B (clerical) and C (commercial)
   in the English group. When the figures in the table are examined
   statistically using the chisquare test, they reveal a relation
   between occupation and first language in this area which is
   greater than may be due to chance. Beyond that it is unsafe to
   draw conclusions.(3)

   The SCRE survey was incorrect in stating that category E was
'also the most important category connected with either language'.(4)
   For the English mother-tongue group, this was not the case so
far as absolute numbers were concerned, for category D (technical)
contained the highest number of native English-speakers (162),
whilst category C (commercial) contained the highest proportion of
this group (77.6 per cent).(5)

TABLE 5.6 Strength of Gaelic language-maintenance amongst sampled
Harris schoolchildren by occupational class of parent

Occupational class	Harris schoolchildren		Total		
	1972-3 and 1973-4			Gaelic-speaking %	English-speaking %
	Gaelic-speaking	English-speaking			
A (Professional)	1	9	10	10.0	90.0
B (Public servants)	6	7	13	46.2	53.8
C (Commercial)	4	6	10	40.0	60.0
D (Technical)	17	11	28	60.7	39.3
E (Agricultural)	37	6	43	86.0	14.0
F (Manual)	52	7	59	88.1	11.9
G (Unemployed)	6	1	7	85.7	14.3
Totals	123	47	170	73.4	27.6

χ^2 = 43.0281 Significant below 0.001 level at 6 degrees of freedom

The results for Harris are given in Table 5.6. Here the sample comprises each of the school-aged groups surveyed in 1972-3 and 1973-4 aggregated together. These children represent with hardly any exceptions each child in attendance at Harris schools in 1972-3 at the PI and PII (infants) stage (aged 5-7), the PVII (top junior stage (aged 11-12) which proceeded to secondary education as SI in 1973-4) and the SI stage (12-13 years). Although a complete sample of all Harris primary schoolchildren was not obtained in this study it may be felt that these samples comprising the age-groups spanning the extremes of the primary stage may be regarded as representative.

The weakest categories for Gaelic mother-tongue maintenance are the three highest groups in terms of occupational prestige-rating (A - professional, B - public servants, C - commercial). As it is from these occupational categories that the majority of the non-native incoming element of the resident population is drawn we may not be justified in discussing Gaelic language-maintenance for such cases as these families are of English mother tongue and hardly ever acquire Gaelic. If the children of these incoming families are removed from the sample, the remainder comprises the native Harris population amongst whom the incidence of Gaelic is thus understandably strengthened. This relative strengthening affects the groups in terms of percentage points improvement as follows: A (professional) 6.6; B (public servants) 3.8; C (commercial) 17.2; D (technical) 4.7. The numbers involved are small and it would be unjustifiable to adduce any great significance to these comparisons. The improvements within categories A and C are owing to the sample containing the children of local ministers and shopkeepers. Table 5.7 indicates the relative strength of Gaelic language-maintenance across the occupational social spectrum.

TABLE 5.7   Incidence of Gaelic mother tongue for native Harris school population, 1972-4 samples

Occupational class	Gaelic-speaking	English only	Total	Gaelic-speaking %	English only %
A (Professional)	1	5	6	16.6	83.3
B (Public servants)	6	6	12	50.0	50.0
C (Commercial)	4	3	7	57.2	42.8
D (Technical)	17	9	26	65.4	34.6
E (Agricultural)	37	5	42	88.1	11.9
F (Manual)	52	5	57	91.2	8.8
G (Unemployed)	6	1	7	85.7	14.3
Totals	123	34	157	78.3	21.7

$\chi^2 = 31.723$ Significant below 0.001 level at 6 degrees of freedom

Statistical tests confirmed that the most significant split
between occupational levels occurs between the occupational categories of group D-technical (together with 'higher' groups) and
group E-agricultural (together with 'lower' groups). This result
suggests that the most significant social division for the incidence
of the two mother tongues lies between the middle class and skilled
working class on the one hand and the unskilled and lower working
classes on the other.

Having now considered various factors affecting the maintenance
of Gaelic as a mother tongue amongst primary-aged children, we shall
turn next to consider the usage of Gaelic by these children in
various social situations including the use of Gaelic within the
schools.

TABLE 5.8   Use of Gaelic in Harris primary schools 1957-8 and 1972-3

No. of schools	No. of schools in 1957-8	No. of schools in 1972-3
	16	8
PI and PII taught by same teacher	16	8
Gaelic-speaking teaching of PI and PII	16	8
PI and PII mainly taught in Gaelic	2	1
Gaelic and English	6	1
English	8	6
Some subjects taught in Gaelic only	4	2
Period set aside to teach Gaelic	8	7
Gaelic used in helping English speakers	16	8
Religious instruction given in Gaelic	11	6
Gaelic services for children	16	8
Language of playground: Gaelic	16	3
Gaelic and English	-	3
English	-	2
Language of community: Gaelic	16	7
Gaelic and English	-	1
English	-	-

A similar comparison may also be made concerning the use of Gaelic
by Primary I and II children in specific situations.

In comparison with the 1957-8 primary school survey, the use of Gaelic in the schools has improved in certain respects, and is summarised in Table 5.8. Recent years have seen improvements in the supply of school books in Gaelic. In 1957-8, 8 out of the 16 schools (or 50 per cent) set aside a regular period to teach Gaelic. In 1972-3, 7 out of the 8 schools (or 87 per cent) provided time for Gaelic in this way. There has been little change in the numbers of schools giving religious education in Gaelic — 6 out of 8 in 1972-3 in place of 11 out of 16 in 1957-8. In all other respects a comparison of the conditions reported in 1957-8 with 1972-3 indicates worsening of the situation for Gaelic. However, the schools reported varying degrees of ability in Gaelic amongst 5 (or 55 per cent) of the 9 English mother-tongue children in 1957-8. Fifteen years later the schools reported similar abilities amongst 22 (or 81 per cent) out of the 27 English mother-tongue pupils.

In this respect the schools today may be promoting bilinguality amongst the English mother-tongue pupils more successfully than was the case fifteen years previously. This finding is borne out by the results from the initial secondary stages (see Table 5.4).

Table 5.9, which gives details of first- and second-language abilities of Harris schoolchildren in the initial two years of primary education, indicates the overall decline in numbers from 110 to 86 over the fifteen-year period: a decline to 78 per cent of the earlier total. Within this reduced total a reduced proportion of the age-group spoke Gaelic as a first language: 67.4 per cent in 1972-3 as against 91.8 per cent fifteen years earlier. The proportion of all fluent speakers of Gaelic were 68.6 per cent and 94.5 per cent respectively. Gaelic has thus considerably weakened as a mother tongue. Acquisition of Gaelic by English mother-tongue children in the pre-school years although slight in both cases was more so in 1972-3.

The use of Gaelic as a home language is illustrated in Table 5.10, where it can be seen that Gaelic is less generally used even by Gaelic-speaking parents to their children. Changes will also be seen in those cases where only one parent is Gaelic-speaking, to the detriment of use of Gaelic in the home. Cases where neither parent was Gaelic-speaking had by 1972-3 begun to occur within the community.

The results of Table 5.10 show clearly that there is an increasing number of cases where thoroughly Gaelic-speaking households have chosen not to use Gaelic as the language of socialisation for their children. There were only three such cases in 1957-8 (representing 2.7 per cent of the age-group). These instances had increased to eleven cases in 1972-3 (representing 12.8 per cent of the age-group). It may also be significant to note that whereas in 1957-8 there was only one case of an English mother-tongue child of whose parents the father alone spoke Gaelic, fifteen years later there were eleven such cases, indicating a much greater propensity for a local father to bring an outsider or non-Gaelic-speaking wife into his home.

Table 5.11 examines the use of the two languages in home and school domains amongst the younger primary-aged children over the fifteen-year interval. It will be seen that the changes in language used with siblings and peers is more strongly in favour of English

TABLE 5.9 First- and second-language abilities: Primary I and II children in Harris, 1957-8 and 1972-3

Question	First language of pupil and language ability in second language	Harris 1957-8		As % of all PI and PII pupils	Harris 1972-3		As % of all PI and PII pupils
		Number	%		Number	%	
	First language Gaelic, knowledge of English:						
A	No knowledge of it	23	22.8	20.9	0	0.00	0.0
B	Understanding but unable to speak it	19	18.8	17.3	2	3.4	2.3
C	Understanding simple lessons and able to conduct conversations in it	48	47.5	43.6	22	37.9	25.6
D	Fluent in it	11	10.9	10.0	34	58.6	39.5
Total		101*	100.0	91.8	58	100.0	67.4
	First language English, knowledge of Gaelic:						
A	No knowledge of it	4	44.4	3.6	5	17.9	5.8
B	Understanding but unable to speak it	1	11.1	0.9	11	39.3	12.8
C	Understanding simple lessons and able to conduct elementary conversations in it	1	11.1	0.9	11	39.3	12.8
D	Fluent in it	3	33.3	2.7	1	3.6	1.2
Total		9	100.0	8.2	28	100.0	32.6

Question	First language of pupil language ability in second language	Harris 1957-8	As % of all PI and PII pupils	Harris 1972-3	As % of all PI and PII pupils.
	All PI and PII children: knowledge of Gaelic	Number		Number	
A	No knowledge of Gaelic	4	3.6	5	5.8
B	Understanding Gaelic but unable to speak it	1	0.9	11	12.8
C	Understanding simple lessons and able to conduct elementary conversations in Gaelic	1	0.9	11	12.8
D	Fluent in Gaelic	104	94.5	59	68.6
Grand total		110	100.0	86**	100.0

*   These returns were not complete in 1972-3.

** A PI child in 1972-3 whose first language was Urdu is included within this table as an English-speaking child.

Sources: 1957-8: SCRE Report (1961), 'Gaelic-speaking Children in Highland Schools',
Table VI, p. 37, The Knowledge of the Second Language.
1972-3: Own survey (returns of questionnaires to primary school teachers).

TABLE 5.10 Home language situation of primary I and II schoolchildren: Harris, 1957-8 and 1972-3 (based upon 'GSCHS', Table VIII, p. 40, The Language of the Home)

First language of pupil	Number of pupils in Primary I and II classified according to first language and language used at home					
	Harris 1957-8			Harris 1972-3		
	Number	%	As % of all PI and PII pupils	Number	%	As % of all PI and PII pupils
First Language Gaelic						
Language of home: Gaelic	101	100.0	91.8	57	98.3	66.3
English	–	0.0	0.0	–	0.0	0.0
Both	–	0.0	0.0	1	1.8	1.2
Parents as Gaelic speakers:						
Father only	–	0.0	0.0	–	0.0	0.0
Mother only	–	0.0	0.0	1	1.8	1.2
Both	101	100.0	91.8	57	98.3	66.3
Neither	–	0.0	0.0	–	0.0	0.0
Total	101	100.0	91.8	58	100.0	67.4
First Language English						
Language of home: Gaelic	–	0.0	0.0	6	21.4	7.0
English	9	100.0	8.2	21	75.0	24.4
Both	–	0.0	0.0	1	3.6	1.2
Parents as Gaelic speakers:						
Father only	1	11.1	0.9	11	39.3	12.8
Mother only	5	55.6	4.5	3	10.7	3.5
Both	3	33.3	2.7	11	39.3	12.8
Neither	–	0.0	0.0	3	10.7	3.5
Total	9	100.0	8.2	28	100.0	32.6

	Harris 1957–8		Harris 1972–3	
	Number	As % of all PI and PII pupils	Number	As % of all PI and PII pupils
All PI and PII children				
Language of home: Gaelic	101	91.8	63	73.3
English	9	8.2	21	24.4
Both	–	0.0	2	2.3
Parents as Gaelic speakers:				
Father only	1	0.9	11	12.8
Mother only	5	4.5	4	4.7
Both	104	94.5	68	79.1
Neither	–	0.0	3	3.5
Grand total	110	100.0	86	100.0

Note: A PI child in 1972–3 whose first language was Urdu is included within this table as an English-speaking child.

Sources: 1957–8 SCRE Report (1961), 'Gaelic-speaking Children in Highland Schools', Table VIII, p. 40, The Language of the Home.
1972–3: Own survey (return of questionnaires to primary school teachers).

TABLE 5.11 The use of Gaelic and English in home and school domains by Primary I and II schoolchildren, Harris, 1957-8 and 1972-3

	Numbers of children in Primary I and II with language used										
	Harris 1957-8				All PI and PII pupils, Harris, 1957-8		Harris 1972-3*				All PI and PII pupils, Harris, 1972-3	
	Number of pupils whose first language was						Number of pupils whose first language was					
	Gaelic		English				Gaelic		English			
	number	%	number	%	number	%	number	%	number	%	number	%
Number of pupils	101	100.0	9	100.0	110	100.0	58	100.0	28	100.0	86	100.0
Language used												
At home: Gaelic	99	98.0	–	0.0	99	90.0	50	86.2	–	0.0	50	58.1
Both	2	2.0	–	0.0	2	1.8	8	13.8	1	3.6	9	10.5
English	–	–	9	100.0	9	8.2	–	–	27	96.4	27	31.4
To sisters and brothers: Gaelic	98	97.0	–	0.0	98	89.1	44	75.9	–	0.0	44	51.2
Both	3	3.0	2	22.2	5	4.5	7	12.1	–	0.0	7	8.1
English	–	–	7	77.8	7	6.4	2	3.4	24	85.7	26	30.2
No sisters or brothers	not ascertained				not ascertained		5	8.6	4	14.3	9	10.5
To other children: Gaelic	83	82.2	8	88.9	91	82.7	26	44.8	–	0.0	26	30.2
Both	14	13.9	1	11.1	15	13.6	26	44.8	–	0.0	26	30.2
English	4	4.0	–	0.0	4	3.6	6	10.3	28	100.0	34	39.5
In playground: Gaelic	84	83.2	–	0.0	84	76.4	10	17.2	–	0.0	10	11.6
Both	13	12.9	3	33.3	16	14.5	38	65.5	1	0.0	38	44.2
English	4	4.0	6	66.7	10	9.1	10	17.2	28	100.0	38	44.2
To teacher: Gaelic	54	52.5	–	0.0	54	49.1	21	36.2	–	0.0	21	24.4
Both	14	13.9	–	0.0	14	12.7	24	41.4	–	0.0	24	27.9
English	33	32.7	9	100.0	42	38.2	13	22.4	28	100.0	41	47.7

* The Urdu-speaking child is not included.
Sources: SCRE Report (1961), 'Gaelic-speaking Children in Highland Schools', Table IX, p. 42; and questionnaires of present study.

as compared with language usage between parent and child already
examined in Table 5.10

It will be noticed in Table 5.11 that by 1972-3 Gaelic as a sole
language of the home had contracted to some 58.1 per cent of cases
as compared with 90.0 per cent of cases in 1957-8. However, it was
in use together with English in some 10.5 per cent of cases addi-
tionally in 1972-3 (compared with 1.8 per cent in 1957-8). Thus in
aggregate 91.8 per cent of the age-group were accustomed to use
Gaelic at home in 1957-8 but only 86.6 per cent of the age-group
in 1972-3.

In 1957-8 almost all Gaelic-speaking children used Gaelic with
sisters or brothers (97.0 per cent). Fifteen years later only
three-quarters of the Gaelic-speakers did so (75.9 per cent).
However, if a correction is made for those cases where the child
had no brothers or sisters this proportion was of the order of 83.0
per cent in 1972-3.

Outside the home there is a similar decline in use of Gaelic to
other children. In 1957-8 96.1 per cent of the Gaelic-speaking
children used Gaelic either solely or together with English in
speaking to other children. In 1972-3 this proportion was 89.6 per
cent. If Gaelic as a sole language for communication with other
children is taken by itself, the decline is even more dramatic:
from 82.2 per cent to 44.8 per cent, i.e. virtually halved. It is
noteworthy that eight English mother-tongue children habitually
used Gaelic alone to other children in 1957-8. None did so fifteen
years later. The decline of Gaelic in the school playgrounds is
the most pronounced decline of all. In 1957-8 83.2 per cent of the
Gaelic-speaking children used only Gaelic in the playground. Only
17.2 per cent did so in 1972-3. However, taking the age-groups as
a whole 90.9 per cent were regarded as using Gaelic either alone or
together with English in the playground in 1957-8. Fifteen years
later only 55.8 per cent of the age-group was still regarded as
using Gaelic similarly.

In speaking with teachers only 53.5 per cent of the Gaelic-
speaking children used only Gaelic in 1957-8; still fewer fifteen
years later, 36.2 per cent. However, in terms of the proportions
using Gaelic alone or in combination the fifteen-year interval
evidences a proportional increase from 67.4 per cent to 77.6 per
cent.

The results illustrate the considerably strengthened position of
English in all aspects of the school and home life of Harris
children. The sole exceptions to this tendency are the improvements
of abilities in Gaelic amongst the English mother-tongue group and a
greater incidence of usage of Gaelic bilingually with teachers.
Teachers are very conscious of the pressures to use English in the
social life of the child and see the school as an agency for conserving Gaelic language and culture. At the same time they see the
school as of necessity imparting other aspects of the culture.
Instrumentally there is felt to be a greater need to teach reading
as such, number skills and English as a second language. The importance of these aspects of education may be seen as being more
instrumentally necessary for children, and where there is conflict
of interests or competition for teachers' time and resources, Gaelic
may take second place. One Harris primary teacher felt that the

coming of television some seven years previously had tipped the
balance. Until that time Gaelic had held its own in school and
community. Another teacher felt the predominating use of English
in the playground was unfortunate. She attempted to provide a
strong supportive Gaelic atmosphere in her classroom, but the children switched to English outside: 'Yet they have plenty of Gaelic
in school and they are encouraged to use it all the time.' At
Tarbert where the playground is overwhelmingly English (the domain
of play being in English for virtually all the children) two boys
from one of the outlying villages remained steadfastly loyal to
Gaelic, using it exclusively during play throughout their time in
the primary school.

In two rural primary schools in South Harris non-Gaelic children
typically became effective Gaelic-speakers within about two years.
This undoubtedly is due to particular teachers' implementation of
the official policies. However, it was to one of these schools
that the authority appointed a non-Gaelic-speaking second teacher.
In the other case closure was threatened, and was effectively resisted chiefly as the result of the efforts of two outsiders who
organised the opposition at a public meeting. Here the school
roll is very small and closure probably cannot be indefinitely
postponed.

Centralisation of educational facilities clearly is to the
detriment of Gaelic language-maintenance and its usage amongst
schoolchildren. The presence of English monoglot children rein-
forces other social pressures and almost inevitably results in the
switch to English.

CONCLUSIONS

Fifteen years have considerably weakened the incidence of Gaelic
as a mother tongue amongst Harris primary-school children, but this
is far less marked in rural areas. The acquisition of English as
a second language now occurs readily at the pre-primary stage
amongst Harris children. On the other hand there is now a quite
definite phenomenon of Gaelic second-language acquisition amongst
the younger primary-aged children — at least in so far as passive
familiarity is concerned. Table 5.4 indicates the extent of effective command of Gaelic by English-speaking primary-school children
as they enter the secondary stage.

As the principal language of the home, it will be seen from
Tables 5.9 and 5.10 that Gaelic has declined from 91.8 per cent
to 66.3 per cent of cases amongst the younger primary children;
although Gaelic was used in the homes of 75.6 per cent of the age-
group in 1972-3 either exclusively or bilingually. Amongst Gaelic-
speaking children the use of Gaelic amongst sisters and brothers
was well maintained in 1957-8. By 1972-3, however, two out of the
fifty-eight Gaelic-speakers were using only English to their sisters
or brothers, 12.1 per cent of the children were using both languages
and only 75.9 per cent (as compared with 97.0 per cent) using only
Gaelic. In 1957-8 two of the nine English mother-tongue children
used both languages to sisters and brothers. None did so fifteen
years later. The use of Gaelic to other children has considerably

weakened. Almost half of the Gaelic group used both languages in 1972-3 (44.8 per cent) and six (10.3 per cent) used English only, as compared with 13.9 per cent and 4.0 per cent fifteen years earlier. A more pronounced weakening of usage in the playground was reported. However, in conversations with the teacher the results indicate rather a greater degree of bilinguality in usage.

Concerning the relationship between children's language and occupation of parent, direct comparison between Harris in 1957-8 and 1972-3 is unfortunately not possible. In 1957 (whether in the bilingual area as a whole or merely in the bilingual area of Inverness-shire) the agricultural category ('E') comprised the group with the highest maintenance-rate for Gaelic. The two lowest categories ranked second and third, indicating that a more pronounced shift towards English is occurring within the lower socio-economic categories. The rank ordering was the same for the 1972-3 Harris sample. It would seem that there are indications that this deliberate choice of English as a home language amongst the non-crofting 'working' or 'lower' class may be made as the result of a belief that Gaelic may 'hold back' the children in terms of their life-chances.

As this phenomenon is most pronounced in Tarbert, the principal commercial centre of the Isle of Harris, it can be seen that taken together with the centralisation of educational facilities and the concomitant bussing and mixing of the school children there is a reinforcement of the pressures causing Gaelic to be shifted out of such domains of usage as communication with age-peers and recreational activities.

Chapter 6

GAELIC IN SECONDARY AND FURTHER EDUCATION

There are three secondary schools in Harris: all junior secondaries with primary departments. Only Sir E. Scott school at Tarbert had an 'academic' secondary stream at the period of the survey. An academic curriculum was not provided at Leverhulme Memorial School, Leverburgh nor at Scalpay.

There was some variation between the Harris schools concerning the time devoted to Gaelic in the secondary curriculum. This varied from one hour thirty-five minutes per week at Leverburgh and two hours per week at Scalpay to three-and-a-half hours per week at Tarbert. At Leverburgh and Scalpay Gaelic as a specific subject formed part of the common course and was taken by native and non-native speaking children. At Tarbert non-Gaelic children were not necessarily taking Gaelic as a subject in their secondary course.

The 1972-3 surveys produced an impression of strongly persistent use of Gaelic amongst the younger secondary-aged children (Table 6.1).

TABLE 6.1 Use of Gaelic by secondary I pupils, 1972-3

School	Language used in speaking to other children				Language used in the playground			
	Gaelic	Both	English	Total	Gaelic	Both	English	Total
Tarbert	17	0	9	26	13	0	13	26
Leverburgh	6	2	0	8	0	8	0	8
Scalpay	7	0	1	8	7	0	1	8
Total	30	2	10	42	20	8	14	42

χ^2 = 12.5462 (Significant below 0.025 level at 4 degrees of freedom)

χ^2 = 46.3875 (Significant below 0.001 level at 4 degrees of freedom)

There are three principal areas within Tarbert from which come
the children without Gaelic as a first language: Scott Road,
MacQueen Street and Sunnyhill. Although these are 'council house'
areas, the children from the other 'council house' area of West
Tarbert are predominantly Gaelic-speaking.

Amongst secondary-aged children there are higher proportions
speaking Gaelic as a first language. This is in itself a measure
of the rapidity of shift from Gaelic amongst school-aged children.
Seventy-nine per cent of Harris children attending secondary schools
on or off the island spoke Gaelic as a first language in 1972-3.
A comparison with the Secondary I pupils of 1958-9 is possible. In
that year 49 out of 58 SI Harris pupils were native Gaelic-speakers
(84.5 per cent). In 1972-3 35 out of 46 children were native Gaelic-
speakers (76.1 per cent). The comparable figure over the fifteen-
year period for SI pupils in 1973-4 was 28 Gaelic-speaking children
out of 41 (68.3 per cent) (see Table 6.2).

However, an outside visitor might not gain an overall impression
of the generality of Gaelic as a predominant medium of communication
amongst the secondary schoolchildren. At Tarbert English strongly
predominates as the language of the playground and it would take a
sharp ear, searching for the differences, to detect the cases of
children speaking amongst themselves in Gaelic. At Scalpay, and in
large measure Leverburgh too, the playground is more strongly Gaelic.

Amongst the older secondary-aged pupils use of Gaelic within the
school domains is widely claimed — except for communication with
teachers (Table 6.3).

It is clearly the case that although Gaelic is maintained amongst
Harris children throughout the secondary stage and conspicuously
amongst the academically brighter Harris children at school away
from home, Gaelic does not enter into relationships of pupils to
staff in any marked degree. The official language of the school
(even of the most strongly Gaelic schools in Harris) is English. As
one headmaster observed: 'The younger children will converse quite
freely in Gaelic with the teacher — but the older secondary pupils
are somewhat reticent to do this. English is generally accepted as
the official language of communication between pupils and teachers'
(Scalpay).

Yet it is clearly the case that Gaelic enjoys greater confidence
and status in the secondary schools at the present time as compared
with a generation or more ago. During the past fifteen years
literacy in Gaelic has become general amongst schoolchildren and
since about 1960 the school leaver within the Gaelic communities has
typically left school with the ability to read and write in Gaelic.
John Murray, the Editor of the Gaelic Books Council(1) regards
illiteracy in Gaelic as a phenomenon associated with the middle-aged
categories within the population (although this is not borne out in
the 1971 census results), the oldest age-groups having acquired
Gaelic literacy through studies of the scriptures in the church and
Sabbath School and the younger adult groups becoming literate in
Gaelic at school. The questionnaire amongst the older secondary
children is also encouraging with respect to the indications of
confidence shown in the use of Gaelic.(2)

The situation of Gaelic in the schools of Harris in 1972-3 certainly still bears out the claims made ten years earlier by the then

TABLE 6.2 First language of secondary-aged children at school on Harris, attending school or technical college elsewhere on full-time school-level courses, 1972-3

Secondary class or college equivalent	Attending school on Harris		Attending school elsewhere		Attending technical college		Total: all Harris school-aged children		Total	% Gaelic-speaking
	Gaelic	English	Gaelic	English	Gaelic	English	Gaelic	English		
SI	35	10		1			35	11	46	76.1
SII	26	10					26	10	36	72.2
SIII	30	6	6	3	3		39	9	48	81.3
SIV	18	3	5	1			23	4	27	85.2
SV			9	1	4		13	1	14	92.9
SVI			8	1	1		9	1	10	90.0
Totals	109	29	28	7	8	0	145	36	181	80.1

TABLE 6.3   Use of Gaelic within school by older secondary pupils.
Secondary III upwards, 1972-3

School or college	No. of children	Use of Gaelic in specific situations			
		To a teacher in a Gaelic lesson	To a teacher in any other lesson	To other pupils	In the playground
Scalpay	4	3	O	4	4
Leverburgh	11	10	O	10	8
Tarbert General	15	12	O	8	3
Tarbert Academic	15	13	1	13	11
Nicholson (Lewis)	10	9	1	4	4
Portree (Skye)	5	4	O	2	1
Inverness Royal Academy	17	14	2	7	4
Inverness High School	2	1	O	1	1
Inverness Technical College	8	7	O	7	5
Totals	87	73*	4**	56***	41****

*	(Not significant)
**	(Not significant)
***	$\chi^2 = 19.5574$ (Significant below 0.025 level at 8 degrees of freedom)
****	$\chi^2 = 22.19$ (Significant below 0.005 level at 8 degrees of freedom)

Schools Gaelic Supervisor for Inverness-shire, in an address to the
Gaelic Society of Inverness concerning the place of Gaelic in the
schools:

> The general effect of the introduction of the Gaelic Education
> Scheme has been to ensure for Gaelic a wider sphere of influence
> and a more imaginative presentation in the schools of Inverness-
> shire than it ever did before, to provide in some degree the
> benefits of a bilingual education for bilingual children, to
> enliven the activities of the schools by the addition of fresh
> interests, and to awaken in many of the pupils a new sympathy
> and respect for their mother tongue. How far these results can
> be extended in the face of an ever-increasing process of angli-
> cisation is uncertain, but the improved status of the language is
> in itself some criterion of success.(3)

At the secondary stage the Gaelic lesson represents the only
substantial occasion whereby Gaelic enters into the school life of

the secondary child. Until recently, though, English had been in
general use as the teaching medium even for the Gaelic lesson.
Naturally enough now Gaelic is at least in general and frequent
use within the Gaelic lesson — except in circumstances away from
the island in academies where there is an admixture of non-native
speakers studying the language. Here at any rate there is something
of a bilingual approach to education, bearing out the continued progress of the Gaelic Education Scheme cited by Macleod in 1963. Apart
from the Gaelic lesson, the language may enter into the curriculum
for religious education. The Gaelic lesson has also been the means
of awakening 'fresh interests'. Harris schools have, for example,
undertaken surveys of local placenames: traditional lore records
an exceptionally close-textured toponymy carrying the names of even
the most minor topographical features. These have been of value as
important source collections for the national linguistic survey
undertaken by the School of Scottish Studies, Edinburgh University.
Taped interviews with local people have explored oral history and
personal biography in Gaelic. Studies of the origins of the Harris
tweed industry, folk medicine, internal migration and land-
resettlement (*tuineachas*), and the fishery revival on Scalpay have
been undertaken as projects in the Gaelic lesson and Harris schools
have been conspicuous in winning awards by An Comunn Gàidhealach
and other bodies for schools projects in local studies. It is noteworthy also that as 'traditional' Gaelic themes (crofting practices,
tweed industries and folklore) have been 'used-up', schools have
turned to more contemporary themes for Gaelic project work. This
is important if it is desired 'to promote the status of the language
and to persuade the pupils in a natural, informal manner that Gaelic
is as appropriate to the classroom situation as English', as
Macleod would wish.(4)

There has been a noticeable transformation of teaching approaches
from the traditional practice of the Gaelic lesson comprising little
more than translations from Gaelic into English: a practice having
had as its chief later effect the rendering of English as the chief
referent for the bilingual child (the meaning of a Gaelic text
becoming its literal translation in English rather than its explication in Gaelic). In this connection a lecturer in the Celtic
Department, Glasgow University, reports that being asked in Gaelic
for the meaning of the Gaelic bird-name '*Gille Brìghde*' (literally
'servant of (St) Bride', the oystercatcher) his students typically
responded by giving the name in English. The lecturer observed to
his students that in psycholinguistic literature it is commonly
observable that bilinguals take as their referent their mother tongue
but here they were taking their second language as their standard of
reference.

Another alienative effect of the separation of the Gaelic lesson
from the remainder of the curriculum is to emphasise the importance
of English as a teaching medium. English comes to be seen as the
appropriate medium for handling such aspects as science, mathematics, technical subjects, art and crafts, geography, history,
games, natural history and environmental studies and the discussion
of current affairs. Gaelic is used for the 'Gaelic' lesson itself,
religious education and for local study project work within the
Gaelic lesson. One junior secondary headmaster conducts current

affairs discussions in Gaelic so that pupils can see that Gaelic
is just as appropriate for this type of activity as is English and
to accustom them to the use of Gaelic in the discussion of public
affairs. This practice, though, seems to be rare. In general, the
classification and framing of the curriculum(5) separates the school
subjects rigidly as a 'collection code' at the secondary stage:
except in the case of Gaelic, within which a great deal of subject-
matter is integrated. Bernstein explains the *classification* of a
curriculum in terms of 'The degree of boundary maintenance between
contents'(6) and *framing* as referring to 'The degree of control
teacher and pupil possess over the selection, organisation and
pacing of the knowledge transmitted and received in the pedagogi-
cal relationship'.(7) (Integration of the curriculum has often
been held to signify low status of the educational area: as with
Liberal Studies in technical colleges, infant education and, in
this instance, of Gaelic.)

The results of this process may be in defining a domain for Gaelic
within the school where none existed before, but a domain which
firmly associated Gaelic with local life, local solidarity and folk-
life studies which may be moribund in the present age. Where Gaelic
is being used to educate in terms of contemporary problems and conditions this, of course, need not necessarily be so. Many pupils
naturally enough do not see Gaelic as appropriate for handling the
whole range of school subjects. In the senior secondary survey
numbers of respondents felt Gaelic should not be used to teach other
subjects 'because there might be other children who do not understand Gaelic' or 'because we shall have to take the examinations in
English'. Unlike Wales, where it is now possible to take school
examinations in Welsh, Gaelic Scotland has little realisation that
it could be possible to teach and examine to O-grade and Higher-
grade levels through the medium of Gaelic. As there has been no
move to provide Gaelic papers for the range of school examination
subjects, so there has been no response by schools to extend the
use of Gaelic as a teaching medium. In discussion with local teachers the impression may be formed that there is still a strong
residual respect for the 'rightness' of the situation whereby Gaelic-
speaking children should undertake their secondary education essentially through the medium of English so that examination success
shall not be hindered by the possession of Gaelic as a first
language. Some secondary children saw in Gaelic an advantage as 'it
gives you the second language which you need in order to gain university entrance'. Another Harris pupil away from the island entered for Higher-grade Gaelic, taking the 'learners' paper although
being in fact a native-speaker, as he felt this would ensure for him a
better grade.

In these ways attitudes towards Gaelic are developed by the school
at the 'latent' level or the level of the 'hidden curriculum'. Ostensibly the school 'does a good job' for Gaelic but in other respects
it 'keeps it in its place'. The development of bilingual education
within the Gaelic areas still means that Gaelic enters into the
school curriculum in very limited ways. It is not surprising that
the Gaelic Education Scheme has had limited success in holding
Gaelic as the community language in marginal areas such as Skye.(8)
There is a detectable shift in the use of Gaelic as a community

language even in such 'strongholds' as Harris at the present time.
Official policies are strongly supportive of the role of the school
as an agency of societal language-conservation. For example, the
1964 Inverness-shire Scheme of Instruction in Gaelic cites as a
prime aim 'The perpetuation of Gaelic as a spoken language'(p. 2),
and the 1965 Scottish Education Department Primary memorandum
states, 'it is the duty of the primary school to maintain and
develop Gaelic as a living means of communication . . .' (p. 199).
Similarly the 1955 Junior Secondary memorandum had urged 'complete
mastery of the spoken language' and Gaelic courses 'which will . . .
continue its use in the future'. The school is, of course, only
one means whereby society transmits or re-creates its culture
amongst the growing generation. Whatever importance is attached to
formal education in the local culture, undoubtedly such influences
as television, popular newspapers, comics, pop music, broadcasting —
and even local administration and local clubs, associations and uni-
formed organisations — are all strongly anglicised and anglicising.
In the face of these aspects of the culture (chiefly intrusive but
nevertheless well represented and well taken up by local people) the
school is not particularly well-equipped to reverse very strong
national pressures.

Recent years have witnessed a resurgence of concern for the
Welsh language in Wales. The school is being consciously utilised
as a means of conservation of the language and its effective learning by non-native-speaking children. Also in Wales there is a
number of patterns of bilingualism in the school in operation. Such
a well-developed image of bilingualism diffused throughout the
teaching profession and into the community has secured a measure of
success for the school as an effective agent within the field of
language-shift. Gaelic Scotland lacks a well-developed image of
bilingualism in the school. Its elements seem to comprise:

1   use of Gaelic instrumentally, as a means of explaining school
    work to the younger primary child;
2   the allocation of a regular time and place for Gaelic for the
    older primary and the junior secondary child;   and
3   the provision of Gaelic as a specific subject on 'modern
    language' lines for the more academic secondary child, en-
    abling him to profess Gaelic at O- and H-grade Scottish Certi-
    ficate of Education examinations.(9)

Schools in Harris develop a 'Gaelic atmosphere' by the production
of wall-display material in Gaelic. This is useful for the promotion
of Gaelic Studies and its appearance is almost always well-maintained,
bright and interesting. However, almost invariably display material
in English preponderates and the Gaelic material is almost always
restricted to those areas of the schools where Gaelic is taught. The
spirit of bilingualism is rarely carried as far as, say, visual
displays in the technical room of the Gaelic names of tools, Gaelic
material displayed in science laboratories illustrating Gaelic
scientific terms and Gaelic names of processes, or Gaelic sporting
terminology and rules of the games displayed in Gaelic in gymnasia
and changing rooms. Historical, geographical and natural history
material is frequently displayed in Gaelic — as the official
reports suggest — but this is almost inevitably in the Gaelic room.
A lot of printed material comes into the schools from local

authorities, public boards and official bodies and from commercial firms. Apart from some use of Gaelic by the National Savings Movement, this material during the survey period was entirely English in content. Often it was not only English in language but English in origin and illustration — even in aspects of life where Scottish conditions are physically, administratively, historically and legally very different from English conditions. Some of this could be very misleading to a Gaelic — or Scottish — child (e.g. a National Savings poster, illustrating the 'British' monarchy from William the Conqueror onwards!). The school notice-boards are virtually entirely English in content. The English material is professional in appearance but the Gaelic, of course, is inevitably 'home-grown'. Exposure to this visual background to education probably has the consequence of encouraging unarticulated attitudes of double standards regarding Gaelic as a component of official life. Schools broadcasting is almost entirely in English. The weekly twenty-minute Gaelic programme is on general interest topics. The schools programmes having specific subject-matter are inevitably in English. There is no provision of a range of subject-matter through the local language as in Wales. The school within the home community is anglicising in its effects. Still more so in the situation for the child who proceeds to selective education outside the home area: a case which we shall now turn to consider.

The 'academically brighter' Harris child is selected (on the basis of a 'verbal reasoning test' at eleven years and school records) for academic education — generally away from home at Inverness, Stornoway or Portree. Since about 1970 parents have had the option to send the child to Nicholson Institute at Stornoway (although on the same island land-mass, administered by a different county education authority, an anomaly which ceased in 1975 with local government reorganisation). In 1972-3 parents of eleven Harris children had taken this option. It had the advantage of enabling children to return home to Harris at weekends. The rector of the Nicholson Institute believed that this was an option taken up by the 'middle class' of Harris.(10) Boarding at Portree on the adjacent island of Skye has no advantage over Inverness in enabling children to return home for the weekends as the timings and days of sailing of the Hebrides ferry would not make the weekend trip feasible. Four Harris children were boarded at Portree and 27 at Inverness (17 at the Royal Academy, 2 at the High School and 8 on school-level courses at the Technical College). Thus some 43 (25 per cent) Harris secondary-aged children out of a total of 173 were attending selective secondary-school level courses away from the island.

Children from remoter areas of Harris itself and from the adjacent islands of Berneray and Scalpay may be boarded at Tarbert to attend the Sir E. Scott Junior Secondary school, the only one of the Harris schools which has an 'academic stream' leading to the Scottish Certificate of Education O-grade examination at the end of the fourth year of the secondary stage. The school hostel can accommodate approximately 20 boys and 20 girls. During 1972-3 the girls' accommodation was full — with some girls boarded out in the village — and the boys' accommodation was almost full. Approximately (for numbers varied from time to time) 18 boys were being accommodated away from home at Tarbert and about 22 girls. These children will

comprise most of the children from the remoter villages of North
Harris, together with the brighter and older children (from the
second year onwards) from Scalpay and South Harris.

   Secondary education for the brighter Harris child is almost
inevitably associated with a move away from home to board, generally
at a school hostel, for a term or a half-term at a time. The sailing which brings children home for the holidays or for the long mid-
term weekend is a joyous passage eagerly anticipated by the children
and awaited with expectation by parents upon the quay. This phenomenon in itself may be viewed as a form of anticipatory socialisation, for a few of these children will be able to return home to
work in their home area. Their form and level of education is preparing them for university and college of education entry or for
higher professional or technical education. During the period
1969-72, of some 27 Harris selective secondary-school leavers it
has been possible to trace, 13 proceeded to university, 2 into professional education, 2 to college of education, 2 into nursing
training, 5 directly into employment and 1 into higher technical
education.(11) The impression is strong that the more academically
able Harris children follow the traditional path to the older Scottish universities, often to undertake the MA Arts course. Educational success and improved life-chances for the Harris child are
inevitably associated with a permanent move away from home. The
nature and pattern of secondary education accustom the child to
this necessity.

   A contributor to the Aberdeen College of Education Journal
'Education in the North' and herself a teacher in training from a
Gaelic area(12) describes the process of selection and transfer
to boarding education for the children of the Gaelic area as a
'junior clearance'. In Sutherland these children 'fail to fulfil
the promise of their primary attainment'. But the system is criticised for a more fundamental reason: 'The first and most obvious
result . . . is the unhappiness of the child. Parents . . . dread
the end of each holiday with its resultant tearful partings on the
arrival of the school bus.'(13) The author also draws attention to
effects within the local economy of diminished attractions of a
workforce to fisheries and industries in the area as families are
split up when children reach secondary age: 'the impossibility of
repopulating an area where full educational facilities do not
exist'.(14) Furthermore teachers would be attracted back to the
area, restoring balance to the age and occupational structure. The
author argues for a restructured pattern of education in which
children largely remain in their home area, where travelling and
accommodation expenses are saved and where modern teaching media
are utilised by teachers who may spend part of their time travelling to teach in the remote area schools. This is to reverse the
present dominant pattern through the Highland area of the child
travelling to the teacher.

   In Harris it would be feasible for a restructured pattern of
education to be established upon these lines. There was in the
1972-3 session a total secondary contingent of 173 children of whom
10 were undertaking five-year studies and 9 six-year studies (together comprising the equivalent of an English sixth form of nine-
teen students). At third- and fourth-year levels an 'academic'

stream proceeding to SCE O-grade examination would have totalled a
third-year class of 18 and a fourth-year class of 12. The six non-
academic subject teachers (for physical education, art, homecraft
and technical subjects) do in fact travel between the three Harris
junior secondary schools, but the ten academic subject teachers
stay put. Were the academic teachers to travel to the children a
common comprehensive course could be maintained at each school to
fourth-year level, specialist subjects being taught by visiting
specialist teachers and the facilities of the school hostel and
Sir E. Scott School at Tarbert used as a fifth- and sixth-year
centre for Higher-grade SCE and Certificate of Sixth Year Studies.
For this purpose it would be necessary for specialist teachers to
travel from Stornoway to Tarbert (36 miles) for specialist subjects.
However, it was decided earlier in 1974 to recommend a '2-2-4'
pattern of secondary reorganisation for Harris. The Isle of Scalpay
had always strenuously represented a desire to maintain its own
secondary school. Parents had threatened a school strike some years
previously when closure had been mooted — and another 'strike' was
threatened for autumn 1973 over various delapidations of the school
building. In the recommended pattern of reorganisation all Harris
children will attend a common comprehensive course in local schools
in the first two secondary years. Leverburgh and Scalpay will be
12-14 year comprehensive and Tarbert 12-16 year. As specialist subjects such as French and Latin will be available at Tarbert only,
its status will be that of a 'comprehensive-plus'. There would seem
to be little option for children desirous of the 'full' secondary
course to do other than to proceed to Tarbert at twelve as at
present. The streaming will still operate but self-streaming rather
than streaming on the basis of a test of verbal reasoning ability.
Fears were expressed in the local press that the new system to be
introduced when the new Western Isles authority takes over local
education in 1975 would effect the closure of the secondary departments except at Tarbert over the issue of provision of specialist
languages.

   If such a scheme is adopted for Harris, it will bring the island
more closely into line with the system coming into operation in the
contiguous area of Lewis. For the system to work equitably in
Harris further consideration will necessarily have to be given to
the provision of specialist secondary subjects — namely languages.
This could be solved by the expedient of appointing part-time staff
to travel around the schools for this purpose. There were qualified
local teachers in French and Latin on Scalpay and on Harris who were
not employed in education in 1974 and who might work part-time in
these subjects in future years.

   One of the older secondary students boarded at Stornoway felt
that the Lewis pattern of secondary reorganisation would be the
means of 'saving' Gaelic within the schools. As all secondary-aged
children outside Stornoway are in future to remain at their local
comprehensive school for the earlier secondary years, the 'academic'
children are to be educated within their own home area. Hostels
are strongly anglicising and the above respondent stated that when
they first came to the hostel at the age of twelve, 'the older boys
soon knocked my Gaelic out of me'. Older boarders set the tone of
the establishment and as far as language was concerned this would

be English. The same informant believed that Gaelic would become
the language of the hostels as these would in future only be
catering for the older students, by that time well used to using
their Gaelic throughout the pre-16 secondary stage. If this is so,
the custom of the use of language as a marker of the superiority
of the older residents over the younger would die out. The need to
prove superiority by inducing language-shift amongst the younger
children should disappear. As Harris came within the same local
authority area as Lewis from 1975, it may be expected to function in
administrative terms in similar fashion to one of the larger rural
parishes of Lewis.

For boarders, hostel life can be something of a privation. There
are comfortable new hostels for girls and younger boys in Stornoway.
The older boys' hostel there and the hostel at Tarbert are somewhat
more spartan — as are the older hostels at Inverness. There are
hostels of varying age at Portree. What at least may be said in
favour of the more spartan hostels with older equipment — as at
Tarbert — is that it is impossible to fall out of bed no matter
how uncomfortable it may be: the sag of the mattresses renders
this very much an uphill task! The children will be without home
comforts and will live communally under close common discipline
for between nine and ten months of the year.

One hostel warden was critical of the island girls using Gaelic
amongst themselves. As they could speak English, she felt the use
of Gaelic was unnecessary and divisive as there were many non-Gaelic-
speaking girls from other areas. Generally Harris children are
submissive, tolerant, polite and will accept everything a teacher
or other educational authority-figure may give out or require —
however bizarre (as my own researches indicate). They will be more
prepared to write their private views than to voice them. In one
hostel where I recorded the conversations of Harris girls boarding
there I was stunned by the strong collective opinion amongst the
Harris girls of all the age-groups represented there that they were
despised by teachers for being Gaels, subject to abuse from other
pupils and called 'teuchtars'.(15) These girls felt strongly that
they were singled out for special treatment by some of the teachers
and made to feel different if not inferior compared with the local
pupils. This was, they felt, chiefly on account of their being
Gaelic-speakers. They complained that back in Harris they had never
encountered this type of attitude amongst the teachers there.

Harris children in general show reasonable confidence in their
community language. Although often regarded as 'dying' or 'fading
away', there seemed to be a widespread desire that it should be
'kept up', 'revived' or 'given more importance'. A measure of
confidence in the language was obtained from the seven questions in
the questionnaire relating to whether the respondent was pleased or
sorry about his ability to speak Gaelic, whether it should be taught
as a school subject, whether it should be used as a teaching medium,
whether the respondent wished future children of his own to speak
Gaelic, whether he would use it in his own future home, whether he
wished it to continue in use as the community language and whether
he thought Gaelic would die out in the foreseeable future. The
answers to these seven questions were scored and the mean values
were converted to a ten-point scale to enable comparisons to be made

with other aspects of attitude to and use of Gaelic by these
children. The results are detailed in Table 6.4. There appeared
to be little overall variation between the confidence in Gaelic
expressed by the children away at hostels compared with the home
group, although the home group was younger and less 'academic'.
The group boarded away registered a group mean index of 5.24 compared with the home group at 5.81. The academic group registered
5.57 compared with the non-academic group at 5.37. A greater degree
of difference showed up between the native speakers of Gaelic and
the non-native and non-speakers of Gaelic: 5.77 as compared with
3.71. However, as there were only ten respondents in the non-
Gaelic group out of a total of 87, little can be said about this
differentiation except that it is in an understandable direction.
The results of this enquiry are detailed more fully in Table 6.4
in terms of sex, academic 'stream' and residence on or away from
the island of the 87 Secondary III-IV-aged Harris pupils.

TABLE 6.4 Confidence in Gaelic amongst older Harris secondary
pupils (Secondary III-VI) 1972-3

Sex	Language ability	Location of school	Academic stream	Number	Total score	Mean score*	Confidence index**
Girls	Native Gaelic-speakers	in Harris	General	12	46	3.83	5.48
			Academic	6	33	5.50	7.86
		boarded away	Academic	19	74	3.89	5.56
			Technical	5	20	4.00	5.71
	non-native and non-speakers of Gaelic	in Harris	General	1	0	0.00	0.00
			Academic	1	3	3.00	4.29
		boarded away	Academic	4	8	2.00	2.86
			Technical	–	–	–	–
Totals: Girls							
Gaelic-speakers only				42	173	4.12	5.88
Non-Gaelic-speakers only				6	11	1.83	2.62
General courses only				13	46	3.54	5.05
Academic courses only				30	118	3.93	5.62
Technical courses only				5	20	4.00	5.71
Harris residents only				20	82	4.10	5.86
Boarders away only				28	102	3.64	5.20
All girls				48	184	3.83	5.48

TABLE 6.4 contd

Sex	Language ability	Location of school	Academic stream	Number	Total score	Mean score*	Confidence index**
Boys	Native Gaelic-speakers	in Harris	General	14	54	3.86	5.51
			Academic	8	34	4.25	6.07
		boarded away	Academic	10	37	3.70	5.29
			Technical	3	13	4.33	6.19
	Non-native and non-speakers of Gaelic	in Harris	General	2	9	4.50	6.43
			Academic	1	4	4.00	5.71
		boarded	Academic	1	2	2.00	2.86
			Technical	–	–	–	–

				Number	Total score	Mean score*	Confidence index**
Totals: Boys							
Gaelic-speakers only				35	138	3.94	5.63
Non-Gaelic-speakers only				4	15	3.75	5.36
General courses only				16	63	3.94	5.63
Academic courses only				20	77	3.85	5.50
Technical courses only				3	13	4.33	6.19
Harris residents only				25	101	4.04	5.77
Boarders away only				14	52	3.71	5.31
All boys				39	153	3.92	5.60
Boys and girls together							
Gaelic-speakers only				77	311	4.04	5.77
Non-Gaelic-speakers only				10	26	2.60	3.71
General courses only				29	109	3.76	5.37
Academic courses only				50	195	3.90	5.57
Technical courses only				8	33	4.13	5.89
Harris residents only				45	183	4.07	5.81
Boarders away only				42	154	3.67	5.24
Grand total				87	337	3.87	5.53

*   Mean score of responses to the seven questions (maximum possible score 97).

** Conversion of the mean score to a ten-point scale (maximum possible score of 10).

Although this measure cannot be argued as statistically significant, it may be interesting and suggestive to note that the boys
evidenced a greater degree of confidence in Gaelic than did the
girls. The 'academic' girls boarding away from the island were in
discussion markedly more confident in Gaelic than were the corresponding group of boys. This may be associated with the tendency
of the girls, particularly, perceiving something of the process
whereby they are in course of extrusion from their home community,
to come to seek in Gaelic and its associated culture something of a
'prop' or 'support' that they can carry into the new surroundings.
   We may appropriately next turn to what use the older secondary-
aged pupils regarded themselves as making of their Gaelic in their
school and extra-curricular life. The results are summarised in
Tables 6.5 and 6.6.
   In terms of the use made of Gaelic by children boarded away from
the home community in school hostels, of 42 such students, 35
reckoned to use the language to teachers in a Gaelic lesson, 3 to
teachers other than teachers of Gaelic and 21 to other students.
Fifteen of these students reported using it 'in the playground'
although, of course, this aspect of the school domain is not so
important for this age group. The results are summarised in Table
6.5 comparing the home-based and the boarding groups.

Table 6.5 School dominance-configuration: use of Gaelic by older
Harris secondary-aged pupils (Secondary III-VI) in specific
situations, 1972-3

	To teacher in a Gaelic lesson		To other teachers	To other pupils	In the playground
Harris residents	45	38	1	35	26
Boarders away	42	35	3	21	15
Totals	87	73*	4**	56***	41****

*   Not significant
**   Not significant
*** χ^2 = 7.30847 Significant below 0.01 level at 1 degree of
       freedom
**** χ^2 = 4.24412 Significant below 0.05 level at 1 degree of
       freedom

   As English predominates in the school, the academic pupils
boarding away will not necessarily return to a Gaelic atmosphere
after school hours. Hostel life is predominantly anglicising.
Most pupils will use Gaelic at some point in the school day, but
in hostel different constraints operate. There are no Gaelic-
speaking parents to maintain a Gaelic home atmosphere. In Portree
and Inverness, the Gaelic boarders are likely to be a minority. Even
in Stornoway and Tarbert there are likely to be strong social pressures in favour of English. Of the 55 Gaelic-speaking Harris
boarders, some 45 claimed to use Gaelic to others after school hours
(e.g. to close friends, Harris and island pupils). Harris children,

girls especially, could develop a firm symbolic attachment to Gaelic.
In discussions with all pupils boarding away, it became clear that
girls would readily articulate their identity as Gaels. Nevertheless both boys and girls might develop commitment to their home
language as a symbol of identity, as the following quotations
indicate:

'It's a friendly language to speak' (boy at Inverness).
'It is the mother tongue and I would feel a foreigner without it'
(boy at Stornoway).
'It should be taught as on equal to other languages, as it
probably would not be dying out if it wasn't for the influence
of other languages' (girl at Inverness).
'Gaelic is really the Scottish language and it is an advantage
to have it. It is a language to be proud of' (girl at Inverness).
'If you are away from home and you hear someone talking Gaelic
you think they are one of you' (girl at Stornoway).
'It is an asset to have two languages and it forms a bond between
people who can speak it' (girl at Inverness).
'What would draw me back to Harris? People speak Gaelic there'
(boy at Inverness).
'It (Gaelic) equips them for a way-of-life. It gives you something to look back on. I would not have missed my childhood for
anything. It really gave me something I can come back to any
time: something secure' (girl at Stornoway).
'Gaelic creates a more homely atmosphere' (boy at Inverness who
claimed to use it with the warden, masters and other pupils).

The use of Gaelic can be a support in the strange surroundings:
'My friends speak Gaelic so we usually speak it amongst ourselves'
(girl at Inverness). 'It is the language of my childhood' (girl at
Inverness). A boy at Stornoway reported that he always spoke in
Gaelic to the hostel cooks, whilst a girl, also in Stornoway, re-
ported on using it with the hostel maids.

There may be a variety of instrumental reasons for keeping up
one's Gaelic away from home. Frequently reported was the reason
that the language counts as a 'modern' or 'foreign' language for
university entrance. Hence it is an advantage for a native Gaelic-
speaker as an 'easy option'. Otherwise Gaelic may function as a
'secret' or 'underground' language: 'Being able to speak two
languages you can say some things among friends which you don't want
English-speakers to pick up' (girl at Inverness).

Another girl at Inverness used Gaelic 'very rarely' except with
friends when 'on our own and when we don't want anyone else to hear
our conversation'. A boy at Inverness used his Gaelic 'to baffle
pupils who cannot understand me'. Another boy reported that 'some
people used Gaelic in front of strangers to their advantage as a
"code language".'

The situation in the hostels at Stornoway was explained by an
older Lewis boy as follows: 'There's people . . . after some ten
years in the place they speak nothing but English. Yes, we influence them to it. Without knowing yourself to do it. We do it
without even realising it. We don't know about it but we do it.
When we were first years we would speak in Gaelic or English. First
of all it's Gaelic for the first few days. It didn't take long to

adapt to speak English between ourselves.'   Another older Lewis boy
reported: 'There's much more Gaelic being spoken in the next two
grades after our two years — fourth years.   We were let go.   They
have gone three years in the MacRae Hostel speaking Gaelic and they
are not liable to change at once anyway.'

The situation at the MacRae Hostel at Stornoway is unusual
amongst the hostels where Harris children might find themselves.
It is a bright, modern and comfortable hostel, recently established
in Stornoway for older secondary girls and younger secondary boys.
This combination seems to have had a noticeable effect in retaining
Gaelic in use amongst the pupils.   As between girls and boys away
at the various hostels the reported usage of Gaelic amongst the
Gaelic-speaking pupils is given in Table 6.6.

Table 6.6   Language-usage amongst Gaelic-speaking Harris pupils
boarded away from home, 1972-3

Hostel	Girls using Gaelic in hostels or lodgings	Total girls	Boys using Gaelic in hostels or lodgings	Total boys	Total
Inverness	16	18	5	9	27
Portree	2	2	2	3	5
Stornoway	8	9	1	2	11
Tarbert	7	7	4	5	12
Totals	33	36	12	19	55

Significance of differential usage between boys and girls:
χ^2 = 6.7946   Significant below 0.01 level at 1 degree of freedom

Eighty-two per cent of Gaelic-speaking Harris pupils boarded
away claimed some usage of Gaelic in after-school contacts: 92
per cent of the girls and 63 per cent of the boys — a significant
difference which may indicate a tendency for girls to maintain their
Gaelic better than boys.

Stornoway pupils claimed in discussion that this was so at the
MacRae Hostel for senior girls and younger boys.   In comparison the
Gibson Hostel for senior boys at Stornoway had developed the tradition of predominating use of English.   A Lewis boy explained, 'In
the MacRae Hostel the young people there are speaking nothing but
Gaelic.   Up till now — well up till three years ago, was it? —
people have been coming straight to first year, and all the years
above them were English-speaking amongst themselves, but now they
go to MacRae.   First, second and third year in MacRae — three
years — and it's Gaelic-speaking there because it was, you know,
a sort of fresh lot from the country that went to fill it up at
once and they were Gaelic-speaking amongst themselves.   That means
they were all Gaelic-speaking and that means three years speaking
Gaelic among themselves and that means they are not liable to change
at once even if there were pressure from us.   I would not be

surprised if Gaelic in the next couple of years it will be the
language they will be talking there.'
     If there is substance in these observations, it would seem that
hostel life is not necessarily anglicising — providing the conditions are right. As Lewis and Harris are on the point of going
over to a comprehensive system in which the critical years of
secondary education are spent in the local community (formerly
junior secondary) schools, the prospects for maintenance of Gaelic
amongst the secondary-aged pupils is likely to improve.

THE FURTHER EDUCATION AND EMPLOYMENT PROSPECTS OF HARRIS CHILDREN

It is very difficult to substantiate claims which are sometimes
made that the Highland area is contributing a greater proportion
of university students and graduates than the country as a whole.
For example, Farquhar Macintosh (Rector of the Royal High School,
Edinburgh, and Chairman of the Highlands and Islands Development
Board Consultative Council Panel on Education) in an address to a
recent annual conference of An Comunn Gàidhealach said:
     Are there not indications that the proportion of an age-group
     which obtains passes on the Ordinary and Higher Grades of the
     S.C.E. examination is higher in the Highlands and Islands than
     in the cities of Scotland? Similarly is it not a fact that the
     Western Isles with their comparatively small population, pro-
     vide a very high proportion of University graduates and pro-
     fessional people?
     Unfortunately, it is very difficult to answer these questions
owing to the difficulty of obtaining satisfactory statistics relating to the flow of Highland school leavers into higher education.
Since the Scottish Education Department and not the county education authorities (as in England) is responsible for the granting
of awards to students proceeding to higher and advanced further
education, statistics are not available for the Highland counties.
In the presentation of official statistics within this field the
breakdown is apparently not in terms of county of origin but of
city or county within which the students' education takes place.
There is no university, central institution, college of education
or higher education centre of any kind operating within the seven
Highland counties.(16)   Hence the official statistics available
give no indication of the proportion of the school-leaving age-
cohort proceeding to such institutions. Some estimation of this
flow may be obtained indirectly from statistics of school leavers,
assuming that the majority of school leavers in the 17+ and 18+
categories will be proceeding to some form of advanced further
or higher education. In 1971 there were 821 leavers in the age-
cohort 17+ and 172 in the age-cohort 18+ from the seven Highland
counties.(17)
     In terms of the proportion of the total age-cohort remaining at
school beyond statutory leaving age in 1971 this total of 992
represented a percentage of 13.8 per cent out of a total of 7,205
eighteen- and seventeen-year-olds enumerated in the 1971 Census
within the seven Highland counties. So far as Inverness-shire as
a whole was concerned, 272 seventeen-year-olds 57 eighteen-year-

olds were remaining at school out of a total 17-18+ age-cohort of 2,440 (or 13.5 per cent).(18) Focussing more closely upon Harris, as we have seen, some 19 remained in full-time education beyond SIV in 1972-3 (the year in which children reach the age of 16 or sit SCE O-grade examinations). As children may be leaving the island for work elsewhere at this age, it is difficult to compare this number directly with the total age-cohort brought up and educated in Harris. In 1972-3 the total age-cohort of SIII and SIV (the last two years of compulsory attendance) produced 72 pupils of whom the 19 would comprise some 26.4 per cent. The 1971 Census indicates some 50 fifteen- and sixteen-year-olds resident in Harris of whom the 19 remaining at school in 1972-3 would comprise some 38 per cent (or 30 per cent if some 26 per cent of these age-groups are in fact enumerated elsewhere as the result of boarding away).

A study of school achievement, boarding away from home and employment prospects in remoter areas of the north Highland mainland is suggestive of a relationship existing between school leaving, examination success and local availability of work.(19)

There was an interesting difference in tendency to stay on in secondary school between south west Ross at one extreme and north Sutherland at the other. In south west Ross many pupils initially allocated to the lower streams actually stayed on for five years or more, possibly because the children in the area went to one relatively small comprehensive school where transfer from one class to another was easily arranged. In north Sutherland children were allocated either to a junior secondary school in the area or to a senior-type school on the east coast. Those who were not initially enrolled in the senior school were unlikely ever to come there. But the difference may also be accounted for by different opportunities for work after leaving school. Development in the Thurso area has made it easy for north Sutherland youths to get jobs within daily travel of home thus offering a temptation to leave school early. In south west Ross prospects of jobs within the area are worse.(20)

Harris has much in common with the situation described here for southwest Ross with the variation that a Harris child not selected at 12 or 14 for senior secondary education off the island has been able to proceed to Tarbert and to the 'academic' O-grade course from SIII to SIV.

Lee draws attention to the comparable position in Wales where in similar areas to the Scottish Highlands and Islands — the predominantly rural and Welsh-speaking counties(21) — between 40-50 per cent of the children in full-time attendance at schools may be continuing in full-time education beyond school-leaving age. Lee believes this phenomenon in Wales and Scotland

to derive from tradition and to be bound up with the existence of a separate culture and identity. It is also a tradition which, so far as one can tell, takes many of the ablest youngsters into higher education and into professional and technical employment outside the region itself. In the further education sector at least, juvenile migration can take some alarming forms. . . .

Within Scotland itself, Synge has drawn attention to significant regional differences in school achievement and entry into further education.(22) She concludes that 'Despite the generous financing

of the rural school system, boys from country districts were less
likely to gain good certificates and enter full-time education
than were boys from cities.' However,
    among girls, contrary to our expectations, rural upbringing
    was associated with *high* rates of school achievement and entry
    into higher education. Generally, the achievements of girls are
    below those of boys; in Scotland, however, those of rural
    girls match and often surpass those of rural boys. We suggest
    that poor local employment opportunities for rural girls and
    the limited social life in rural districts encourages girls to
    seek 'escape routes' through further education.
Of the 50 Harris pupils on selective courses between SIV-SVI, 30
were girls and 20 were boys. In addition, of the 8 Harris students
on full-time school-level courses at Inverness Technical College,
5 were girls and 3 were boys: ratios which strongly bear out
Synge's conclusions. Of those staying in full-time education after
16 years of age, 9 were boys and 15 were girls.
    It has already been noted that amongst Harris girls boarded
away from home for selective secondary education, there is a greater
tendency to retain Gaelic in active everyday use (Table 6.6). There
is little discernible difference between 'academic' and 'general'
pupils or home residents and boarders away regarding confidence in
Gaelic (Table 6.4). Differences in confidence in Gaelic between
'academic' boys and girls (indices of 5.79 and 6.01 on the ten-
point scale) cannot be regarded as statistically significant and
it would be unwarranted to infer from these data that actual use
of and claimed confidence in Gaelic amongst academic girls boarding
away from home tends to be higher than among the boys. However, in
discussions, particularly strong and sustained views to this effect
were voiced by the girls.
    More girls than boys board away for secondary education. It
would be valuable to know whether this was because girls performed
better on selection tests or whether parents, teachers or pupils
themselves promoted this differential pattern between the sexes.
These brighter girls will almost inevitably be lost to the island
community. The census results suggest, very significantly, that
young women remaining within the island community do so largely
because they are married. In 1971, 150 (or 67 per cent) out of the
225 women aged 20-39 in Harris were married. In contrast only 155
(or 48 per cent) of the 320 men in this age-group were married. The
analysis of the census results concerning young adults in Harris in
some detail yielded χ^2 results significant below the 0.001 levels —
even after adjusting for the military establishment on St Kilda.(23)
It would be valuable to compare Harris with other island, rural and
Gaelic communities in this respect.
    It is therefore noticeably the case that the local culture pro-
motes the extrusion of the academically brighter young people and
of these the girls in significantly greater numbers than the boys.
It is ironic that these young women demonstrate a conspicuous attachment to their home language and culture and yet are placed in the
position of finding a career and a husband elsewhere. The local
culture promotes a 'success-oriented' pattern of educational achievement more greatly pronounced among the mothers of the future generation than amongst the potential fathers.

The Gaelic language, Gaelic culture and the island way of life viewed in retrospect can together form an important cultural 'prop' for young people leaving the home community for institutional life in a school hostel, a college or university, a hospital or the merchant service. It would seem that girls at any rate will admit to this or claim adherence to this to a greater extent than may boys. There may, therefore, be a causal relationship between symbolic adherence to Gaelic culture, access to and achievement of success through the educational system, sex, marriage chances and fertility. As girls in selective secondary education or higher education away from the island may feel themselves to be in process of extrusion from the home community, so their attachment to the symbolic culture — exemplified by the language — may be the stronger.

The principal occupational opportunities open to young people on the island are limited. They comprise principally manual labour, skilled trades such as electrical work, joinery and construction, agricultural work and employment in transport. These openings are exclusively for young men. There are very few prospects for young women such as work in catering, shops, offices and banks. Hence there is a greater relative migration of girls leaving school and the principal perceived opportunities for Harris girls include hotel work and catering, the nursing service, the women's services (e.g. as policewoman or 'Wren') but notably and in the first instance into selective secondary and into further education. There is an economic factor at work here which was criticised by at least one warden of girls' school hostels, namely that the county supports scholars at these institutions or pays the boarding allowance for lodgings. Hence in a low-income crofting family it is an attractive prospect for a mouth to be fed and a child supported at a hostel rather than within the home. This is a mechanism operating within the economy of the remote rural areas of Scotland having an important effect upon the local economy and social structure.

As young women are away from home in their later teens and early twenties, attachments develop with boyfriends out of the home community and these young women marry out of and away from the island. Very few return either from further and higher education away from home and virtually none resettle into the home area with a husband from elsewhere. This is in accordance with the patrilocal nature of the family as an institution in Harris anyway.

The young men who remain at home are those who have employment prospects or the likelihood of succession to the family croft. But there is a shortage of young women in their own age-groups, hence the marriage-rate is lower than average and the age of marriage is higher than the national average. The operation of these factors together has resulted in the imbalance of the ages and the sexes, low fertility and a low birthrate, decline in population and restricted local employment prospects. In the schools, school rolls have shrunk, rural schools have been closing at the rate of one every two years and so far as Gaelic is concerned there has been a perceptible lessening of confidence in the language amongst the families of the more 'urbanised' lower socio-economic groups.

The population contracts and changes are induced into its symbolic culture and physical composition. Without the utilisation of sophisticated computer simulation it would be difficult on simple trend prediction to calculate by which year the majority of the adult population might cease to be Gaelic-speaking and Gaelic may be said to have ceased to be the community language, for there has been a recent increase in live births within Harris and this trend against the national average has been associated with a higher incidence of knowledge of Gaelic amongst infants and younger children. From the lowest recorded level of live births of six in 1964, numbers of live births increased to forty in 1972. The incidence of Gaelic amongst children born at that time (and aged seven to eight in Primary III in 1972-3) was the lowest recorded in the two surveys: 51.7 per cent. Subsequently the incidence has increased to 61.7 per cent and 74.4 per cent in the age-cohorts of the two successive years. Whether this trend of a higher birth rate and higher incidence of Gaelic used in upbringing will continue is, of course, problematical. As the trend is at present, prediction or estimation is rendered difficult. This increase in live births may be accounted for by the stimulation of fishery (especially in Scalpay) and the return of younger families to the community.

The island community may be regarded as essentially a manpower reservoir for mainland Britain. The principal economic value of such remote rural areas may be in their functioning as a nursery for the supply of entrants to the professions, public services and skilled trades in Britain as a whole.(24) The school has contributed to the creation of a local culture supportive of this role. Gaelic and its associated culture assists the transition from home to school, from local school to boarding away from home and provides a source of identity for the young person in process of being 'exiled'. An older boy at Stornoway said: 'You know I was down in Glasgow last week — and went into a few bars (laughter). You know there are thousands of Lewismen in Glasgow and it's nothing but Gaelic they speak in the bars.' Another Harris pupil said of Gaelic: 'It makes you feel more of an individual.' Thus the young exiled Gael may take some comfort from his culture in strange surroundings.

ATTITUDES TO GAELIC AND ENGLISH AMONGST SECONDARY-AGED CHILDREN

Through their socialisation, education, exposure to the media and contacts with visitors and incomers, the Harris children have access to a wide selection of speech varieties in English and Gaelic. As the preponderant majority of Harris children are bilingual and as almost all of the non-native speakers of Gaelic have some degree of ability in Gaelic, Harris children may be regarded as having a greater range of speech-varieties within their repertoire as com- pared with monoglot English children generally. An examination was, therefore, made of the attitudes towards speech variants commonly encountered or utilised by the Harris children, in order to estimate whether there might be ascertainable associations of subjective values with regard to speech variation, by a 'verbal guise' test.

Four speech samples were prepared in order to illustrate, respec- tively, (1) 'received pronunciation' formal Gaelic, (2) relaxed colloquial local Scottish English, (3) received pronunciation formal English, and (4) relaxed colloquial local Harris Gaelic. The content of the samples was, in terms of information, identical: between

2-3 minutes on a theme familiar to all Highland schoolchildren in 1972: the centenary of the 1872 Education Act (which had been featured throughout the year by public ceremonies and exhibitions in each of the region's secondary schools). A formal broadcast talk in Gaelic was recorded from Radio 4, translated into formal English and recorded by a speaker of received pronunciation in a similarly formal manner. Matching for age, sex, status, occupational role, timbre of voice, a local Harris man having heard the recordings then spoke in a relaxed and colloquial manner covering the same content in the accustomed variety of local English and then similarly in Gaelic. These samples were separated as number (2) and number (4) in sequence of play in order to reduce the effect of the identity of the speaker interfering with the results.

The recordings were used with 80 Harris secondary-aged children in the upper forms of secondary schools both on and away from the island. The investigation was not undertaken in one of the Harris junior secondary schools where the identity of the speakers would have been obvious and the sample also failed to include three older Harris boys at school on Skye. The sample thus omitted four 'non-academic' and three 'academic' children within the Secondary III to Secondary VI age-range and comprised 80 out of the 87 children in this group.

By means of a questionnaire the study attempted to investigate what the hearers perceived as the speaker's level of education, intellectual ability, status and personality. Similarly measures were derived for intelligibility, identification of the hearer with the speaker, and familiarity with the speaker's speech-variety.(25) Table 6.7 presents the results for each of the four speech samples.

In terms of ratings of the speakers' likely educational levels, the RP English-speaker was perceived by almost all respondents as 'well educated'. The two Gaelic-speakers were ranked next — and the speaker using local Scottish English was ranked as the least 'well educated'. In contrast, the criterion of intellectual ability (as explored by the question 'Quick-thinking and clever' versus 'Slow-thinking and dull') produced contrasted results. The local Harris Gaelic-speaker had the highest rating for these qualities, followed by the formal Gaelic-speaker, whilst the 'slowest-thinking and dullest' speakers were respectively the RP English and the local Scottish English-speakers.

The perceived status and prestige of these speakers was explored by the questions concerning their 'importance', their supposed 'good' or 'poor' jobs, whether they possessed a 'lot' or 'little' money and whether they were 'in charge of things' or 'had little authority'. The differences resulting from the question on 'job' were small and not significant. Concerning 'importance', the RP English-speaker was very strongly perceived as 'important', with minimal differences amongst the other speakers (Scottish English rated least). Regarding possession of money, the results were similar for the RP English-speaker. However, the local Harris Gaelic-speaker was regarded as least likely to possess a 'lot' of money, and next to him the Scottish English-speaker. This issue produced the greatest indecision and uncertainty amongst respondents, over half not committing themselves regarding the two informal speakers. On the issue of 'authority' the differences were not

TABLE 6.7 Reaction to speech variety: Harris pupils in secondary years III-VI, 1972-3 (number in Sample: 80)

Description of speaker	Speaker 1 ('RP' formal Gaelic)		Speaker 2 (colloquial Scottish English)		Speaker 3 ('RP' formal English)		Speaker 4 (colloquial Harris Gaelic)		Significance of the difference between the correlated proportions of the two most extreme cases (z)
	No.	%	No.	%	No.	%	No.	%	
Well educated	72	90.0	65	81.3	79	98.8	74	92.5	z = 3.742 Significant below 0.01 level
Poorly educated	7	5.0	12	15.0	1	0.0	5	6.3	
Undecided	4	5.0	3	3.8	0	0.0	1	1.3	
Quick thinking and clever	57	71.3	46	57.5	50	62.5	62	77.5	z = 3.1568 Significant below 0.01 level
Slow thinking and dull	15	18.8	27	33.8	25	31.3	13	16.3	
Undecided	8	10.0	7	8.8	5	6.3	5	6.3	
Important	36	45.0	36	45.0	69	86.3	39	48.8	z = 5.5155 Significant below 0.01 level
Not very important	32	40.0	35	43.8	4	5.0	24	36.3	
Undecided	12	15.0	9	11.3	7	8.8	12	15.0	
Has a good job	68	85.0	66	82.5	68	85.0	59	73.8	z = 1.1766 Not significant
Has a poor job	7	8.8	4	5.0	1	1.3	9	11.3	
Undecided	5	6.3	10	12.5	11	13.8	12	15.0	
Has a lot of money	35	43.8	28	35.0	61	76.3	19	23.8	z = 6.7823 Significant below 0.01 level
Has little money	11	13.8	10	12.5	2	2.5	18	22.5	
Undecided	34	42.5	42	52.5	17	21.3	43	53.8	
In charge of things	52	65.0	56	70.0	56	70.0	52	65.0	z = 0.7559 Not significant
Has little authority	20	25.0	17	21.3	8	10.0	17	21.3	
Undecided	8	10.0	7	8.8	16	20.0	11	13.8	

TABLE 6.7 contd

Description of speaker	Speaker 1 No.	%	Speaker 2 No.	%	Speaker 3 No.	%	Speaker 4 No.	%	Significance
Honest	56	70.0	64	80.0	35	43.8	65	81.3	$z = 5.3033$
Untrustworthy	0	0.0	2	2.5	14	17.5	2	2.5	Significant below 0.01 level
Undecided	24	30.0	14	17.5	31	38.8	13	16.3	
Generous and kind	50	62.5	51	63.8	20	25.0	48	60.0	$z = 5.3964$
Mean and unkind	4	5.0	5	6.3	22	27.5	1	1.3	Significant below 0.01 level
Undecided	26	32.5	24	30.0	38	47.5	31	38.8	
Friendly and likeable	68	85.0	64	80.0	20	25.0	70	87.5	$z = 6.9488$
Unfriendly and unlikeable	2	2.5	5	6.3	33	41.3	4	5.0	Significant below 0.01 level
Undecided	10	12.5	11	13.8	27	33.8	6	7.5	
Easy to understand	68	85.0	68	85.0	49	61.3	69	86.3	$z = 3.6566$
Difficult to understand	11	13.8	10	12.5	24	30.0	6	7.5	Significant below 0.01 level
Undecided	1	1.3	2	2.5	6	7.5	5	6.3	
Desiring to speak like speaker	53	66.3	42	52.5	10	12.5	59	73.8	$z = 6.9488$
Not desiring to speak like speaker	21	26.3	22	27.5	65	81.3	12	15.0	Significant below 0.01 level
Undecided	6	7.5	16	20.0	5	6.3	9	11.3	
Meeting such speakers rarely or sometimes	51	63.8	32	40.0	70	87.5	19	23.8	$z = 6.3013$
Meeting such speakers often or regularly	24	30.0	45	56.3	6	7.5	51	63.8	Significant below 0.01 level
Undecided	5	6.3	3	3.8	4	5.0	10	12.5	

significant. (It may be suggestive that the RP and Scottish English-speakers were rated marginally more likely to be 'in charge of things' than the Gaelic-speakers.)

The 'halo' effect of speech variety in terms of personality or behaviour characteristics was explored by the descriptions 'honest' versus 'untrustworthy', 'generous and kind' versus 'mean and unkind', and 'friendly and likeable' versus 'unfriendly and unlikeable'. The speakers of local Harris Gaelic and Scottish English were those most readily seen as 'honest'. Fewer than half the respondents thus regarded the RP English-speaker and some 38 per cent were undecided. Even less confidence was shown with this speaker concerning 'generosity and kindness'. High and positive responses were shown here to the other speakers: 60 per cent and over in each case as against only 25 per cent of the respondents regarding the RP English-speaker as 'generous and kind'. Over 27 per cent regarded him as 'mean and unkind' whilst almost half were undecided. Results regarding friendliness and likeability were similar. The colloquial Harris Gaelic-speaker was regarded as 'friendly and likeable' by the largest proportion of the sample (over 87 per cent), the formal Gaelic-speaker closely following (85 per cent), and the colloquial English third (80 per cent). The RP English-speaker was rated 'friendly and likeable' by 25 per cent whilst one-third of respondents were undecided how to describe him.

In terms of claimed intelligibility there were minimal differences between the Gaelic- and non-RP English-speakers. However both for the non-native Gaelic-speakers and for the sample as a whole the colloquial Harris Gaelic-speaker was regarded as easiest to understand. The RP English-speaker was again significantly less positively rated. Concerning identification with the speakers, most respondents (74 per cent) desired to speak like the colloquial Harris Gaelic-speaker. Closely following was the formal Gaelic-speaker (66 per cent), over half the sample wished to speak like the local Scottish English-speaker, and only one in eight to emulate the RP English-speaker. Familiarity with these speech varieties was estimated by the extent to which respondents regarded themselves as meeting such speakers in everyday life. Naturally enough, the most familiar was local Harris Gaelic, closely followed by local Scottish English. Formal Gaelic was rated quite low: less than one-third of the sample reckoned to meet such speakers 'often' or 'regularly'. Only 7 per cent of the sample similarly claimed to encounter RP English-speakers.

If the three non-speakers and seven non-native speakers of Gaelic are removed from the sample the results remain very closely similar in all material respects.(26) The results are broadly similar to those of the study by Giles of 'upward convergence' undertaken in Bristol and Cardiff(27) and to the study of Welsh language as a factor in Welsh ethnicity reported by Bourhis and Giles.(28) As with the earlier 'convergence' study, the present findings corroborate the attribution of 'prestige' to RP English. With older Harris schoolchildren the playing of the third speech sample almost always raised general reactions of amusement. This speaker, though, was the most highly rated so far as 'education' was concerned and was outstandingly highly rated in terms of such status factors as being an 'important' person, having a 'good job',

earning a 'lot of money' and being 'in charge of things'. This
speaker was the lowest scored on such factors as desirable personality traits (honesty, generosity, friendliness), intelligibility and familiarity. The RP English-speaker was the second-
lowest scorer so far as intellectual ability was perceived. In
terms of identification, a strong negative result indicated an
overwhelming antipathy towards RP English. (The 'convergence'
study reported that RP-speakers were perceived amongst Bristol and
Cardiff adults less favourably than regional dialect-speakers in
terms of personal integrity and social attractiveness.) Although
the speaker of colloquial local Gaelic (No. 4) was rated lowest in
terms of status, this speaker was the highest scored in terms of
intellectual ability, desirable personality traits, intelligibility,
identification and familiarity.

As with the Welsh-language study, which reported the identification of language as a principally determinating aspect of ethnicity, so the present study showed that the only positive index of
identification made by the ten non-native-speakers or non-speakers
of Gaelic was with the speaker of local colloquial Gaelic. Strong
antipathy was shown to the RP English-speaker, mild antipathy to
the speaker of local colloquial English and ambivalence regarding
the 'formal' Gaelic-speaker. In the follow-up questionnaire each
of these non-Gaelic-group children agreed with the statement that
they were sorry not to have Gaelic as a native language and added
as reasons for this such statements as:
'I would like to speak to the rest of the pupils and friends
in Gaelic.'
'. . . because there are a lot of people who speak Gaelic nearly
all the time.'
'. . . because anyone having Gaelic has the advantage of being
bilingual from the start. One can get to university with "A" level
Gaelic (sic) and no other language.'
'. . . because other people are saying it and you aren't.'
'. . . because most people in the island speak it.'
'. . . because I find it complicating now.'
'. . . as I would like to learn it.'
Here are a variety of reasons: instrumental, intrinsic, but
above all, social identifying. As will be seen with the Gaelic
group there is a strong feeling of the value of Gaelic as above all
the principal means of identification with the island community.
Although this may not be bound up with a developed idea of ethnicity,
as in the Bourhis and Giles study(29) there is evidenced here the
operation of the factor which Fishman terms 'groupness'.(30)
Quite definitely Gaelic is perceived as an essential component —
even as a distinguishing component — of community identity, and
of social functioning within the peer group.

As the non-Gaelic group comprised only ten individuals out of
the sample, there are no significant conclusions concerning them.
It is interesting to note that six of the ten desired to speak like
the colloquial Harris Gaelic-speaker, four desired to emulate the
formal Gaelic-speaker, three the colloquial Harris English-speaker,
and only one the 'RP' English-speaker. As the results for this
group were not markedly different from the whole, it might be
valuable to explore the attitudes of the entire non-Gaelic group

throughout the secondary range to ascertain the extent to which it takes the Gaelic group as its reference group and identifies with its values and cultural traits.

Fishman has drawn attention to attitudes towards and behaviour with respect to a language as a social institution within a language-contact situation in the following terms: 'Three major categories of behaviour towards language are discernible. . .: Attitudinal-Affective Behaviour. . . . Overt Behavioral implementation of Attitudes, Feelings and Beliefs. . . . Cognitive aspects of Language Response.'(31)

> We know all too little about language-oriented attitudes and emotions (running the gamut of language loyalty . . . to language antipathy . . .) as distinguished from attitudes and emotions toward the 'typical' speakers of particular language variants. The features of language that are considered attractive or unattractive . . . have largely remained unstudied. However, in multilingual settings, particularly those in which a variety of 'social types' are associated with each language . . . languages per se (rather than the customs . . . of their model speakers) are reacted to as 'beautiful' or 'ugly', 'musical' or 'harsh', 'rich' or 'poor', etc.(32)

In the present study something of the 'language-stereotypes' of the commonest speech variants in use within the speech-community of Harris children have been illustrated. By way of comment upon them or as justification or explanation of their attitudes, the respondents are likely to make such observations as:

'I should very much like to speak like speaker number three (RP English) because of his ability to string together good and proper words in their correct place. His vocabulary was also impressive.'

'I would hate to speak like number three because he sounded *too* important and business-like.'

'. . . his voice sounded very up-up.'

'Speaker three spoke rather as though he classed himself above others — yet he was difficult to understand.'

'Three, dull voice, too many ineffective stops.'

'The third speaker was too educated for my liking and I think he thought a lot of himself, as though everyone should listen to him.'

'I should hate to speak like (3) because of the poshness in his voice.'

'No. 3, very friendly, overdoing it a little.'

'Speaker three gave me a horribly English impression.'

'. . . the third speaker is too aristocratic.'

Similar observations were made regarding the other speakers in terms of their speaking like local people, in terms of their being easy to understand, friendly, unassuming, pleasant to listen to, and so forth.

Fishman cites the case of older Polish immigrants in Australia identifying strongly with English yet speaking it poorly.(33) This phenomenon is well exemplified with the non-Gaelic group. These respondents on the whole were not able Gaelic-speakers yet almost all of them identified strongly with the local speakers and numbers of them even professed to find the colloquial Gaelic speaker more intelligible than the speaker of RP English. As Fishman continued, in the Polish-Australian case cited above, 'many young immigrants spoke English faultlessly and yet identified strongly with Polish, although they spoke it poorly'.

Within the contemporary Gaelic situation there is little 'overt behavioural implementation of attitudes, feelings and beliefs'.(34) As Fishman observes, 'Language reinforcement may proceed along voluntary as well as along official routes and encompasses organi- sational protection, statutory protection, agitation and creative production.' As we have seen, Gaelic does receive a certain amount of recognition, status and time within the education system. Vir- tually all respondents had experience of Gaelic in school and through classwork or contributions to school projects and journals would have participated in some measure in creative production in Gaelic. Since Gaelic does not enjoy the type of official status accorded to Welsh as the result of the Welsh Language Act 1967, official promotion of the language did not seem to figure strongly as part of the general awareness of the respondents with respect to language. This aspect was explored in the questionnaire and res- pondents were asked whether they would wish to see Gaelic used (whether or not together with English) on public signs and notices such as on road and street signs, official notices, advertisements, for announcements on public transport, on name-boards over shops and on official forms, licenses, tickets, etc. On the whole this was not seen as a significant aspect of public life into which Gaelic should be brought. The impression was strong that in asking these questions the matter was being raised in many minds for the first time. Many respondents left these questions unanswered or stated English should be used so that everyone should understand the message. The general attitude towards language within this domain was strongly instrumental: there did not seem to be any general awareness of the use of language as a symbol or expression of local solidarity. In discussions, news of the Welsh roadsigns campaign (although well-reported in the English media) did not seem to have entered the awareness of secondary schoolchildren in Harris to any marked extent. Some of the older students at Stornoway were fami- liar with the issue and commented: 'Well, the difference between the two countries here is that in Wales most of the country seems to want to preserve Welsh and the Welsh language. Whereas here it's the only people who are for the Gaelic language are up here in the Highlands. I mean if we started to concentrate as the Welsh do, the rest of Scotland would look down on us, not merely the rest of Britain — the rest of Scotland. The rest of the Welsh don't look down on their own people.' Generally, these students thought that the Welsh activities were 'crazy'; for example, bidding in Welsh at an auction: 'If any person did that (sort of thing) here even to save the Gaelic language, by the majority of the people he would be branded a lunatic and it would be suggested that he should be "taken away" right away. Those religiously-minded they would see to it right away. They will refuse to see any point of view but their own and therefore they brand the younger people who would be doing such crazy things in their opinion. They would say, "those are the people we are going to leave Scotland to?"'

On raising this point with a religious leader in Harris (a good
Gaelic-speaker, well-used to using his Gaelic expressively in
church), the observation was made that such activities in Wales,
even although led by ministers of similar religious views, were
'sheer fanaticism'.

Of the voluntary associations concerned with Gaelic language
and culture few had heard of any except An Comunn Gàidhealach and
Comunn na h-Oigridh, even though the latter is virtually defunct.
Both were readily reckoned to be effective and having some success
in keeping the language alive.

Agitation as an aspect of behaviour regarding language is absent
in the Gaelic context. Although in discussions older pupils might
state that they had firm commitments towards Gaelic, and the majority desired its perpetuation in the community and the home, this
represents a more passive aspect of language-loyalty. Typically
secondary students would like their children to be Gaelic-speaking
provided their future husband or wife would speak Gaelic. An older
student at Stornoway observed: 'We have a defeatist attitude. What
we need is someone — even one person who has got a purely optimis-
tic attitude about the future of Gaelic — and someone who is a
strong enough leader to get the people behind him in this way. That
is what you need!' (Said against some persistent interruption and
disagreement.) The image is persistent of activists and leaders
coming from the outside. An outsider who had effectively learned
Gaelic and who participated in — and in some measure led — in
local affairs in Harris left the island shortly after my arrival.
I was explicitly asked by a number of people whether I would be
taking his place. Reluctance to initiate activism and agitation
within a small community is common and understandable. In Harris
local people may stand aside, whether consciously or not, for outsiders or even gently encourage them into taking leadership positions: as officers or committee members of local organisations and
the like, even into council membership.

Fishman lists 'cognitive aspects of language response' as
'consciousness of mother-tongue as an entity separate from folkways
more generally; knowledge of synchronic variants, language history
and literature; and perceptions of language as a component of
"groupness".'(35) To some extent the second category of promotion
of knowledge regarding the language, its history and its literature
is the field which the school seeks to develop through the Gaelic
lesson. More detailed knowledge of 'synchronic variants' and
language history and literature is really taken to be the province
of higher 'Celtic' studies in the universities. In the community
there are, however, tradition-bearers and self-taught 'Gaelic
scholars' and one girl at Inverness reported using her Gaelic for
speaking with friends when trying to imitate their accents. At the
secondary-school level, however, the older pupils at any rate show
a very strong 'perception of language as a component of "groupness"':

'It gives you a sense of heritage' (girl, at Stornoway).

'I only wish I was a true "Hearrach" and that I could speak
Gaelic fluently. I took Gaelic in school for two years but in that
time learned very little except grammar' (girl, at Stornoway).

'It [Gaelic] has been part of our life for hundreds of years and
it should not be thrown away through lack of interest' (girl, at

Stornoway).

'I would not like being unable to speak Gaelic coming from a Gaelic-speaking island' (girl, at Inverness).

'I'd be ashamed if I could not speak the language of my island — as it is such a lovely language to listen to and to speak. Having the language tends to make you more of an individual' (girl, at Inverness).

'Adults try to learn Gaelic but they will never succeed in capturing the originality of the language or in developing a Gaelic dialect, which I think makes the Gaelic language' (girl, at Inverness).

'I'd be ashamed to come from the islands without Gaelic. People should carry on tradition' (girl, at Portree).

'One would feel out-of-place if he didn't speak Gaelic on an island like Harris' (boy at Tarbert).

'I would have liked to learn it. It would help . . . to get along with other people' (boy at Tarbert).

'Gaelic is really the Scottish language and it is an advantage to learn it' (girl, at Inverness).

'It is an advantage over others, being able to understand the country's first language and the people on the islands, etc. who deserve more appreciation than they get' (girl, at Inverness).

'I think people have an entirely wrong concept of the Gaelic language. They consider it inferior to English, where to my mind it is superior, I think if Scotland had their own government, the language would have a much better chance of survival together with the Gaelic culture' (girl, at Stornoway).

'It's up to us to start the other people speaking Gaelic.' 'Are you prepared to?' 'That's it — you need to combine.' 'Aye, but will they?' 'Stornoway is an English-speaking community — you can't change that.' (Discussion amongst boys at Stornoway.)

'If I spoke English at home they'd just look at me. Like this — I know — if any of the older people spoke English it would just seem strange' (girl, at Stornoway).

'It wouldn't be right to speak in English' (at a home funeral service) (girl, at Stornoway).

'If an Englishman were speaking Gaelic would you resent that?' 'No.' 'But if you knew that when you were speaking Gaelic amongst yourselves that an Englishman could understand you?' 'Oh yes!' 'I'd admire him if he had taken the trouble to learn it — a dying language.' (Conversations between girls at Stornoway.)

In a study of the Catholic island of Barra in the early 1950s(36) the social anthropologist Vallee concluded that the Gaelic language and its associated lore and culture had an important function in providing symbols of in-group identification. This being particularly noticeable at such events of island-wide solidarity as 'funerals, visitations and celebrations'. This awareness of the phenomenon which Fishman terms 'groupness' mediated through awareness of the Gaelic language as a distinctive entity seems as true and as strong for Calvinist Harris in the 1970s as it did for Catholic Barra in the 1950s. Unlike Wales, there is no very great sense of linkage of language and nationality. Neither is there any pronounced sense of Gaelic or a Highland or Island ethnicity. Yet there is definitely a sense of group of community identity with the

Gaelic language. It is difficult for those in the secondary age-
group adequately to articulate these feelings, but they nevertheless appear to be felt. One girl at Stornoway said, 'I would
never marry an Englishman. I am very race conscious. They are
very snobbish.' When asked what was the difference between an
Englishman and an English-speaking Scotsman, she replied, 'Nothing —
hardly anything — just the accent.' She was further asked what
she regarded as being the difference between a Gaelic-speaking
Scotsman and an English-speaking Scotsman. She thought they were
different but she could not express the difference in words.
   Although there is little overt language-consciousness there is
evidence for the continuation of a warm affective tone associated
with the language amongst the young people of Harris. By themselves the internally-generated attitudes and supports for the
community-language in the home and in some measure also in the
school, would assure its continuance into the next generation. But
as we have seen, there are now families who are in fact not trans-
mitting Gaelic to their children, and the secondary-aged child as
he leaves school to join the adult community is surrounded by
particularly strong anglicising pressures in his hostel, away at
college or university and in industrial training. As the more
academically- and occupationally-mobile children leave the island
they are dispersed throughout the educational and occupational
system of Scotland, of Britain, of the armed forces and merchant
navy, and overseas. If they return at all, they are not likely to
be married to a member of their home community. If their attachment to and favourable attitude to Gaelic are retained, it is on a
personal level alone. The language and the identifications with
the home community are unlikely to be passed on through their
families.

LANGUAGE-SHIFT AMONGST HARRIS SECONDARY I CHILDREN (1958-9 - 1973-4)

The updating of the 1958-9 Survey results of the Scottish Council
for Research in Education Study, 'Gaelic-Speaking Children in
Highland Schools' enables fairly exact comparisons to be made over
the 14-15 year period between 1958-74 concerning the language-
situation of Secondary I-aged pupils.
   The results of re-issuing copies of the earlier study's questionnaires to the Harris secondary schools and to the Secondary I
pupils are given below (Tables 6.8-6.15). References are made to
the published tables in the 1958-9 Survey and copies of the questionnaires may be found in its Appendices.

TABLE 6.8 The incidence of Gaelic and English as first languages and knowledge of Gaelic amongst Secondary I pupils in Harris schools 1972-3 (and 1973-4) (frequencies for 1973-4 are shown in brackets in each case)

School	SI pupils of 1st language Gaelic	SI pupils for 1st language English	Total with effective knowledge of Gaelic C + D + E	Total year group	% with knowledge of Gaelic
Tarbert	19 (12)	7 (12)	25 (18)	26 (24)	96 (73)
Leverburgh	8 (5)	0 (0)	8 (5)	8 (5)	100 (100)
Scalpay	7 (11)	1 (1)	8 (12)	8 (12)	100 (100)
Totals	34 (28)	8 (13)	41 (35)	42 (41)	98 (100)

	1st language Gaelic Extent of ability in Gaelic*						1st language English Extent of ability in Gaelic*						Grand total	Total with effective knowledge of Gaelic (C + D + E)
	A	B	C	D	E	Tot.	A	B	C	D	E	Tot.		
Tarbert	0(1)		4(8)	15(3)		19(12)	1(2)	0(4)	5(4)	1(2)		7(12)	26(24)	25(18)
Leverburgh			2(0)	6(5)		8(5)						0(0)	8(5)	8(5)
Scalpay	0(1)		7(10)			7(11)	1(0)			0(1)		1(1)	8(12)	8(12)
	0(1)		6(9)	28(18)		34(28)	1(2)	0(4)	5(4)	2(2)	0(1)	8(13)	42(41)	41(35)

* Coded as in Table 6.13 below

TABLE 6.9 The incidence of Gaelic and English amongst parents of Secondary I pupils in Harris schools 1972-3 (and 1973-4) (frequencies for 1973-4 are shown in brackets in each case)

School	First language of Secondary I pupils									
	Gaelic Pupils with parents as Gaelic-speakers					English Pupils with parents as Gaelic-speakers				
	Father only	Mother only	Both	Neither	Total	Father only	Mother only	Both	Neither	Total
Tarbert	1(0)		18(13)		19(13)	0(2)	1(2)	4(7)	1(1)	6(12)
Leverburgh			8(5)		8(5)					
Scalpay			7(10)		7(10)	0(1)		1(0)		1(1)
Total	1(0)		33(28)		34(28)	0(3)	1(2)	5(7)	1(1)	7(13)

TABLE 6.10 The use of Gaelic in specific situations amongst Secondary I pupils in Harris schools 1972-3 (and 1973-4) (frequencies for 1973-4 are shown in brackets in each case)

School	No. of pupils	To parents Gaelic	Both	Eng.	To siblings Gaelic	Both	Eng.	No. Sib.	To other children Gaelic	Both	Eng.	In playground Gaelic	Both	Eng.
Pupils whose first language was Gaelic														
Tarbert	19(13)	19(12)	0(1)		16(8)	0(2)	3(1)	0(2)	17(4)	0(6)	2(3)	13(5)	0(8)	6(0)
Leverburgh	8(5)	8(5)			8(5)				6(3)	2(0)	0(2)	0(3)	8	0(2)
Scalpay	7(10)	7(10)			7(10)				7(13)	0(7)		7(8)	0(2)	
Totals	34(28)	34(27)	0(1)	0	31(23)	0(2)	3(1)	0(2)	30(10)	2(13)	2(5)	20(16)	8(10)	6(2)
Pupils whose first language was English														
Tarbert	7(12)	1(1)		6(11)		1(1)	6(11)				7(12)		0(1)	7(11)
Leverburgh	0(0)													
Scalpay	1(1)		0(1)	1(0)			1(1)		0(1)			0(1)		1
Totals	8(13)	1(1)	0(1)	7(11)	0	1(1)	7(12)	0	0(1)	0	8(12)	0(1)	0(1)	8(11)

TABLE 6.11 The study of Gaelic in secondary schools: first year classes in Harris secondary schools 1972-3 (and 1973-4) (frequencies for 1973-4 are shown in brackets in each case)

School	Pupils of first language English						Pupils of first language Gaelic					
	Primary Gaelic course		Secondary Gaelic course		Periods per week	No. of pupils	Primary Gaelic course		Secondary Gaelic course		Periods per week	No. of pupils
	Yes	No	Yes	No			Yes	No	Yes	No		
Tarbert	7(12)		5(10)	2(2)	0-3½ hrs (3-3.20)	7(12)	15(11)	4(1)	19(11)	0(1)	2 hr. 40m - 3 hr. 30m (3 hr. 20m)	19(12)
Leverburgh							8(5)	0(1)	8(6)	0(0)	1 hr. 25m (2 hrs)	
Scalpay	1(1)		1(1)		2 hrs (3-4 hrs)	1(1)	7(9)	0(1)	7(10)	0(0)	2 hrs (1 hr. 40m - 4 hrs)	7(10)
Totals	8(13)		6(11)	2(2)	0-3½ hrs	8(13)	30(25)	4(3)	34(27)	0(1)	1 hr. 25m - 3 hrs 30m (1 hr. 40m - 4 hrs)	34(28)

TABLE 6.12   GSCHS Table XI (p. 49),   The Gaelic-speaking group in Secondary Schools (First Year)

	Number of Gaelic-speaking pupils in SI		
	Harris 1958-9	Harris 1972-3	Harris 1973-4
First language Gaelic ('Col.1')	49	34	28
First language English ('Col.2')	6	8	13
Total with knowledge of Gaelic ('Col.3')	55	41	35
Total year group ('Col.4')	58	42	41
Percentages:			
% of year group with 'Col.1' first language Gaelic 'Col.4'	84	81	68
% of year group with 'Col.3' knowledge of Gaelic 'Col.4'	95	98	85

	Number of Gaelic-speaking pupils in SI whose first language was					
Responses to statements concerning ability in Gaelic	Harris 1958-9		Harris 1972-3		Harris 1973-4	
	Gaelic	English	Gaelic	English	Gaelic	English
'A' I have forgotten all of it	–	–	–	1	–	2
'B' I understand but am unable to speak it	–	2	–	–	–	4
'C' I understand simple lessons and can conduct elementary conversations in it	–	1	–	5	1	4
'D' I express myself with fair fluency in it	–	2	6	2	9	2
'E' I express myself with considerable fluency in it	49	1	28	–	18	–
Total	49	6	34	8	28	13
Total, whole year group	55		42		41	
Corrected totals of Gaelic-speaking children ('C' + 'D' + 'E')	49 / 53	4	34 / 41	7	28 / 35	7
do. as % of year group	82 / 91	7	81 / 98	17	68 / 85	17

TABLE 6.13 GSCHS Table XIII (p. 54), The use of Gaelic at home (Secondary I pupils)

Pupils with parents as Gaelic-speakers	Number of pupils in secondary schools (first year) claiming some knowledge of Gaelic whose first language was					
	Harris 1958-9		Harris 1972-3		Harris 1973-4	
	Gaelic	English	Gaelic	English	Gaelic	English
Father only	2	3	–	–	–	3
Mother only	–	–	1	1	–	2
Both	47	–	33	5	28	7
Neither	–	–	–	1	–	1
Total	49	3	34	7	28	13

Note: Definitions of parents' ability in Gaelic as in GSCHS Table VIII (primary scholars)

TABLE 6.14 GSCHS Table XIV (p. 55), The Study of Gaelic in Schools

		Number of pupils in secondary schools (first year) claiming some knowledge of Gaelic, with details of Gaelic studies for pupils whose first language was					
		Harris 1958-9		Harris 1972-3		Harris 1973-4	
		Gaelic	English	Gaelic	English	Gaelic	English
Primary course:	Yes	47	3	30	8	15	13
	No	2	3	4	–	3	–
Secondary course:	Yes	49	5	34	6	27	11
	No	–	1	0	2	1	2
Periods per week		2-7	3-5	1 hr. 25m - 3 hr. 30m	0 hr. - 3 hr. 30m	1 hr. 25m - 4 hr.	3-4 hrs
Number of pupils		49	6	34	8	28	13

TABLE 6.15   GSCHS Table XV (p. 58), The use of Gaelic in specific
situations

Specific situation:		Number of pupils in secondary schools (first year) with language used, whose first language was					
		Harris 1958-9		Harris 1972-3		Harris 1973-4	
		Gaelic	English	Gaelic	English	Gaelic	English
Number of pupils		49	6	34	8	28	13
To parents:	Gaelic	46	–	34	1	27	1
	Both	3	1	–	–	–	1
	English	–	5	–	7	–	1
To brothers and sisters:	Gaelic	47	–	31	–	23	–
	Both	2	–	–	1	2	1
	English	–	6	3	7	1	12
No brothers or sisters		Not ascertained					
To other children:	Gaelic	32	1	30	–	1o	1
	Both	17	2	2	–	13	–
	English	–	3	2	8	5	12
In playground:	Gaelic	23	1	20	–	16	1
	Both	26	2	8	–	1o	1
	English	–	3	6	8	2	11

CONCLUSIONS

In general the secondary school has a neutral position regarding
Gaelic. It supports and continues language-development in Gaelic
where the child enters secondary school as a native-speaker or
with effective knowledge of Gaelic. Otherwise the school at this
stage does not attempt to promote the bilinguality of monoglot
English-speaking children.
    Gaelic 'first-language' and maintenance amongst the younger
secondary group has greatly declined over the fifteen-year period.
The age-group has declined to 72 per cent of its size between
1958-9 and 1972-3 (or 71 per cent over the fifteen years to 1973-4).
The incidence of first-language ability in Gaelic has dropped from
84 per cent of the age-group to 81 per cent and 68 per cent.
Effective ability in Gaelic, however, improved between 1958-9 and
1972-3 from 95 per cent of the age-group to 98 per cent. However,
this maintenance was not sustained in the following year-group.
A decline to 85 per cent is most noticeable.
    The thirteen non-'first-language' speakers of Gaelic in SI in
1973-4 comprised one Scalpay boy who was fluent in Gaelic but
whose mother was non-Gaelic-speaking and twelve children attending
Tarbert. Both parents of seven of these children were claimed as

Gaelic-speakers. Of the remainder there were two cases in which
the father also spoke Gaelic, two of the mother alone and one
case of an incoming professional family where neither parent spoke
Gaelic. The 'mixed' families appear to comprise either a local
woman married to a higher-technical incoming man or a manual-
working man marrying from off the island. The seven cases of 'first-
language' English-speaking children include two cases of professionals and the remainder of lower-status parental occupations. However,
only one child in 1972-3 and two in the following year had no
ability in Gaelic at all, although in 1973-4 four children as
against none in the preceding year and two 15 years earlier were
restricted to passive ability only in Gaelic.

   Thus the school is supportive of ability in Gaelic whether
native or acquired. However, as in the later primary years, the
educational programme is not truly bilingual.

   As brighter older secondary children are required to move away
from the home area for higher secondary, academic, technical and
further education, the institution of the school within the island
community has a significant physical function in controlling the
size, internal structure and composition of the society. There is
a selective 'creaming-off' of the brightest children - and of girls
compared with boys. The residual population structure is distorted
by the diminution of younger age-groups, the diminution of an internal 'intelligentsia' or leadership cadre, and by the relative scarcity
of younger women of marriageable and childbearing age.

   The institution of the school also has a significant symbolic
function within the Gaelic speech-community in placing the native
language and its associated culture into a special position. The
initial stages of education treat Gaelic instrumentally as a means
of acquiring literacy and as a 'bridge' to ease the transition to
school. Subsequently Gaelic is separated from the remainder of
the curriculum, whose classification and framing(37) is otherwise
strong, and integrates the 'subject' in ways comparable with low-
status areas elsewhere in the educational system. As Gaelic
ceases to be the medium of education and becomes a 'subject', the
promotion of ambilinguality and biculturalism within the school is
diminished. Gaelic may be reified, as it were, into a 'thing' apart
from the main endeavours of the everyday life of the children and
thus they experience an alienation with regard to 'Gaelic', as
imparted by the school.

   The studies of confidence in and attitudes towards language
support the impression that children maintain a good image of Gaelic
and its culture. As an institution within the extra-curricular and
informal life of a young person it may function as a personal support in the process of the socialisation of the 'academic' student
into higher education and career in mainstream society.

Chapter 7

LANGUAGE-CONSERVATION AMONGST THE HARRIS ADULT POPULATION

The place of language within the schools and patterns of language-usage amongst schoolchildren have been illustrated and discussed in the foregoing chapters. Social processes have been outlined affecting language usages, attitudes, careers and life-chances of the contemporary school population.

In order to present a more complete picture of social processes as they have affected the population as a whole, it is now necessary to turn to the adult population and consider the social functions of language within the local culture. Although a synchronous study such as this is not able categorically to argue concerning the ways in which patterns of social behaviour amongst young people may work themselves through the age-structure, comparisons of the attitudes and behaviours of the children and the younger and the older adults may be suggestive of diachronous processes which a longitudinal study might reveal more substantially. Something of such a diachronous view has been possible amongst the schoolchildren. As there has been no previous study of the adult community, a future study providing comparisons over time will be very valuable.

The enumerated adult population of Harris of eighteen years and above in 1971 approximated some 2,195 persons. (The Census included returns from Berneray and St Kilda with this total.) As the 1971 Census presents data only to the nearest five persons, the computation of precise numbers from the published reports is rendered impossible. The electoral roll compiled later in the year contained some 2,265 names. Discrepancies also result from the administration of electoral registration at Inverness. Considerable benefit of doubt is extended in the case of electors not included in subsequent returns in a following October. Hence the register contains not only numbers of persons known locally to have died or left the island in recent years but also double entries in the case of persons who have moved home locally. The 1972-3 electoral roll contained the names of 2,243 electors aged eighteen and over.

The study of attitudes towards language and language behaviour was undertaken by means of questionnaire amongst a 4 per cent sample of the registered electors. A 5 per cent random sample was made up in proportion to the size of each of the four electoral division units (Table 7.1).

TABLE 7.1

Electoral area unit	Registered population	5% sample	Rounded sample	Sample respondents
26 Tarbert and North Harris	907	45.35	45	35
27 Isle of Scalpay	397	19.85	20	18
28 Mid-Harris and Bays	381	19.05	19	13
29 Leverburgh and South Harris	558	27.90	28	25
Totals	2,243	112.15	112	91

Response rate: 81.2 per cent of sample, comprising 4.06 per cent of population

In practice it was only possible to secure an effective response rate of 81 per cent of the sample for a variety of reasons. The 91 contactable respondents comprised a 4.06 per cent sample of the electoral roll. Amongst the sample were 3 deceased, 2 away at sea, 4 of limited understanding or substantial deafness, 9 out or away from home (despite several repeated calls) and only three refusals. It was, therefore, impracticable to include these 21 individuals in the sample. Of the 91 in the effective sample 86 (or 94.5 per cent) were Gaelic-speaking and five spoke English only. The sample thus corresponds very closely in this regard with the adult population as a whole. (In 1971 91.6 per cent of the population aged 15 and over was bilingual. The addition of Gaelic monoglots would render the fit even closer.) The sample also corresponds closely with the age- and sex-structure of the population as a whole at the 1971 Census (Tables 7.2 and 7.3).

TABLE 7.2 Age-cohorts as percentage of totals: Harris adults 1971 and 1973

Age-group	Sample 1973	Whole population 1971
18-29	12.1	13.6
30-39	13.2	13.4
40-49	14.3	17.1
50-59	19.8	14.4
60-69	19.8	20.7
70-79	15.4	13.9
80+	5.5	6.8

TABLE 7.3   Sexes as percentage of totals: Harris adults
1971 and 1973

Sex	Sample 1973	Whole population 1971
Males	51.6	49.7
Females	48.4	50.3

Within the present-day patterns of social behaviour in Harris
Gaelic alone does not enable an individual to function adequately
within all the domains of social interaction. As we have seen, the
broadcast news and entertainment media are almost entirely English
and English dominates such other important areas as administration,
education and many other aspects of public affairs. The Census
returns indicate 38 Gaelic monoglots amongst the Harris population.
These comprise chiefly young children and older women who may be
housebound in less accessible areas.(1)   During the course of the
survey one elderly man was encountered who was a very ineffective
speaker of English. Also two older women living in isolated conditions were monolingual in Gaelic only. There are probably Gaelic
monoglots whose relations would be unlikely to return them as
'Gaelic-only' on a census form. They would be able to count, give
the date and exchange a greeting in English and would be likely to
be put down as 'Gaelic-and-English-speaking' on a Census form. The
language question on the Scottish Census has never attempted to
gauge the degree of proficiency in Gaelic or English possessed by
the speaker. However, in 1971 for the first time the Census sought
information regarding ability to read and write in Gaelic. Thus it
will be possible to ascertain some idea of 'media-variance' amongst
the Gaelic-speaking communities.
    Fishman(2) draws attention to the situation whereby bilinguals
may have differing abilities or levels of performance between their
two languages within the various media of communication such as
speaking, reading and writing. A study was made within the sample
of the adult population and respondents were asked to rate themselves
concerning their ability in Gaelic for understanding, speaking and
reading and writing. Respondents were asked to state whether they
believed their ability in Gaelic to be very good, quite good, not
always sufficient, usable only with great difficulty or unable to
use Gaelic at all in respect of each of the four media. Thus a
profile of what Fishman terms 'media-variance' can be derived and
the results are illustrated in Table 7.4.
    No significant differentiation of abilities to understand, read
or write Gaelic was obtained for the various age-groups. Had a
larger sample been possible, it might have been the case that the
principal difference in pattern of abilities, namely that of the
youngest age-group compared with the remainder, could have proved
significant. However, the population Census of 1971 for the first
time sought information concerning abilities in reading and writing
as well as speaking Gaelic and as this information is now available
for the whole of the adult population it will be useful to compare
the findings of the census regarding literacy in Gaelic with the

TABLE 7.4 Literacy in Gaelic: Gaelic-speaking Harris adults, 1973 (sample survey)

Age-group	Number speaking reading, writing Gaelic	Number speaking and reading Gaelic only	Number speaking Gaelic only	Total	% reading and writing Gaelic	% reading Gaelic
18-29	4	2	4	10	60.0	40.0
30-39	2	3	7	12	83.3	58.3
40-49	2	2	8	12	83.3	66.7
50-59	5	5	7	17	70.6	41.2
60-69	5	5	7	17	70.6	41.2
70+	5	6	7	18	72.2	38.9
All ages	23	23	40	86	73.3	46.5

Not significant

TABLE 7.5.1 Gaelic literacy in Harris in 1971 and 1973 by ages

| Age-group | From population Census 1971 Speaking Gaelic and English | | | | From sample survey 1973 Speaking Gaelic and English | | | |
	Total	Total (with % of total age-group)	Reading Gaelic (and as % of all Gaelic-speakers)	Reading and writing Gaelic (and as % of all Gaelic-speakers)	Total	Total (with % of total age-group)	Reading Gaelic (and as % of Gaelic-speakers)	Reading and writing Gaelic (and as % of Gaelic-speakers)
15-24	235	205 (87.2)	175 (85.4)	135 (65.9)				
25-44	595	505 (84.9)	450 (89.1)	300 (59.4)	25	24 (96.0)	18 (75.0)	13 (54.2)
45-64	740	645 (87.2)	625 (96.9)	370 (57.4)	31	30 (96.8)	23 (76.7)	14 (46.7)
65+	690	665 (96.4)	570 (85.7)	245 (36.8)	29	27 (93.1)	19 (70.4)	10 (37.0)
Totals	2025	1865 (92.1)	1645 (88.20)	915 (45.19)	85	81 (95.29)	60 (70.5)	37 (43.5)

χ^2 = 143.073 significant below 0.001 level at 6 degrees of freedom

χ^2 = 19.4548 significant below 0.001 level at 4 degrees of freedom

present sample obtained two years later. It seems unlikely that any
material difference had occurred over this period except a slight
contraction and ageing of the population. Unfortunately, it was
not clear at the time of the fieldwork precisely in what form the
Census would present its findings. As its results are grouped
in the age-bands 15-24, 25-44, 45-64 and 65 and over, the younger
adults are difficult to compare between these two studies.

The sample indicates a pattern of lesser abilities of reading
and writing amongst young adults, higher abilities amongst the
middle-aged and a lesser ability amongst the older age-groups.
Table 7.4 sets out the results. The contingencies are not significant but it will be seen that in the case of the 1971 population
census results a similar pattern is discernible.

Since the population census represents the whole population the
numbers involved enable a highly significant result to be obtained.
Unfortunately, the presentation of the census results does not enable
the abilities of the youngest age-group of the adult population to be
compared between the sample and the census. If there is a consistent weakness of reading and writing abilities in Gaelic amongst
these individuals (within the age-range 18-29 or more particularly
18-24), as the sample might suggest, the significance of this cannot
be supported statistically. So far as abilities to read and write
Gaelic are concerned, both the census and the sample indicate that
from a modest level of ability of a little over half of all Gaelic
speakers in the 25-44 age range, the ability both to write and read
Gaelic consistently declines to a little over one-third of all
Gaelic-speakers in the over-65 group. However, it is encouraging
that the more highly significant and reliable results of the census
provide a pattern which corresponds with that of the findings
amongst the 1973 sample. There may, therefore, be some justification in arguing the validity of the sample results on these grounds.
The results are summarised in Tables 7.5.1 and 7.5.2.

It can be seen that the results of the sample survey follow
fairly closely the results of the population census carried out two
years previously. (The true incidence of ability in Gaelic amongst
the younger adult age-groups in Harris is higher than that given by
the census, owing to the fact that some sixty-five service personnel
stationed on St Kilda are enumerated in with Harris. This fact
probably accounts for the ostensibly lower proportion of Gaelic-
speakers mainly in the 25-44 age-group in 1971 as compared with the
sample survey in 1973.) The method of presentation of the Census
statistics makes it impossible to compare the younger adult groups
in the 18-24 years age-range. It must also be borne in mind that as
the Census gives totals only to the nearest whole five persons a
measure of random error may thus be brought in. In the case of
small populations, as we have here, such errors may be proportionately greater than in large populations.

The pattern of reading and writing abilities within these age-
groups requires some comment. Taken separately the contingencies of
reading ability and writing ability across the age-groups of the
census results prove to be significant. (The χ^2 value for readers
yielded 7.7617: significant below the 0.01 level at 3 degrees of
freedom; that for readers and writers of Gaelic yielded 14.1269 and
was significant below the 0.005 level.) The similar patterns within

TABLE 7.5.2   Gaelic literacy in Harris 1973 by age and sex (sample survey)

Age-group	Sex	Total	Total Gaelic-speaking		Reading Gaelic		Reading and writing Gaelic	
			No.	%	No.	As % of speakers	No.	As % of speakers
18-29	M	5	5	100.00	3	60.00	1	20.00
	F	6	5	83.33	3	60.00	3	60.00
30-39	M	6	6	100.00	5	83.33	3	50.00
	F	6	6	100.00	5	83.33	4	66.67
40-49	M	6	6	100.00	4	66.67	3	50.00
	F	7	6	85.71	6	100.00	5	83.33
50-59	M	8	7	87.50	4	57.14	2	28.57
	F	10	10	100.00	8	80.00	5	50.00
60-69	M	10	9	90.00	7	77.78	4	44.44
	F	8	8	100.00	5	62.50	3	37.50
70-79	M	9	9	100.00	6	66.67	3	33.33
	F	5	5	100.00	5	100.00	2	40.00
80+	M	3	2	66.67	0	00.00	0	00.00
	F	2	2	100.00	2	100.00	2	100.00
Total	M	47	44	93.62	29	65.91	16	36.36
	F	44	42	95.45	34	80.95	24	57.14
Total all ages and sexes		91	86	94.51	63	73.26	40	46.51
			Not significant		Not significant		Not significant	

the 1973 sample proved not to be significant, but it must be borne in mind that the sample is small. Why should there be a higher incidence of reading ability amongst middle-aged groups compared with younger adults, and as compared with the old? An answer may be found within the religious culture of the community whereby family devotions lay upon the middle-aged groups the instrumental necessity of reading aloud from the Gaelic Bible. Yet such skills should have been retained by the old even if not as yet acquired by the young. Concerning the ability to write, the higher incidence of this skill amongst the young may be attributed to the improved place which Gaelic has gained in the schools. The oldest age-groups would all have passed through primary school stages before the 'permissive clause' of the 1918 Education Act enabled Gaelic to be taught as part of the normal school curriculum. The youngest age-groups would even have been benefited by the bilingual policies introduced into Inverness-shire schools from 1958 onwards. Hence the seemingly sequential decline with increasing age of abilities of reading and writing together may reasonably be regarded as reflecting the place of Gaelic in the schools which individuals attended in their childhood.

No significant differences were discernible between males and females regarding abilities to read and write Gaelic. This was the case concerning the whole population aged three and over at the 1971 Census as well as for the sample of Harris adults aged 18 and over in 1973. The results are presented in Table 7.6.

TABLE 7.6 Gaelic literacy in Harris in 1971 and 1973

Sex and age categories	Numbers able to speak Gaelic	Numbers able to read Gaelic	Numbers able to read and write Gaelic
Census 1971			
Males aged 3 years and over	1,210	1,010	595
Females aged 3 years and over	1,250	1,075	615
Totals	2,460	2,085	1,210

χ^2 = 3.6619: only significant below 0.250 level at 2 degrees of freedom

Sample 1973			
Males aged 18 years and over	44	29	16
Females aged 18 years and over	42	34	24
Totals	86	63	40

χ^2 = 4.0778: only significant below 0.250 level at 2 degrees of freedom

In a community such as Harris, where there is a more noticeable differentiation of the role between the sexes than in a more urban contemporary society, some differences in claimed ability between the sexes would not have been surprising. However, no highly-marked or significant differentiation of literacy in Gaelic between the sexes has emerged.

There is little instrumental necessity for Gaelic to be used in writing. Official business of all kinds is undertaken in English. Even in church services there is no necessity to have to read Gaelic — although the practice of following the readings and singing the Metrical Psalms from the Gaelic Psalter are common. In any case the Psalms are precented: the precentor first giving out each line and the congregation repeating it, with variations. Scripture references and Psalm numbers and verses are generally cited first in Gaelic and then in English at Gaelic services. Congregation members who are more used to the English system of numeration than the Gaelic would be at no disadvantage. Posters of Gaelic events are invariably in English, not so much for the benefit of speakers of English only, but for the 25-30 per cent of Gaelic-speakers unable to read their own language effectively. This inability is generally regretted. As most Gaelic-readers are self-taught, this inability is largely due to personal inactivity. There is hardly a house without at least a Bible in Gaelic. One respondent said, 'The teacher hadn't any Gaelic. If I had had a Gaelic teacher I would have been proficient.'

The use of Gaelic in personal letter-writing is rare. In response to the question concerning which language was used when writing a letter to a member of the family, it was almost entirely the case that English alone was used. Out of 85 competent Gaelic-speaking respondents only ten responded that they used Gaelic to any extent for this purpose. One respondent (a younger teacher) claimed to use mainly Gaelic for this purpose, two respondents claimed to use Gaelic and English to about the same extent, and five used mainly English. Two octogenarians claimed to use Gaelic alone for letter-writing. At least one of these respondents was an ineffective speaker of English. Neither might have been habitual letter-writers anyway in either language. English, is, therefore, almost universally seen as the appropriate language for this purpose: even though the activity may be between members of a family who otherwise utilise Gaelic for all other family purposes. Although this question was included in order to elicit information on language-use within the family domain, it might be better regarded as an activity separate from the face-to-face interaction of family life. One respondent, a retired skipper, commented: 'You need practice. When you write on business, you use only English.'

The use of Gaelic was explored in a number of 'prima facie' domains. The questionnaire sought to elicit information regarding the language used 'intra-personally' (in dreaming, personal prayers, swearing and counting), within the family (to spouse, to others at home, for community affairs, at work, at township meetings, in quarrels, at church) for commercial transactions (at garages, shops, at the Post Office and on public transport), and for official purposes (in local government business, in discussions with teachers, the district clerk and crofting assessor).

TABLE 7.7   Extent to which Gaelic is used in various prima facie domains by Gaelic-speaking adults in Harris, 1973

Age group	Number	Percentage of respondents claiming always to use Gaelic within the following domains				
		Personal	Familial	Communal	Transitional	Official
18-29	10	43.6	67.7	54.5	42.5	42.9
30-39	12	40.5	68.6	39.4	52.6	31.6
40-49	12	43.2	85.4	77.8	65.6	55.0
50-59	17	54.0	91.1	90.0	59.3	44.2
60-69	17	50.8	83.6	62.7	53.6	50.9
70+	17	70.2	93.7	83.9	75.0	78.9
All ages	85*	51.6	84.0	71.1	58.2	50.6
Correlation of age with usage of Gaelic		r=+0.891	r=+0.818	r=+0.565	r=+0.758	r=+0.825
Significance level (4 df)		Below 0.02	Below 0.05	Not sig.	Below 0.10	Below 0.02

* One male respondent in the 70+ age group was omitted owing to his mental inadequacy.

Respondents were asked whether they always used Gaelic, generally used Gaelic, used Gaelic and English to about the same extent, generally used English or always used English in respect of each of the activities comprising each domain. The results are summarised in Table 7.7 for the various age-groups and the population as a whole. On the basis of the questions asked, the study attempted to explore the extent to which Gaelic functioned as a sufficient medium to support the typical activities within the various ostensible domains of social life.

Very little difference either to the results themselves or to their significance was obtained by aggregating respondents using 'Gaelic only' with those using 'Gaelic generally'. Tests of significance yielded good results of differentiation of usage of 'Gaelic only' across the age-groups of the sample. However, the results must be interpreted with caution. The concept 'domain' is to a great extent an artifical and exterior categorisation of the language-behaviour of an individual or a community. It is of course made up from numbers of typical speech-situations and interpersonal behavioural patterns. These may or may not be seen as related or as functionally clustered together by the speakers or by the speech communities themselves. In this situation it may have been more explicit to have separated the component activities and to have discussed their characteristics separately. However, one difficulty here is that without a very much larger sample it becomes difficult meaningfully to discuss the significance of such results. Only the most differentiated usages across the age-range produce results which are statistically significant.

Amongst the speech-situations comprising the domains utilised in Table 7.7 the statistically significant age-differentiated usages were as follows: within the 'personal' domain, only 'swearing'; within the 'familial' domain, 'talking to spouse' and 'work on the croft'; within the 'communal' domain, 'church', 'talking to people at work' and 'to a foreman at work'; within the 'official' domain, 'discussing local affairs with a councillor' (in which latter case younger people were more inclined to use 'Gaelic only' than were older people).

Various writers have quite differently categorised the concept domain. Schmidt-Rohr cites nine (family, playground, school, church, literature, press, army, courts, administration). In contrast Baker cites merely four (familiar, informal, formal and inter-group).(3) The number, contents and extent of the domains are very much open to the individual investigator and no more validity may be claimed for the domains utilised here than for those distinguished by any other investigator.

With these reservations in mind, it may be justifiable to draw some limited conclusions from the general character of the results in Table 7.7. Older respondents are much more likely to claim usage of Gaelic only than younger respondents within each domain. These differences show up the most strongly between the under-50s and over-50s within the 'personal' domain, and between the under-40s and over-40s within the 'familial', 'communal' and 'transactional' domains. Gaelic is more strongly represented as a predominating language of social intercourse within the 'familial' and 'communal' domains. It is weakest in the 'official' and 'personal' domains. It must be remembered that in discussing 'domains', as such, in these respects what is really being signified is a sort of average language behaviour amongst the particular usages which have been brought together to comprise the particular domain. On these measures the use of Gaelic stands up very well in communal life (except amongst the 30-39 age-group — the principal age-group, it would seem, of parents with young families).

In the case of the 'communal' and 'transactional' domains it will, however, be noted that the differentiation of claimed language use across the generations is not particularly high. The correlation of age with maintenance of Gaelic, whilst positive and moderate, is not statistically significant — thus arguing for a fairly homogenous pattern of societal language-usage in the more public aspects of everyday life.

Gaelic is maintained at a high level of usage as a family language. There are, however, significant shifts to English amongst the younger respondents for such personal usages as 'swearing', 'church affairs', 'talking to one's spouse', 'talking to older people', 'croft work', communications to 'people at work' and 'foremen'. In this analysis we might conclude that there were definite social pressures at work weakening the place of Gaelic in personal language usages, although there are still strong social pressures to maintain Gaelic in everyday communal affairs. Church and work represent two fields of activity in which Gaelic is being shifted out in favour of English amongst younger age-groups. Gaelic is thus weakening as the language of the symbolic value-system and as the language of transactional and instrumental

aspects of life. In contrast the shift in favour of Gaelic in the
usage with local councillors may indicate the beginnings of some
shared social feeling that Gaelic should have greater significance
in local political affairs.

The patterning of this last usage is in some contrast to the
other situations comprising this domain — hence the less marked
trend across the age-groups in the overall results. It may, therefore, be questioned concerning how far the concept domain may be
empirically useful in this type of analysis. In order more meaningfully to discuss social processes and language-use it may be
more revealing of social processes which are internally significant
to the speech-community to take a wider variety of more particular
speech-situations and to consider the language-usage claimed for
each. The problem of external as contrasted with internal significance of language-usage has been raised within sociolinguistic
literature. Although it was first discussed in relation to phonological phenomena, the distinction may be carried over onto other
levels of linguistic analysis.

Pike draws attention to 'emic' and 'etic' significance of a
social event or pattern of behaviour.(4) These terms are adapted
from the terms 'phonemic' and 'phonetic' as used in linguistics.
A phonological feature may be demonstrably differentiated at a
'phonetic' level but yet not be capable of discernment by a native-
speaker, who will be unlikely to discern or make any 'phonemic'
distinction between the 'phonetically'distinguishable sounds. Pike
extends these distinctions by analogy to the level of social behaviour. An objectively discernible and measurable social feature
may possess 'etic' significance in similar manner to an outside
observer but have little internal subjective or 'emic' significance to a member of the society or group exhibiting the feature in
question. Hence in so far as a particular socio-linguistic domain
may be concerned, it may have 'etic' significance only as external
relationships alone are concerned with it or are involved significantly with regard to it. The 'emic' domains may be aligned along
different social patterings and it may be hypothesised that within
a bilingual community congruence in the use of each of the two
languages may be the key to making explicit the extent, the boundaries and the relationships of the domains which are internally
significant or 'emic' for the community in question.

With this reservation in mind, it might nevertheless be possible
to argue from the patterned usage of Gaelic within the community at
large in contrast with its patterning within the 'intra-personal'
and 'familial' domains that at this particular stage of language-
shift there is a mutual support for the language as the medium for
the exchange of community meanings even though in more private
aspects of life people may tend to forsake the language. In other
words a differential loyalty towards the language may be evidenced
between private and public usage.

Although the use of a language for counting to oneself may be
regarded as an indication of the language of 'inner speech' it must
be remembered that for various reasons counting may very readily
be undertaken in English even within a completely Gaelic context.
So much so has English numeration been taken over into Gaelic that
it might no more be regarded as a conscious example of code-switching

than say a loanword taken over from English like 'garage', 'room'
or 'chair' and thoroughly Gaelicised as *'garaids'*, *'rùm'* or
'seathair' and used unconsciously in a Gaelic sentence. To an
English mind the Gaelic vigintal system of numeration seems clumsy —
perhaps old-fashioned, imprecise, unbusinesslike or unscientific.
(The numbers run in digits and the 'teens' to twenty and thence as
it were, twenty-and-one to twenty-and-ten and twenty and one-teen
to two twenties up to one hundred. Fifty may often be expressed as
a half-hundred — and a hundred may be expressed as five twenties.)

As numeracy and mathematics have not been taught through the
medium of Gaelic in the schools, few persons today could perform
advanced mathematical computation in Gaelic. Gaelic has also
dropped out of use for counting change, stating prices, counting
out items of merchandise, measuring, numbering the year, and
giving the date. In this latter connection the English names of
months are in general use in Gaelic. Commerce and education may
chiefly be responsible for this supersession of Gaelic. Thus this
aspect of the 'intra-personal' domain might from an emic viewpoint
be more properly regarded as part of the domain of 'commercial
transaction'. Letter-writing and counting as typical activities of
family and personal life weaken the incidence of Gaelic usage thus
measured within these domains.

The results from the questionnaire illustrate examples of weakness of Gaelic in the home and private lives of a number of respondents. Nevertheless these respondents score quite highly concerning use of Gaelic with other community-members for everyday
affairs. Although they may be exercising a certain choice within
their own family circles — or responding to particular social
pressures in the language which they use at home, these choices
are not altogether so free outside the home and the pressures are
certainly contrary to what may be felt when withdrawn as a private
person from the community.

Concerning the delineation and delimitation of the internally-
significant sociolinguistic domains of language-use from the point
of view of the speech community, Fishman observes: ' . . . there
are classes of events recognised by each speech community such
that several seemingly different situations are classed as being of
the same kind'.(5) It may be added that conversely within a bilingual speech-community ostensibly similar and ostensibly associated speech situations may be shown through their separation into
the spheres of usages of the different languages to be distinctly
constellated in terms of social behaviour patterns or social attitude. In fact it would be practicable to turn the concept 'domain'
inside-out for this purpose. In any case, by means of the concept
'domain' a view of language as a social institution is obtained
through the investigation of particular constellations of social
behaviour. As Fishman further observes:

> *Just where the boundaries come* that do differentiate between the
> class of situation generally requiring one variety and another
> class of situation generally requiring another variety must be
> determined by the investigator and constitutes one of the major
> tasks of descriptive sociology of language. Such classes of
> situations are referred to as *domains*. The various domains and
> the appropriate usage in each domain must be discovered from the

data of numerous discrete situations and the shifting or non-
shifting which they reveal. This is a central task of descriptive sociology of language . . . to reveal the behavioural
parsimony of members of speech communities all of whom inevitably
come to rely on a relatively functional sociolinguistic typology
to guide them through the infinite encounters of daily interaction.(6)

If the focus of interest is transferred away from the concern
with language as a social institution for which domain-usage is the
marker or index, to domain constellation or the significantly associated patterns of social behaviour for which language may serve as
an indicator or index, then the language used in typical situations
the extent of shift and the proportions of the speech community
using one language rather than another may provide keys or clues as
to the significant patterning of social behaviour for that speech
community. Although the concept 'dominance-configuration'(7) has
been advanced by Weinreich to express the relative strength with
which one language rather than another enters into the speechways
of a bilingual individual or speech-community, the concept is unsatisfactory for the present purpose, chiefly for two reasons. First,
focus of interest here was primarily linguistic rather than sociological. Weinreich was principally interested in how language contact is a psychological phenomenon — and interaction essentially
within the speakers' minds — and what may be the circumstances
leading towards 'interference' of one language with another or the
various linguistic levels (phonology, lexis, morphology, syntax,
idiom, etc.) Language-use within the community is influenced by
social factors and the bilinguality of the community is exemplified
by the extent to which each mother-tongue group may bear the 'burden
of bilingualism'. Profiles of language-use may be drawn up and
used comparatively to elucidate what may be happening to language.
Second, as taken up with the literature, the concept of 'dominance-
configuration' had strengthened the focusing of interest upon
language as a social institution. Its properties as an index of
dominance of one group over another, its 'halo of prestige', its
indications of how far across the field of social interaction one
language or another can carry a speaker, mean that the concept
'dominance-configuration' should be adapted or changed for the
present purpose. As it stands it is more indicative of hegemony
of one language over the other with respect to 'commanding heights'
of social prestige or to suzerainty over typical reified domains.

What might be analytically and empirically valuable in addition
to such a view, might be a measure which attempted to associate
together the situations which predominantly call for one particular
language and distinguish those other situations predominantly calling for the other language. In such an exercise language becomes
the index distinguishing the significances of one cluster of social
behaviours from another with regard to the integration of social
institutions with group life. The term 'demesne-extension' is
advanced to signify this concept of language 'occupying' or 'owning'
particular 'hereditaments' within social life and extending its
ownership to link these together into an integrated 'estate'. Such
an image of legitimate occupancy of estate may be more helpful than
the image of domination/subjugation of one language over another,

especially in the type of contact situation as we have here, where
one language is generally and outrightly prestigeful and the other
is not. It may also be valuable in describing what is really a
special case of such a situation in which the less prestigeful
language actually gains ground, producing a language-shift at the
expense of the 'dominating' language (a case in which Weinreich
found the applicability of the concept 'dominance-configuration'
difficult to apply).

As Wittgenstein observes, 'The limits of my language mean the
limits of my world',(8) so here we might adapt this insight and
propose that in a language-contact situation the use of one language
rather than another signifies the limits of an integral set of
social relationships which here symbolise the limits of the internal
'world', 'estate' or 'demesne' of group-life versus the external
'world' of mass-society. In the cases illustrated by the rank-
ordering of Table 7.8, the local or 'Gaelic' 'estate' or 'demesne'
extends from family relationships as far as discussing a child with
a teacher at school. Religious relationships, business with local
people, transactions at the Post Office (but not the bank), communication with a district nurse (but not a doctor), business at a
township meeting or grazing committee (but not with a local councillor), business with the district clerk (but not a policeman) come
well within the Gaelic 'demesne'. Conspicuously, letter-writing,
dealings with telephone operators, inspectors, salesmen and waiters,
lie well outside it. It is noteworthy also that such aspects of
language-use generally associated with 'inner speech' lie marginally
outside the Gaelic 'demesne': dreaming, swearing and counting.
So, too does the discussion of local government affairs, local
club and society life and public transport. The use of Gaelic
within these various activities symbolises the degree of distance
or of the closeness which they have to the solidary and integral
values of local life. On this score, letter-writing (albeit to a
family member) is an activity very much to be distinguished from
everyday face-to-face relationships.

Thus the incidence of language used is capable of indicating
something of the quality of the structure of events making up the
pattern of everyday life.

The process of language-shift may be illustrated in the case of
each of these activities by means of an inter-generational comparison of incidence of language-use. As in Tables 7.4, 7.5 and 7.6
illustrating inter-generational differences in literacy, so in like
manner can inter-generational comparison suggest within which
aspects of everyday life Gaelic is best being retained or extended.

Alternatively, if language is regarded as an index of measurement of social significances, these inter-generational differences
may suggest which aspects of everyday life best retain their
vitality as features of integral local life, behavioural and value
systems.

Figures 7.1 and 7.2 illustrate the results of comparing the
incidence of use of Gaelic only for particular activities between
the older age-groups (60+ years) and the younger (18-39 years).
Varying differences are shown between the various activities and
social situations. These inter-generational differences are
greatest for dealings with people generally at work, conversations

TABLE 7.8   'Demesne-extension' of Gaelic amongst Gaelic-speaking adults, Harris 1973 (N = 85)

Rank order	Speech activity in which Gaelic may be used	% members of sample engaging in the activity who claim to use Gaelic alone	Inter-generational language-shift*	Number of individuals engaging in the activity
1	to older relations	96.0	2.8	74
2	to parents	95.8	2.6	71
3	to spouse when alone	92.1	25.0	63
4	to older people locally	86.5	19.0	74
5	when on own croft working	84.5	22.4	71
6	for family prayers and worship	83.8	11.6	80
7	when on croft work with others	79.4	17.8	63
8	to a missionary	78.1	4.2	73
9	to family at home (generally)	78.1	23.4	82**
10	to a church elder	78.1	5.7	72
11	to other members of family (not spouse or parents)	77.8		
12	for praying to yourself	76.8	22.8	73**
13	at township or grazing meeting	74.7	19.4	83
14	to younger people locally	72.2	20.5	54
15	to younger relations	69.9	21.9	73
16	to minister	68.5	18.0	73
17	at church meetings	68.5	9.5	73
18	for quarrelling or 'telling-off' locally	68.0	31.3	78
19	in Post Office	66.7	2.4	75
20	to shopkeepers or van-drivers	66.3	10.5	83
21	for getting messages in a shop	66.2	6.6	74
22	to a Gaelic-speaking stranger same age and opposite sex	65.5	23.0	84
23	to a Gaelic-speaking stranger same age and same sex	64.3	10.8	70
		63.4	11.2	71

#				
24	for explanations to children	63.0	6.6	73
25	to misbehaving children	63.0	12.2	73
26	to fellow-workers at workplace	62.9	11.5	62**
27	to others at work	62.9	48.1	70**
28	to children about morality	62.9	21.0	70
29	to a foreman at work	62.8	27.3	43
30	to a nurse	59.5	10.4	74
31	when buying petrol	58.6	16.7	58
32	to a schoolteacher	55.6	16.3	72**
33	at a public entertainment	54.7	-1.7	75
34	to the district clerk	54.2	28.0	72
35	when discussing a child with teachers	50.0	4.8	70**
36	when dreaming	49.4	21.3	81
37	on public transport	49.4	2.4	81
38	in a club or society meeting	45.9	4.0	66
39	to a workman at your door	45.5	-17.6	66
40	to a local councillor	47.2	9.5	73**
41	for swearing	44.6	8.5	56
42	at a sports or recreation meeting	43.1	14.6	58
43	for discussing local problem with a councillor	42.3	-15.6	78**
44	to a shopkeeper you do not know	42.5	21.5	73
45	when counting to yourself	36.2	16.9	83
46	to a crofting assessor	24.6	2.6	57
47	to waiter in hotel or cafe	23.2	0.6	69
48	to travelling salesman	22.4	0.9	67
49	to an inspector	17.4	-6.9	69
50	to a telephone operator	16.4	-4.3	73**

TABLE 7.8 contd

Rank order	Speech activity in which Gaelic may be used	% members of sample engaging in the activity who claim to use Gaelic alone	Inter-generational language-shift*	Number of individuals engaging in the activity
51	to a telephone operator on Harris exchange	15.2	-7.7	79**
52	in the bank	13.8	-2.2	80
53	to a policeman	13.0	-6.7	69
54	to a doctor	10.8	7.3	74
55	in a letter to one of the family	2.5	5.9	81
	Mean incidence of use of Gaelic only	55.60		
	Mean extent of inter-generational shift		10.9	

* Inter-generational language-shift represents the difference between the percentages of the older (over 60) and younger (under 40) respondents who claimed to use Gaelic only in each situation. Negative value indicates shift in favour of Gaelic.

** The closeness of results in these cases provides some internal validation of the exercise as the closely synonymous questions are derived from separately administered questionnaires.

and preferred language at church meetings. It would, therefore,
seem that these activities indicate the most pronounced decay in
use of Gaelic over the generations. For the young then, there is
a pronounced and growing rejection of these aspects of life from
the Gaelic point of view. If Gaelic continues to function as the
symbol of group integration then work relationships and the more
formal aspects of religious life are in process of extrusion from
the area of solidary discourse into the area of a more impersonal
and alienated medium.

Also in process in weakening substantially over the generations
is the claimed use of Gaelic only to the district clerk, to a foreman at work (but not to one's workmates) and to one's spouse when
alone and to the family at home and when working the croft. In
these regards, English can be seen as entering into the more intimate social situations amongst the younger age-groups. Gaelic
nevertheless continues to maintain itself quite strongly for such
communal activities as use in family worship and in contacts with
church elders and missionaries, parents and older relations, for
business at the Post Office, to shopkeepers and van drivers,
in quarrelling or 'telling people off', in contacts with strangers
known to be Gaelic-speaking, to a district nurse or a local councillor, to workmates and for explanations and for reproof of one's
own children.

Interestingly, there are situation in which younger people will
claim to use Gaelic — and Gaelic only — to a greater extent than
their elders. These situations include conversation at public
entertainment, in the bank, to a telephone operator (especially on
the local exchange), to a policeman, an inspector, in discussion
with a local councillor over a local problem and to a workman who
calls at the door. These situations and interactions all have in
common an intrusive quality. They all represent modern situations
which have been imported into the traditional Gaelic way of life.
Younger people clearly no longer feel the constraints which older
people had with regard to the propriety of language-use in particular situations. As this language-shift in favour of Gaelic is
recent, none of these social situations as yet figures as a situation of high general use for Gaelic, although moderately high
general rates of use occur in the case of discussions of local
affairs with a councillor and the case of a workman calling at the
door. Younger people are, therefore, not so inclined to maintain
the pattern of diglossia which older people felt to be appropriate
here. A younger person might not be conscious of a constraint to
speak English in the bank. After all, everyone speaks Gaelic at
the Post Office. So that would be the difference? Public entertainments are places to relax, a change from work (where there are
many external encounters requiring English to be used) and in these
circumstances a young person would be in a relaxed, expressive mood:
one in which using Gaelic would be a natural response. Although a
minister might be seen increasingly by the young as outside their
expressive, relaxed area of life, authority figures such as policemen and inspectors might no longer have the aura of awe requiring
English. The younger person is more ready to use Gaelic with them.
(Not that they would necessarily be likely to respond. Neither of
the two policemen stationed on Harris in 1972-3 was Gaelic-speaking.

One of them would become very annoyed when addressed in Gaelic.)
This may be an indication of an incipient development regarding
the relationships of language-usage and authority. As the numbers
of respondents involved are very low, there is no demonstrable
statistical significance.

Although certain situations rate highly regarding maintenance
of use of Gaelic, not all of these are strong in incidence of its
use. For example, the incidence of Gaelic is well maintained over
the generations for such uses as letter-writing, dealings with a
doctor, a travelling salesman, a crofting assessor or a waiter in
a hotel or café. The incidence is well maintained but it is low
anyway. Throughout the age-spectrum very few people use Gaelic or
Gaelic alone for such purposes. One respondent observed of the
crofting assessor, 'He should know Gaelic anyway.' He does, and
is one of the few public officials for whom ability in Gaelic is a
prescribed condition for the job. Yet seemingly few of the sample
claimed to use Gaelic — or Gaelic alone — in dealing with him.
The case is different from that of the district clerk, who is
permanently located within the district and is actually a local man
and Gaelic-speaking. The crofting assessor, although intended, by
law, to be the 'crofters friend' and a figure capable of moving
within crofting society and being accepted as an integral part of
the crofting way of life, is nevertheless on this index of language
use an 'outsider' to the local crofting community. Conversely, the
district clerk who acts as agent for a number of 'external' official
and governmental functions (e.g. social security) is much more
readily acceptable as an integral figure within the community.

There is, of course, a relationship between the incidence of use
of Gaelic generally and its inter-generational maintenance. Logically, of course, a low incidence of inter-generational maintenance
must reduce the overall incidence of use of the language. Thus
the association of low incidence with low maintenance, high incidence and low maintenance, high incidence and language shift from
English to Gaelic must, logically, each be unlikely combinations.
What is suggestive in this distribution is the position within it
which the various activities occupy — and the phenomenon of a
certain amount of language shift proceeding in favour of Gaelic
against the general trend away from it. The distribution is illustrated in graphical form in Figure 7.1 and is summarised in tabular
form in Figure 7.2. A moderately positive and significant correlation exists over the generations between maintenance of use of
Gaelic only and its incidence generally within the population as a
whole. As might be expected, this is in the order of $r = +0.44$.

It must, however, be borne in mind that these data represent
people's beliefs concerning their own language-behaviour. It may
be added that the results are congruent with observations of and
familiarity with the language situation within the Harris community
obtained from over a year's residence on the island and participation in local community life. Although the results may not be regarded as objectified evidence of language-behaviour, the results
are valuable in understanding the patterns of beliefs and attitudes
regarding language-use and something of the language-ideology of
the folk-community.

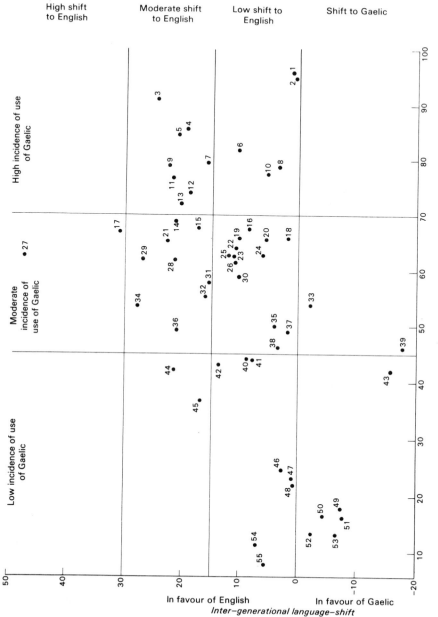

FIGURE 7.1   Inter-generational language-shift: Gaelic speaking adults, Harris 1973

Note: The speech situations are numbered
as in Figure 7.2 (Key to present
figure) and Table 7.8

	High shift to English	Moderate shift to English	Low shift to English	Shift to Gaelic
High incidence of use of Gaelic		3 spouse when alone 9 family at home 11 other family 4 old people 5 when working on own croft 13 township meetings 7 croft (others) 12 personal prayer	6 family prayers 10 church elder 8 missionary 1 older relations 2 parents	
Moderate incidence of use of Gaelic	27 people at work 17 church meetings	34 district clerk 29 foreman 14 young people 21 shopping 28 children (moral) 36 dreaming 15 younger relations 32 teacher 31 buying petrol	26 workmates 27 children (misbehaving) 23 stranger same age and sex 22 stranger opp. sex, same age 30 nurse 19 post-office 40 councillor 16 minister 24 children (explanations) 20 shopkeepers/vandrivers 35 teacher (re child at school) 38 club or society 37 public transport 18 quarrelling	33 public entertainment 39 workman at door
Low incidence of use of Gaelic	44 unfamiliar shopkeeper 45 counting		42 sports meeting 41 swearing 54 doctor 55 letter writing 46 crofting assessor 48 travelling salesman 47 waiter	52 bank 50 telephone operator 53 policeman 49 inspector 51 telephone operator (Harris exchange) 43 councillor (local problem)
Inter-generational language-shift:			In favour of English	In favour of Gaelic

FIGURE 7.2   Inter-generational language-shift: Gaelic-speaking Harris adults 1973 (Key to Figure 7.1)

In view of the size of sample, statistical significance is not
to be expected of those usages showing moderate incidence of use of
Gaelic only and little differentiation of language use across the
generations. Neither can significance be ascribed to those usages
where incidence of the use of Gaelic only is low. However, where
this analysis does indicate the greater differentiations, significant differences better than the 0.05 level across the generations
are demonstrable (as cited in the discussion of Table 7.8) and
these comprised the cases of 'people at work, generally', 'church',
'foreman', 'spouse', 'croft-work with family', 'talking to older
people', 'swearing' and 'discussing a local problem with a councillor'. The use of a more sophisticated test of significance of
contingencies within cases of small sample size(9) yielded some
interesting additional cases of significant inter-generational
claimed differences in use of Gaelic. Significant below the 0.01
level was the use of Gaelic to 'parents' and 'older relations';
below the 0.025 level was the case of 'family prayers and worship';
and below the 0.05 level were the cases of 'people helping on the
croft', 'township and grazing meetings', 'family at home', 'church
elders' and 'missionaries'. It will be clear that these cases
comprise situations very much within the Gaelic 'demesne' involving
private and communal speech-situations and the value-system of
local life.

ATTITUDES TO GAELIC AMONGST THE ADULT POPULATION

Attitudes to Gaelic amongst the adult Harris population were inves-
tigated by means of an attitude questionnaire of some 26 items from
which was derived a Likert scale of ten items: those yielding the
most differentiating results. A satisfactory estimate of internal
reliability was obtained using the split-half reliability coefficient technique (the coefficient of reliability of the ten best
items in the attitude test was 0.68 before, and 0.81 after correction).
  The questions used in this study were:
  1 'There should be an extra radio and TV station all in Gaelic
     to serve the needs of the islands.'
  2 'Education should be given in Gaelic as well as in English
     in all the schools where our children go.'
  3 'The trouble with Gaelic is it has no practical value.'
  4 'Ability to speak Gaelic is the mark of the true islander.'
  5 'We should spend more time improving our English than our
     Gaelic.'
  6 'Gaelic should be used much more on public signs and notices.'
  7 'We should encourage a greater use of English as Gaelic has
     little commercial value.'
  8 'It is more important for children to learn English than
     Gaelic.'
  9 'Official bodies should encourage a greater use of Gaelic.'
  10 'Gaelic is not of great value in this modern world.'
  The compilation of the original twenty-six questions was of
items adapted from issues in the local press or from commonly
retailed sayings amongst the general population. The purpose behind

the exercise was to obtain some measure of attitude towards Gaelic
as a social institution capable of discharging the various functions
of language in social life. In this way an impression could be
derived of favourable or inimical attitudes towards the language as
a social institution, that is to say, feelings of loyalty towards it
as a feature of group life or of confidence in it as a sufficient
medium for the range of purposes of language in social life.

The respondents were able to answer on a five-point scale:
strongly agree, agree, indifferent, disagree, strongly disagree.
The item scores were summarised into an individual overall score
capable of ranging from 50 (signifying exceptionally strong identification with Gaelic) through 30 (signifying complete indifference)
to 10 (signifying exceptionally strong antipathy towards Gaelic).
These scores have been converted to a scale ranging from +100 to
-100 for more ready comparability and comprehension. The distribution of language-loyalty is illustrated in Table 7.9 (and Figure
4.2).

By way of comparison with the sample, the questionnaire was also
used with a local bard (and noted champion of Gaelic culture) who
registered +65 and also with a professional incomer (who learnt
fluent Gaelic for purely instrumental reasons connected with his
profession) and who registered -30.

Interesting relationships may be seen between language-loyalty
on the one hand and upon the other such factors as age, sex, occupation, attitudes to authority, domains regarded as important for
Gaelic language-maintenance, strength of feeling regarding language-
maintenance, beliefs and preferences regarding language-use. The
following tables illustrate the results of the questionnaire amongst
the surveyed sample of the Harris adult population.

As has already been noted in Chapter 4, the Likert scale is
particularly suitable as a measure of language-loyalty. Sharp and
his collaborators have advanced this view in the discussion of the
methodology of their survey of Welsh in the schools of Wales.(10)
The distribution of the measure of language-loyalty within the sample
as a whole, as given in Table 7.9 (and illustrated in Figure 4.2)
evidences some interesting characteristics. The distribution is not
of an evenly normal character. In fact as the intention underlying
the design of the Likert scale is to emphasise differences of degree
of loyalty, a normal distribution of the results is not necessarily
to be expected. The intention of this method is to bring out any
polarisation of attitudes which may be present: to identify clearly
those having antipathetic or very weakly identifying attitudes
towards a language in contrast to those respondents who are very
strong in their identifications with a language.

In this case we can see that there is something of a 'normal'
clustering of respondents about the modal point. This is somewhat
low in terms of value at +40 on the hundred-point scale, the mean
for the sample having a value of 35.5. This is suggestive that
overt loyalties towards Gaelic are not particularly strong — a view
which is substantiated by the analysis of the responses to questions
exploring beliefs regarding community values and the institutionalisation of language within local social life.

There is no highly pronounced polarisation of language loyalty:
relatively few people see language as a special feature of social

TABLE 7.9 Language-loyalty of sampled adult population, Harris
1973 (N = 91)

Language-loyalty score	Number of respondents Whole sample (N = 91)	Gaelic-speakers only (N = 86)
100		
95	1	1
90		
85	2	2
80		
75		
70	4	3
65	4	4
60	2	2
55	8	8
50	6	6
45	8	7
40	15	15
35	13	13
30	2	2
25	1	1
20	5	4
15	5	5
10	3	2
5	3	3
0	2	2
-5	1	1
-10	1	1
-15	1	1
-20	1	1
-25		
-30	1	1
-35	1	1
-40	1	

Mean score: Whole sample 35.5; Gaelic-speakers 36.3

life. Most people have a relatively warm but not a particularly
pronounced affective tone towards the Gaelic language. It is there
within social life, it is well-regarded but few people have developed any particular behaviour or attitudes with regard to it. Yet
the distribution does exhibit some possibly interesting characteristics. The tails of the distribution contain 'humps' at the values
of 65-70 and 15-20, possibly indicating some polarisation of attitudes strongly for and relatively apathetic towards Gaelic amongst
a small proportion of the sample. In Table 7.10 below, the groups
scoring high and low upon the loyalty measure are examined separately
and analysed in terms of age and sex.

From Table 7.10 it will be discerned that there may be an association of language-loyalty with age. The mean scores of language-
loyalty increase with age and scores amongst men are higher than
those amongst women. As we might expect (although the numbers concerned are too small to generalise from) the average score for non-
Gaelic-speakers is lower than for the Gaelic-speaking group.

TABLE 7.10 Attitudes to Gaelic (language-loyalty):
Gaelic-speaking Harris adults, 1973, by age and
sex (N = 85)

| Age-groups | Mean language-loyalty score | |
	Men	Women
18-39	30.5	22.3
(N = 22)	(N = 11)	(N = 11)
40-59	39.6	38.8
(N = 29)	(N = 13)	(N = 16)
60+	42.6	40.0
(N = 34)	(N = 19)	(N = 15)
All	38.6	34.9
(N = 85)	(N = 43)	(N = 42)

The differential loyalty towards Gaelic as between the men and the
women did not prove to be statistically significant. However, the
results of a t-test of the original data comparing the younger
women (under 40 years of age) with the remainder of the sample did
prove to be significant, yielding a t-score significant below the
0.01 level. Similarly a comparison of all the younger respondents
(under 40 years of age) with the remainder produced a result significant below the 0.01 level.

The results here indicate a significant diminution of language-
loyalty amongst young adults compared with the old and the middle-
aged. This phenomenon was the most particularly pronounced amongst
the younger women. It is interesting to contrast the marked differences in attitude towards Gaelic on the part of the younger women
who have remained within the island community, with the strongly
identifying attitudes towards Gaelic amongst the academically

brighter girls boarding away from home in order to attend school and college elsewhere. The fact that the least loyal of all the age and sex categories towards the Gaelic language comprises the young women remaining in Harris does not augur well for the future prospects of Gaelic language-maintenance. These are the mothers or mothers-to-be of the ensuing generation.

There may also be some relationship between language-loyalty and occupational class within the Harris community. The results are given in Table 7.11.

TABLE 7.11   Language-loyalty towards Gaelic: Harris adults, 1973, by occupational class

Occupational class*	Whole sample		Gaelic-speakers only	
	Number	Mean score	Number	Mean score
Professional	8	23.8	6	30.8
Public servants	10	36.0	10	36.0
Commercial	8	25.0	7	22.5
Technical	8	30.0	8	30.0
Agricultural	16	46.9	15	45.3
Manual	11	32.7	11	32.7
Unemployed	2	37.5	2	33.5
Housewives	28	37.5	27	38.5
Total	91	35.5	86	36.3

* Categories are as in tables in Chapter 5 relating to occupational class of parents of primary-school children.

Despite the smallness of the sample the t-score results for the professional and the agricultural groups proved significant. Language-loyalty was highest within the agricultural category, consisting almost entirely of the male crofting 'core' of the local community. The t-test result comparing the 'agricultural' group with the remainder of the sample as a whole was significant below the 0.01 level (and for the Gaelic-speaking group alone was significant below the 0.05 level). The professional group within the total sample yielded a t-score significant below the 0.10 level.

Within the sample as a whole, the professionals evidenced the lowest score (chiefly owing to the number of non-Gaelic-speaking professional incomers). Amongst the Gaelic-speaking group the professionals chiefly comprise local ministers and teachers, and it was amongst the commercial category that the lowest mean loyalty score was evidenced. In neither case did the results prove statistically significant. The manual group yielded below-average mean scores which again did not prove significant. It would be reasonable to expect the commercial and professional groups to evidence greater instrumental attitudes towards language and to show lesser loyalty towards Gaelic. As has been noted earlier, there is

evidence of sections of the manual occupational category having
developed certain attitudes towards Gaelic, regarding it as an
impediment towards educational advancement and mobility of their
children. However, it is most conspicuously amongst the crofting
core of the Harris community that the higher incidences of favourable attitudes towards Gaelic are to be found. Crofting, of course,
represents the continuation of the most typical and traditional of
all the local occupations and it would be reasonable to associate
high rates of Gaelic language-loyalty and language-maintenance with
this group.

Some of the characteristics of those sections of the sample who
evidenced high, moderate, low and antipathetic results regarding
language-loyalty were also studied. The attitudes of these groups
was examined with respect to other institutions of local social
life, especially those which may be regarded as comprising the
agencies of 'authority': district and county councillors, the MP,
lairds, church leaders and public authorities, such as the Highland
and Island Development Board and the local council of Social Service.
Respondents were asked to signify the extent to which they agreed
with statements regarding each of these seven 'authorities'.

The purpose of the questions was to explore whether language-
loyalty followed a similar pattern within the local community compared with attitudes towards other local social institutions within
the political, administrative and religious spheres of life. A
similar measure as that developed for language-loyalty itself would
have proved ideal — and a more thoroughly constructed instrument
might have revealed more of significance. The exercise however,
did not yield any statistically significant result except in the
case of attitudes concerning the Member of Parliament. High favourable attitudes were shown by respondents evidencing loyalty towards
Gaelic, whereas respondents antipathetic towards Gaelic were largely
unfavourably disposed towards the MP.

Also explored were aspects of life such as language-maintenance
in the home and family, interpersonal relationships and relationships at work. Some ten questions were asked within these fields
and the numbers responding were categorised by age and by language-
loyalty. There were no significant differences resulting from age
or language-loyalty regarding the replies (except to Question 9).
The questions and the results, aggregated for the sample as a whole,
are given in Table 7.12.

There proved to be little difference between the percentaged
results of the sample as a whole (89 adults responding to these
questions) and the Gaelic-speakers considered specifically (84
respondents). On no question was there a variation greater than
3 per cent.

From Table 7.12 it will be seen that the belief that children
maintain their Gaelic after absence at school is quite high. This
was strongly felt to be desirable. The mother was generally felt to
be the more important in terms of imparting the language to younger
children. One-third of the sample felt both parents to be equally
important — and there was scarcely any variation across the categories of age or language-loyalty on this question. As to whether
the mother or the father used Gaelic more in the home the majority
regarded both parents as equal. Few respondents regarded girls as

TABLE 7.12   Beliefs and preferences concerning language-use: Gaelic-speaking Harris adults, 1973 (N = 84)*

Question	Replies	Number of Respondents	Percentage of Respondents
1 'When children return home having been away at school do they keep their Gaelic?'	Yes No	57 27	67.9 32.1
2 'How do you feel about your children keeping their Gaelic?'	Important Indifferent Unimportant	75 9 0	89.3 10.7 0.0
3 'Is it more important for a mother or a father to use Gaelic in the home?'	Mother Equal Father	54 29 1	64.3 34.5 1.2
4 'Who tends to use Gaelic more in your home, the mother or the father?'	Mother Equal Father	27 47 10	32.1 56.0 11.9
5 'Do girls tend to keep their Gaelic in use better than boys?'	Yes No	6 78	7.1 92.9
6 'On the whole do women speak more Gaelic than men?'	Yes No	16 68	19.0 81.0
7 'Would you like to see more people on the island even if they were not Gaelic-speaking?'	Yes Indifferent No	61 3 20	72.6 3.6 23.8
8 'Do you think that islanders will have good chances of promotion if new industries come to Harris?'	Yes Indifferent No	75 3 6	89.3 3.6 7.1

TABLE 7.12   contd

Question	Replies	Number of Respondents	Percentage of Respondents
9 'Would you prefer your daughter to marry a Gaelic-speaking boy?'	Yes	41	40.8
	Indifferent	39	46.4
	No	4	4.8
10 'Would you mind very much if your daughter married a boy who could not speak Gaelic?'	Yes	2	2.4
	Indifferent	22	26.2
	No	60	71.4

* Of the 86 Gaelic-speaking respondents within the whole sample of 91 adults, only 84 responded to this section.

maintaining their use of Gaelic better than boys. Many respondents were quite emphatic that boys maintained their Gaelic better than the girls. Similarly concerning language-use between adult men and women, a very similar pattern was reported.

As a distinctive measure of island 'groupness', ability to speak Gaelic was not seen as a particularly important criterion of settlement on the island. A number of respondents stated that it was more important that incomers should respect the Sabbath or be helpful to local people, thus stressing religious values and the tradition of community work-sharing. There was widespread confidence that local people would hold their own economically if new industries were to come to Harris. Whether or not this confidence was misplaced remains to be seen in practice.

Last, as a test of the functioning of Gaelic as a safeguard of group and family traditions, respondents were asked whether they would prefer a daughter to marry a Gaelic-speaker. Here significant differences between the low language-loyalty group and the remainder showed up. Only one-quarter of the low language-loyalty group felt it was desirable for a daughter to marry a Gaelic speaker, but well over half of the moderate and high language-loyalty groups did so. (χ^2 values of 9.7631 for the whole sample and 5.4253 for Gaelic significant below the 0.005 and 0.025 levels respectively at 1 degree of freedom.) There was no significant difference resulting from age. As an 'acid test' of the strength of the responses a further question was asked concerning whether respondents would really mind if the girl married out of the Gaelic speech-community. Hardly anyone (only two respondents in all) maintained that a daughter's marriage to a non-Gaelic-speaker would upset them at all. Responses such as 'It wouldn't break my heart' were frequently volunteered. A commonly-expressed view was that it was more important for the girl to be happy and for the boy to be decent.

The overall picture is of a very favourable attitude towards Gaelic as a desired attribute amongst the coming generation, a view

that it is the mother who is the principally operative link in this
process, coupled with a view that girls are less markedly loyal to
the language than are boys. Confidence exists in the perpetuation
of the island community as an integral entity, but the local language is not seen as a significant institution in this connection
either as a factor in economic life or as a crucial factor affecting
marriage.

Amongst the Gaelic-speakers of the sample there did, however,
prove to be a significant correlation of language loyalty with age.
A value of $r = +0.922$ was obtained (significant below the 0.05
level at four degrees of freedom).(11)

In order to take up more closely the way in which Gaelic is seen
as operating within the institutions of local social life, an
analysis was undertaken by means of questions relating to language-
maintenance and the conservation of Gaelic within various domains.
Respondents were asked within which three out of some eleven domains
they would most wish the use of Gaelic to be maintained. They
were then asked how strongly they felt the importance of preserva-
tion of Gaelic in these situations to be: whether very strongly
or vital, strongly or essential, moderately or desirable. Tables
7.13 and 7.14 categorise the results by age of respondent and by
degree of language-loyalty. There are some slight differences in
the numbers of respondents between Tables 7.12, 7.13 and 7.14,
owing to the reluctance of a small number of respondents to proceed
with these sections of the questionnaire.

Interestingly, the home was not universally seen by all respondents as the most important domain for the retention of Gaelic.
The moderately loyal placed the school first. The middle-aged
group ranked home and school equally within the first two places.

We have already noted how individual language-behaviour might
vary between the home as compared with community insistences upon
a more conforming language-behaviour in public. The middle-aged
group is, of course, the principal group involved in the practical
business of rearing pre-school and school-aged children, i.e. the
coming generation. For the other groups the problem is not so
personal or immediate. Their views may be more prescriptive than
practical.

The church is not ranked third by all groups. Amongst the old
it is seen as next in importance to the home — and strongly so.
Not so with the young who regard the broadcasting media as a much
more crucial area for the retention of Gaelic. When categorised by
language-loyalty, each group within the sample rated the church as
third in importance after home and school, the moderate loyalty
group less markedly so than the others.

No one regarded the use of Gaelic for committee or public meetings
as important for the maintenance of the language.

Younger respondents and the low loyalty group were stronger than
the other categories in regarding the use of Gaelic in public entertainments and by official bodies as important for the language.

They young also rated crofting as more important for Gaelic than
did the middle-aged and older groups, although in terms of the domain
of work generally this relative importance was reversed. As associated with language-loyalty, crofting was seen as less important by the
low loyalty group, as was work generally. However, rather more of

the moderate and high groups regarded work generally as important
for Gaelic language-maintenance than did the low loyalty group.
   So far as local commercial life was concerned, shopping was not
rated as a very important domain for the future of Gaelic, although
younger and middle-aged respondents felt this to be more important
than did the old, as did the high loyalty group compared with the
rest. As this domain fell within the last three places out of the
eleven for each group, the numbers involved here are too small for
meaningful inter-group comparisons to be made.
   The significance of these results was examined by means of a 'z-
test' of the proportional differences between the subsamples of the
younger (18-39 years) respondents and the remainder. The older respondents (60+ years) and the remainder, the low loyalty group (scoring 30 or less) and the remainder, and finally the high loyalty group
(scoring 50 or more) and the remainder. The differences were found to
be significant below the 0.01 level except in the following cases.
   The difference of response regarding 'work' as an important domain for Gaelic language-maintenance was significant only at the
0.05 level in the case of the younger respondents compared with the
remainder. For the low loyalty group the differences resulting from
'school' and 'radio and TV' were not significant. For the high
loyalty group differences arising over the domains of 'crofting' and
'church' were not significant, and the difference regarding 'home'
was significant at the 0.05 level only.
   The details for the Gaelic-speaking group of the sample are given
in Tables 7.13 and 7.14. These results do not markedly differ from the
results for the group as a whole (at the most only by 2-3 per cent).

TABLE 7.13   Relationships between desired domains for Gaelic language-
maintenance and age: Gaelic-speaking Harris adults, 1973 (N = 83)

| Domain | Respondents by age | | | | | |
| | Young (18-39 years) | | Middle-aged* (40-59 years) | | Old (60+ years) | |
	N	%	N	%	N	%
Home	14	66.7	24	82.7	28	84.8
School	13	61.9	24	82.7	25	75.8
Crofting	5	23.8	1	3.4	1	3.0
Work	4	19.0	7	24.1	8	24.2
Shopping	2	9.5	3	10.3	1	3.0
Church	8	38.1	17	58.6	26	78.8
Official bodies	3	14.3	2	6.9	3	9.1
Public entertainments	4	19.0	1	3.4	1	3.0
Radio and television	10	47.6	7	24.1	6	18.2
Number of respondents	21	100.0	29	100.0	33	100.0

* One middle-aged respondent named only two out of three domains.

TABLE 7.14 Relationships between desired domains for Gaelic
language-maintenance and language-loyalty: Gaelic-speaking
Harris adults, 1973 (N = 82)

| Domain | Respondents by language-loyalty* | | | | | |
| | Low**（below 35) | | Moderate (35-45) | | High (above 45) | |
	N	%	N	%	N	%
Home	19	86.4	24	70.6	22	84.6
School	16	72.7	28	82.4	18	69.2
Crofting	1	4.5	4	11.8	2	7.7
Work	1	4.5	10	29.4	8	30.8
Shopping	1	4.5	2	5.7	3	11.5
Church	15	68.2	19	55.9	17	65.4
Official bodies	3	13.6	2	5.9	3	11.5
Public entertainments	3	13.6	2	5.9	0	0.0
Radio and television	6	27.3	11	32.4	5	19.2
Number of respondents	22	100.0	34	100.0	26	100.0

* The indices of language-loyalty are derived from Table 7.9.
** One respondent in the low language-loyalty group named only two
   out of three domains.

The general impression from this analysis is one of younger people
beginning to turn to the more 'modern' as compared with the more
'traditional' domains of usage as being more effective for the retention of Gaelic in community usage in the future. The higher loyalties and strength of feeling of older respondents seem to go along
with belief in the efficacy of the traditional domains of home,
school and church and, to a lesser extent, work as the important
situation for the retention of Gaelic. Use of Gaelic in broadcasting, public entertainments and by official bodies becomes to be
perceived as important by the young and less markedly loyal. Running
counter to this movement is the relative strength of perception of
crofting amongst the young as an important domain for Gaelic. Possibly this reflects the desire of members of this group to acquire
or succeed to a croft and thus to enter into the more stable socio-
economic 'core' of local life.
   The significance of Gaelic within community life is seen essentially as being bound up with everyday behaviour patterns. Language-
maintenance is not perceived as being in any way connected with
political institutions as they are represented locally in the committee structure of the island and in the public meeting (a matter.
of social, political or economic significance) as compared with a
public entertainment (for purposes of relaxation and celebration of
expressive and affectual relationships). This contrasts to the
polarisation of attitudes towards language in Wales where the use
of the local language by official bodies, local committees and public meetings has become an 'issue'. Gaelic language-loyalty and
language-maintenance (which we may subsume under the embracing term
'language-conservation') are maintained as aspects of community or
folk-life rather than at the overt, activist type of level which has
developed in recent years in Wales.

CONCLUSION

In terms of social process the island community is not, as yet, undergoing any substantial degree of economic development or inward migration of outsiders. Nevertheless, a process of language-shift is discernible which would seem to result from the intrusion of such features as the mass-media of communication, the education system, realignments of communications and also perhaps from tourism. Monoglot English-speakers from outside the home community have secured key positions within the committee structure and in public affairs. For such reasons as these Gaelic has been subjected to the process of language-shift out of many domains of public life. This is an index of the extent to which local people have sought to participate — or have been able effectively to participate — in public affairs locally, an index of the extent to which official definitions have been generally accepted of what comprises the education received in school, and the extent to which the use of the 'other tongue' has been accepted as legitimate across many of the public domains.

The 'backwash' of Gaelic into domains which the younger and less-committed Gaels resort for relaxation and expressive needs is an interesting feature running counter to the overall shift of Gaelic in favour of English. Church life as the kernel of the symbolic value-system strongly maintains the use of Gaelic in public worship and religious affairs. As we have seen there is some association between negative attitudes towards Gaelic and negative attitudes towards various 'authorities' in public life — religious authorities included. However, amongst the less markedly loyal towards Gaelic and amongst younger respondents, there was a marked tendency to rate as important for the future use of the language its adoption and use within the 'modern' domains of social life.

Strangely, few saw the instrumental domain of commercial transaction in shopping as important for Gaelic language-maintenance, and no one saw Gaelic as importantly entering the field of local politics.

The pattern of Gaelic literacy emphasises the nature of Gaelic language-maintenance: within the field of community folk-life and essentially as an oral medium for the communication of common-sense meanings of everyday life (as well as for the handling of the symbolic or ideational levels of the local culture in the religious domain).

The results of these analyses taken together with those of earlier chapters on constraint through language (Chapter 2) and Gaelic in the schools (Chapters 4 to 6) depict language-shift as essentially associated with the intimate field of social interaction on a personal and familiar level as much as at the public or community level. In this male-dominated and patrilocal community the differently-apportioned roles of men and women affect language-maintenance at a more subtle and private level. It is believed that boys and young men keep up their Gaelic better than girls and young women. Amongst the younger women remaining on the island language-loyalty is weak. The girls selected for academic education develop a very strong language-loyalty but these are not retained within the island community. Mothers are perceived as the most important for the perpetuation of Gaelic. Sanctions to marry within the Gaelic speech-community are very weak. The shortage of younger women locally results in younger men bringing an outsider back as wife. The operation of these factors together is beginning to weaken the use of Gaelic within the home. These factors may operate more strongly amongst the non-crofting working class and be associated with instrumental images of language-function.

The development of overt language-loyalty within a folk-community whose literacy in the home language is weak would be a rare phenomenon. Although the numbers of English monoglot children of Gaelic-speaking parents entering primary school in recent years have not evidenced a consistently even increase year by year, there must be every expectation that such a consistent trend must shortly develop, failing re-orientations of public awareness concerning language.

It thus becomes clear that such institutions as the education system act as important agencies in social processes which remove from the island community many of its more differentiated members on such criteria as language-loyalty, academic education, and literacy in the home language before they enter fully into adult roles. The residual population continues to evidence a general homogeneity of attitude regarding the ways in which language is articulated with other institutions of local life, whilst at the same time these processes have reduced the numbers of young women of marriageable age resulting in the further diminution of children and young people within the age-structure. The individuals who might possibly change the situation are the ones most likely to leave the island.

Chapter 8

CONCLUSION: LANGUAGE
IN SOCIAL PROCESS

HARRIS: A LANGUAGE-ARENA

The present study has depicted the Harris community as a systemic
whole whose component structures undertake particular social functions. The local community and its component structures are, however, undergoing social processes whose resulting social changes
may shortly transform the local society, as has been the case with
the Gaelic communities of the Highland mainland. Harris may be
regarded as the arena of culture-clash: the conflict of traditional
values and the culture of a local language with the values of a
modern, urban, English-speaking mass society. If the situation is
seen essentially in conflict terms, such a perspective might seem
an unwarranted over-dramatisation of the situation both to the
summer visitor and to the all-year resident. The tempo of life in
Harris is leisurely and community affairs are peaceful, dignified,
courteous and gentle.

I have tried to convey something of this character of community
life in modifying the concept 'dominance-configuration' into one of
'demesne-extension'. I have sought to replace an image of the
dominance of one language over another by an image of legitimate
occupancy of social space by the two languages of societal bilingualism. Bilinguals, within a situation of societal bilingualism,
see both of their languages as having their proper place and do not
necessarily themselves see language-contact in terms of power, domination or conflict.

Nevertheless there is something of a language-arena in the
apparently quiet conformity of island life. There is a sense in
which Harris is a battleground of language issues. Such a battle;
ground may be said to exist at a symbolic level. For the apportionment of social uses of the two languages is a pattern and, over
time, a process which is negotiated under the terms of an unequal
power relationship between two social entities. One is the local
community still possessing strong characteristics of a folk-
community and still strongly Gaelic in speech and culture. The
other is what Vallee has termed 'mass-society'(1) and Deutsch the
'oecumene'.(2) This is the English-speaking core society of modern
Britain, urban in character, socially bonded in terms of a complex

170

division of labour and class-structure, and participating in the
Anglo-American, if not an even more international, culture. Differences exist in degree of division of labour: the local community
remains largely mechanical in solidarity: mass-society is organic.
    To some extent the power conflict is visually signified. The
tourist may traverse the length of the Outer Hebrides and scarcely
see one word of Gaelic written anywhere: on road-signs, shop fronts
or on public notices. Yet he will hear Gaelic spoken at every turn,
particularly in Harris where there are few English monoglot outsiders.
In the Hebrides the clash of cultures is not a divisive phenomenon
in inter-community relations as is literally the case in situations
such as Ulster. The clash occurs intra-communally and, also, in
real measure intra-personally. The community as a whole, together
with the individuals within it, is subjected to a conflictual process of change. The clash of cultures under the unequal power differential, symbolising the influence of one social group on another,
here occurs as the agencies of cultural transmission are intruded
locally. Mass culture is thus promoted and taken up by the local
community as passive recipients of a macro-societal process, over
which they are able to exercise little control or determination.
    A Marxian view of such a process would be developed in terms of
a dominating class securing political control over a dominated
class. The dominating group affects social control by the promotion of its language as the official language and promotes its
culture as the curricular core of the provided education and as
the content of the broadcasting services. It recruits into its
own establishment children of leadership and intellectual potential, distorting and exploiting the local economy to subserve the
interests of the group which commands effective power. Marx had
himself studied such a case of the relationships of a local Gaelic-
speaking community with urban, industrialised bourgeois society in
nineteenth-century Sutherlandshire.(3) Here Marx draws attention
to the essential character of traditional Gaelic society as organised upon the clan principle in the communal ownership of land by
the clan as an extended family. The system was legitimated by the
respect of the clansfolk for the authority of the 'laird' and was
defined in customary tradition rather than by law.
    The island community is often said to be 'classless'. It is
certainly less divisive, socially, than is the class-structure of
urban Britain generally. We are clearly not even today justified
in analysing a community such as Harris in terms of class and a
dialectic of social change based upon it. Local society is still
organised upon a strong underpinning of kinship and a communal
pattern of work-sharing within its economic base. Crofting practice
has replaced the clan system. There are still residual patterns of
respect for the lairds who have replaced the old clan-chiefs. (In
1973 some local people walked out from a public entertainment in
Tarbert when local lairds were satirised.) As the lairds have lost
public credibility, respect has transferred to other authorities:
even to schoolmasters and officials of public authority. The dialectic of social process is being played out in terms of cultures
rather than classes. This may be symbolised in terms of social
values such as the integrity of the local Sabbath and the extent to
which one language rather than the other enters into particular
social usage.

The 'military' differentiation of rank which Marx saw as still
operating in the relict clan-system of the nineteenth-century
Highlands has vanished today. Instead some three forms of status-
system appear to be present. There is a religious system which
accords pre-eminent respect to the ministers, missionaries and lay
elders (all invariably male), but also recognises the respect due
to the upright qualities of communicating full church members –
especially those who are under the cùram — and these may be of
both sexes. There is the cultural status-system (which is weak in
Harris), which recognises those having access to the traditional
culture: village bards, musicians, and the bearers of the oral
tradition of songs and stories. There are few of these in Harris
but there are those who enjoy prestige as 'Gaelic scholars'. Then
there is the politico-communal status system within which the more
organisationally-active of the incomers may find a place. It is
this last of the three systems which articulates best with the
external status system. There are few local professionals. Outsiders form an important stiffening — often the very backbone of
local societies, committees, good causes and political life such
as it is. This last status system represents a weakness in the
integrity of the local socio-cultural system. Local people with
professional, organisational or political talents are scarce, and
those few who are active in this field are often subject to
criticism. Here the mechanical solidarity of the local community
is well evidenced. Within the last of these three systems the
social use of English is a requisite instrumental necessity, as
few incomers have the will or the ability to acquire Gaelic and
local norms of courtesy do not require them to learn it. Gaelic
is maintained as effective only in the religious system. The
cultural status system is weak in Harris life today. It seems, however, to be stronger in the other islands of the Outer Hebrides.

In terms of who meets whom, and for what purpose who uses which
language, Gaelic may be seen as the principal language of face-to-
face relationships, the principal language of moralising, and, in
large measure, of communalising. English, however, takes over for
politicising and commercialising.

Language-variation in Gaelic encompasses a language of the pulpit
and of public prayer. Otherwise an oratorical or public speaking
style is rarely encountered. Language-varieties appropriate to the
religious domain are widely generated and frequently encountered in
the home owing to the custom of family worship, extemporary prayer
and grace before meals. Language-etiquette, however, seems to
break down as the younger and the less language-loyal no longer
accept the traditional diglossic usage which kept Gaelic out of
certain aspects of club and voluntary society life and which required English alone to be used in the presence of certain authority
figures. However, there is little development at local level of
the use of language as a symbol or weapon of group identity as there
is amongst Welsh-speaking youth in Wales today. Language-use
amongst the young often runs contrary to the received wisdom of the
gerontocracy and may be equally posed in opposition to the perceived ineffective quality of traditional life, the 'sacred' tradition of the elders or against the English culture whose intrusion
the 'sacred' tradition chiefly ignores.

BILINGUAL EDUCATION PATTERNS AND COGNITIVE PERFORMANCE

Such cultural transmission agencies as the education and political systems bring in further language-varieties — in English. The mass-media and mainland contacts introduce further varieties of English and Lowland Scots, such that today in Harris the individual may encounter and encompass within his speech repertoire a considerable number of varieties of both languages.

Obviously the school promotes varieties of Standard English in addition to the Gaelic which the beginner brings with him. (Today though this is already in process amongst pre-school children through the medium of television.) Upon entry to school then the Gaelic-speaking child will already have acquired at least passive familiarity with two varieties of Gaelic; in sacred and secular usage. These varieties exhibit differential elaboration and restriction of code. However, for the child at this stage there is no expectation of his being able to generate elaborate code utterances in Gaelic. However, he will be expected to address his parents differently from his peers and know the difference between *thu* and *sibh*. In school he should acquire an elaborated-code version of Standard English. Robinson observes concerning conditions in East Africa that 'in multilingual societies . . . a whole language may function as a restricted code.'(4) This assertion has not as yet been anywhere adequately substantiated empirically. But in terms of Houston's terminology of the 'school register' and the 'non-school register'(5) it may be clearly seen that for the majority of present-day Harris schoolchildren the 'school register' is handled through Standard English and the 'non-school register' in local informal Gaelic. Thus we have an interesting complementary situation compared with the situation which Bernstein has more systematically explored within urban society in England. In the situations which Bernstein has explored, there is a tendency for lower working-class children to enter school having access principally to restricted codes and the middle-class children to enter school having access both to restricted and to elaborated codes.

In Houston's perspective, behind her concepts of the school and non-school registers there lie different orders of meaning. A similar situation can be seen to operate in the case of the Gaelic-speaking child entering school whose 'non-school register' derives from the order of meaning of the local Gaelic community and whose 'school register' will be imparted in English and be embedded in an order of meaning derived from outside mass-society.

In the Harris situation, that of a minority culture in a truly remote rural milieu, is an unequal power relationship with a dominating mass-culture, the circumstances provide an interesting complementary situation so far as speech repertoires are concerned. The working-class children enter school with larger speech-repertoires than do the middle-class children who here may have access principally to one speech variety only: an approximation to elaborate-code Standard English. As children progress up the school it is still rare for English monoglot children of non-Gaelic-speaking parents to acquire an adequate command of spoken Gaelic. The local children rapidly become effective in spoken English and also acquire or develop a local form of Scottish English which shows increasing influence from Lowland Scots. (Amongst the children of the Survey there were some — girls especially — who said they 'admired' the Glasgow accent.) Across these variations of register, social and geographical dialect and discrete language, restriction and elaboration of code can occur. No so with the professional incomer middle-class children: code variation is, of course, present but only within a single variety of a Scottish approximation to Received Pronunciation Standard English.

It may be a useful conceptual extension of Bernstein's hypothesis of sociolinguistic codes that there may exist a polarity of circumstances between the urban society of a single, unitary or centralising mainstream culture on the one hand and on the other a rural or folk community rendered effectively bicultural through the operation of a political power-differential at ideational or symbolic cultural levels. In the first case we might expect a dichotomy of code usage between social classes within the domain of the school (of the pattern working-class restriction, middle-class elaboration). In the second case we might postulate the necessity of a wider speech-repertoire amongst children of the local culture compared with that of the children of the dominating culture.

The literature of the thesis of 'cultural deprivation' and its rebuttal contains many instances of educational 'problems' in providing education for cultural minorities. Interest has focused upon minority sub-cultures: the poor, rural and ghetto blacks, American Indians and immigrant communities of contrasted race or language to that of the host society. Parallels have been drawn between these situations and colonial or 'third world' situations where political or imperial domination has been succeeded by a neo-colonial pattern of economic dominance. Under such processes local cultures have been similarly disvalued and instrumental necessities have been promoted amongst local people through western- or European-type education systems to acquire languages of wider communication and the culture of the political or economically dominating groups. The Gaelic situation illustrated here in Harris has similarities to these situations.

The Gaelic language was seen in the past as a considerable handicap to progress and something of these attitudes may have sedimented down to the lower levels of society in terms of status and access to middle-class mainstream culture. Gaelic may still be seen by some manually-employed parents as a detriment, whilst more enlightened views have entered the currency of educational thought and the official organs of administration. For example, the Scottish Education Department, to judge by its reports, participates in these new attitudes to Gaelic (whereas certain of the older attitudes are still maintained within the Highlands and Islands Development Board).

However, it is often advanced that in terms of cognitive performance Gaelic-speaking children are operating at a lower level than English-speaking children. Or, the same children choose a lower level of cognitive performance when undertaking operations through the medium of Gaelic than when operating through English. Macleod's study of some aspects of bilingualism amongst Lewis schoolchildren is a case in point. (6)

It has often been assumed that children restricted in access to the dominant culture of a society suffer impaired cognitive ability with regard to language performance. Macleod's work indicates this with Gaelic-speaking children in Lewis. However, Labov claims that cognitive performance may depend upon the way in which a child or respondent perceives questioning as meaningful and requiring the calling forth of a particular language-variety.(7)

Labov claimed that his interviewer obtained a higher level of cognitive performance with the Harlem black children when the interviewer was accompanied by the child's friend, sat upon the floor and used informal black speech. Labov claims that the responses he elicited demonstrate an underlying developed structure based upon Aristotelian logic. Labov may well have overstated the situation. He would seem certainly to have happened upon cues which encouraged a previously uncertain child to be less inhibited in generating speech. Inspection of the speech samples Labov quotes seem to indicate that he has probably succeeded in encouraging a child to respond in his everyday, informal 'non-school register'. Whether any higher claims might be entertained for it is debatable. In Macleod's case above, the school situation might have inhibited production of the 'non-school register', which for the Hebridean child would be in Gaelic. A situation in which a visiting educational 'authority-figure' visits a school and encourages children to speak in Gaelic is an unusual event, to say the least. Not surprisingly children might be uncertain of what they should do. The eliciting of speech in the language of the 'school register' is a familiar activity and not surprisingly resulted in more fluent speech.

Houston cites the case of a teacher answering a child's question with another question, thus mistakenly 'cueing' the child that his original assumption (of the teacher putting on her coat in order to go home) was wrong.(8) The uncertainty of the child concerning the intentions of a familiar teacher can affect a child's confidence, speech, and hence its ostensible 'cognitive performance'. When an unfamiliar teacher or other educational 'authority-figure' appears in school the response of children to the situation may well be that this is to be another educational 'exercise'. The uncertainty of the child may be the chief factor depressing cognitive performance. In a school situation where bilingual children take the majority of their curriculum in the 'other tongue' it may not be surprising that in the school situation cognitive performance in the mother tongue should be at a lower level. It is, after all, the less accustomed medium for the child in his school domain. Were a comparative study to be undertaken outside school premises amongst children in relaxed informal circumstances there might be a more eloquent performance within the mother tongue and evidence of more elegant cognitive strategies. In such circumstances, though, it would undoubtedly be the case that the speech-variety of the mother tongue might be that of relaxed informal Gaelic in place of the variety of Gaelic encouraged within the school Gaelic lessons. It may also have been that Macleod's bilingual respondents were performing at a lower cognitive level in Gaelic because school Gaelic required little other of them.

The constraints of the school situation may have made the eliciting of an empathetic bond of language, speaker and respondent difficult. In an exploration subsequent to the present study of the speech of the early school years amongst Harris children of six, seven and eight years of age the elicitation of speech using Trotin cards was not particularly easy — either in Gaelic or English. The description of a busy street or railway station scene often elicited merely 'Bodach . . . cailleach . . . bodach . . . cailleach' ('An old man . . . an old woman . . .') and the model room with dolls often elicited sentences so brief as to be virtually holophrastic or even monosyllabic in content. Relatively few children saw the exercise as an opportunity to do much beyond giving what was hoped to be the most succinct 'educationally-expected' reply in the con- text of the local schools. The station scene was culturally un- familiar. Of some thirty or so children interviewed only one gave as the title the name displayed on the name-board ('Chaville'). Typical replies were 'Tha e trang' ('It's busy') or 'Tarbert', the island 'capital' and ferry terminal. Only one child (daughter of an incomer) took the opportunity actually to play with the toys, comment at large in Gaelic on what she was doing and to interrogate the interviewer. It seemed to me that the exercise was as illumi- nating concerning the interviewer's assumptions of the child within the matrix of the culture of the school as it was of differentials of cognitive performance in the two languages. Any conclusions might say something of children's school performance but it would tell us nothing of the meanings the child would be likely to express in speech within the family or with his peers. In these circumstances the child will be under other forms of social control, will be involved in rather different processes generated by the exercise of other forms of power. We should expect discontinuities to manifest them- selves between the school and non-school life of the child.

It may be apposite here to ask to what extent can a child carry over an elaborated code of English learnt at school into a Gaelic- speaking home. Can an elaborated-code Gaelic that the school requires be applied by the child in a Gaelic-speaking home where it may be assumed that the code of the home is restricted? In contrast can an elaborated-code English monoglot child acquire restricted- code Gaelic from the school, thus enabling him to use Gaelic expres- sively in phatic communion with his Gaelic-speaking peers in relaxed informal social interaction? It may be one thing for such a child to acquire school Gaelic, effectively use the 'school register' in Gaelic, pass his O- and H-grades as a Gaelic-learner but never fully be able to participate in local Gaelic speechways and the full range of social situations using Gaelic. These prob- lems call for much further research at the level of case studies of face-to-face language usage at the family, peer group and dyadic level of social interactions. The situation also calls for height- ened levels of sociolinguistic awareness and insight amongst teachers within teacher education and in-service continuing teacher education and the educational administration of Gaelic-speaking communities.

However, within the home, the child whether bilingual or not has in his pre-school years acquired not only language but a vocabulary and grammar of gesture and expression: a metalinguistic communica-

tion system, language-behaviour and language etiquette, an image of
social reality, and an awareness of the socially structured field
in which he can locate himself. The bilingual situation may render
more obvious to the observer the essentially interrelated way in
which the acquisition of language, behaviour, social processes and
awareness of social structure is concomitantly acquired by the child.
The bilingual experience presents a child with a model of power
relations and social processes derived from the macro-level of
society and interpreted at a micro-level.

Chomsky posits the supposed assumption of a 'language acquisition device'. Through this essential component of the mind, the
infant autonomously constructs his initial and provisional grammars
and undertakes transformations upon the material he absorbs from the
matrix of language surrounding him. Chomsky is unlikely literally
to believe in a discrete or physically separable 'language-
acquiring device'. It is rather better to be understood as a
characteristic of the general powers of the mind. Although too
little is known of such fields as the 'language' of movement, expression and gesture, it may be that in all probability this field
of human behaviour is acquired in an analogous fashion — if not
as part of a more generalised 'language' of social behaviour. Thus
speech, gesture, behaviour patterns generally and the replication of
social structure may be understood as subsuming a continuous area of
human ability of which any particular aspect — such as speech —
may be regarded as a special case.

Some such image seems to be implicit in Chomsky's adoption of
Lashley's model of serial order in behaviour in relation to the
learning of kinaesthetic and motor patterns of physiological movement.(9) There is the latent implication in the work of both
Lashley and Chomsky of an extension of the principle into the field
of social behaviour.

With the bilingual and bidialectal child we can clearly see
how closely-associated language is with social behaviour. The
child who does not have so many speech varieties within his speech-
repertoire may less obviously but no less really be understood as an
autonomous individual formulating not only his own first shots at a
usable grammar but also concomitantly putting them together with
this his own folk- or idio-sociology.

PATTERNS OF DIGLOSSIA AND BILINGUALISM

The socially sanctioned speechways of the adult signify the processes operating within wider society in which he is involved.
Fishman has contributed to the analysis of these problems a conceptual association of diglossia and bilingualism.(10) In terms of
the linguistic culture of urban Britain — especially as regards
working-class speech communities — a situation exists whereby
social dialects are apportioned between the social classes. There
is a middle-class dialect and a working-class dialect which are
socially separate and spoken by different people. True bidialectism
is weak. Relatively few people can generate both dialects effectively and there are relatively few social situations calling for
the same individuals to be able to generate and use either dialect.

Hence a true diglossia is not realised. In London or Newcastle,
Cockney- and Geordie-speakers may not function at all well in the
received-pronunciation Standard English speech variety. Middle-
class Londoners do not speak Cockney at all well.

In contrast, a speech-community such as Harris normally requires
that its members should be able to function in both high and low
speech varieties in terms of diglossic usage (i.e. Standard English
as 'high' and local colloquial Gaelic as 'low'). Here the alternate
speech-varieties are carried in separate discrete languages.
Typically all members whatever their social position have command
over the high and low varieties (the few exceptions comprising
young children who have not yet acquired their second language and
the small number of monoglot middle-class incomers). In the urban
society of modern Britain language is socially divisive. Discontinuities of speech signify social barriers. Not so in communities
such as Harris. Speech variation does not signify a social divide
between persons. It signifies the differentiation of social
function within an individual's behavioural repertoire. The local
language in this diglossic usage preserves the dignity of Gaelic
culture. There is a measure of 'esteem' for the folk culture for
it possesses the stiffening of a recognised language in its own
right. In London 'Cockney culture' on the other hand tends to be
disparaged since it is sustained by a social dialect which is low
in terms of general societal esteem. Such a culture is restricted
to persons who have access only to 'low' speech varieties.

'Cockney culture' in an East London working-class community —
like Gaelic culture in the Harris crofting community — is the sub-
culture of a particular social stratum. Both are discontinuous in
comparison with the 'high' culture of the national society. The
speech of Cockneys is — and always was — the social dialect of a
lower stratum of society. Gaelic was until about eight centuries
ago a national language throughout Scotland and a language which
still preserves something of its 'high' culture. Like Cockney,
Gaelic was under official and educational disparagement until very
recently. Unlike Cockney, Gaelic — and its associated culture —
now enjoys higher esteem both in and out of the Gaelic speech-
community. This may be owing to the fact that Gaelic is now
regarded as a discrete language in its own right — and Cockney
remains in the opinion of its speakers and observers merely a 'low'
social dialect.

Gaelic culture may also enjoy higher prestige both in and out
of the speech-community because the diglossic situation enables
some of its speakers at least to possess both 'high' and 'low'
forms of speech within the Gaelic language. The use of their own
'standard' language (albeit in a relaxed variety) for their own
purposes enables their culture to enjoy a transfer of prestige or
halo effect. Clearly Gaelic language and culture has come to be
seen in Scotland generally as a desirable social phenomenon. The
Gaelic usage of the pulpit and of BBC broadcasts is even providing
something of a standard form of the language. The increase in the
Census returns for Gaelic-speaking ability between 1961-71 may
in some measure be attributable to such attitudes. Between 1961-71
the total number of Gaelic-speakers as enumerated in Scotland as a
whole increased from 80,978 to 88,942: an increase of 9.3 per cent.

The percentage increase of those able to speak both Gaelic and English was 10.5%.(11)   The 1971 Census report attributes these increases to a change in the Census questions (which for the first time included questions on literacy) and the increased number of non-native speakers learning Gaelic.(12)   This phenomenon of the past decade is in marked contrast to the former 'great ill-will of the non-Gael' ('*mi-rùn mór nan Gall*').(13)   Gaelic today is clearly acquiring a measure of prestige and esteem amongst non-Gaelic-speakers.

It is of value to Gaelic culture that there should be a language-usage whereby a language of wider communication may be employed instrumentally in those situations in which wider society makes its demands upon the local community.

For the Gael organic solidarity is realised through English.   On the other hand mechanical solidarity is realised through Gaelic.   In wider English-speaking society we may perceive there to be at work such processes as homogenisation and standardisation of language proceeding alongside an increasing division of labour.   This involves increasingly associative and organic forms of solidarity, disvaluation of non-standard language-varieties and a phenomenon of language-shift which is analogous to that between languages in the Celtic contact-situation types.   In place of a local language of solidarity being shiften out of an increasing number of domains by an intrusive language of power, instead regional dialects or lower-class sociolects as language-varieties of solidarity are being shifted out of domains by 'high' language-varieties of power such as Received Pronunciation Standard English.   There may be a sense in which the sub-culture or 'little tradition' of a local folk-community is 'protected' by a language such as Gaelic and through it members are able readily to communalise and realise relationships of a mechanically solidary character.   Within the 'mass-culture' of wider society such possibilities become more difficult as language-homogenisation and the contraction of speech-repertoires occur.

On the other hand there are processes in society which seek to express local and intra-group values by means of the development of new and socially restricted speech varieties.   There are also changes at the societal level which call for a more mechanically solidary nature of the general social bonding.   The reduction of social alienation which such changes seek to bring about might be aided by a strategy of language-planning.   This concept is generally associated with the creation of a new standard form of a language (such as modern Hebrew, Irish or Norwegian).   It might equally be applied not only to the area of linguistic form but also to the area of social behaviour.   For example, a diglossic bidialectism might in certain circumstances be encouraged — or indeed officially planned — in order to encourage all members of a national society to have access to a wider range of language-varieties.   The object might be to give all or more members access to a language or language-variety of 'power' and also to promote throughout society community languages or language-varieties of 'solidarity'.   In the latter instance regional sociolects such as Cockney or Geordie might receive promotion throughout the social spectrum as media for the realisation of expressive, affective and solidary forms of social interaction.   Received Pronunciation

Standard English in its middle- or upper-class sociolectal form
might receive parallel promotion throughout the social spectrum as
an appropriate medium for the realisation of associative, transactional, non face-to-face and formal relationships. In diglossic
speech-communities such as the German-Swiss a similar social
patterning exists between the German language variants of High
German and Schwyzertüütsch. In the Celtic language-contact situations the social use of the two discrete languages provides a comparable pattern of functioning.

THE PROBLEM OF LANGUAGE-SHIFT

Language-shift proceeds along a number of dimensions. First, we
have noted the dimension of domain. One language is replaced by
another across an increasing range of social situations. Second, we
have noted the displacement of language across the social spectrum.
One language is replaced by another as the vernacular of an increasing range of social groups or strata. Third, we have to consider the displacement of one language by another in a territorial
or geographical sense.

It has been conventional to conceptualise the relationships
between English and the other native languages with which it has
historically been in contact within the British Isles as a process
of the advance or retreat of a 'language-frontier'. (In Wales
Gerald Morgan speaks of the Welsh language-border being swept back-
wards and forwards in medieval Flintshire.)(14) In Ireland the
settlement of an English colony within 'The Pale' surrounding
Dublin, and the 'plantations' of English-speakers across other
regions, reduced the hegemony of Irish vernacular speech to ever
contracting *Gaeltachtaí*. A similar retreat of vernacular Cornish
occurred in historic times. The line of its retreat can be fairly
closely dated and delineated on the ground as 'language-drift'
imparted distinctive characteristics to placenames at various
periods.(15) Contemporary commentators upon the Welsh language
situation such as Cennard Davies and Ned Thomas emphasise what
such an image of language-contact might conceal, namely that the
'line of bilingualism runs along every street in Wales',(16) and
reject the validity of a *Bro-Gymraeg* or Welsh *Gaeltacht* as an
effective strategy for Welsh language-conservation.

The culture-lag hypothesis of language-conservation has been
criticised in Chapter 2 whereby cultural innovation and higher
levels of relative economic development are to be associated with
the early shift to English of areas open to such influences (such
as eastern areas of the Scottish Highlands). Such a hypothesis
regards Gaelic as being conserved in backward areas in terms of
such criteria as difficulty of communications and lower levels of
relative economic development (such as the islands and the western
peninsulas of the Highlands). The Highland counties such as
existed prior to the local government reform of 1975 provided a
convenient means of examining this hypothesis in terms of the
Census results of the 1961 and 1971 Censuses, as the counties
typically extend across the northern mainland and islands from the
almost completely anglicised eastern coastal plain, across mountain-

ous interiors chiefly uninhabited today, to the substantially Gaelic
crofting communities of the western coasts and the predominantly
Gaelic-speaking Hebrides. Whereas such a county as Inverness-shire
does evidence substantial correlation between high relative economic
development and low Gaelic language-conservation, Argyll and
Sutherland do so only to a rather moderate degree and Ross-shire —
ostensibly a comparable case — does not. Such relationships in
Ross-shire are poorly correlated — and in the instance of the
burghs in 1961 the correlation was substantially the reverse of
the expected pattern. In 1971 this was to a moderate degree the
case as between all divisions of the county.

The Lieberson and Hansen(17) have critically examined such models
as Pool's(18) of the relationship between language-diversity and
economic development at societal levels. Pool concluded that
development either requires or results in second-language learning,
and native-language change such that no country is ever able to
maintain a societal pattern of high economic development and substantial diversity of vernacular.(19) Lieberson and Hansen use a
more sophisticated methodology in terms of measure of language
diversity (the use of an index which is that of the statistical
probability of any two citizens selected at random sharing a common
mother tongue) and this is compared with a number of variables
(rather like Deutsch's criteria for mobilisation):(20) urbanisation,
gross national product, newspaper circulation, energy consumption,
statistics on domestic mail, areal size and illiteracy. For
selected countries longitudinal studies over time represent a
dimension which Pool's 'snapshot' synchronous study did not. It
is difficult methodologically to sustain an argument concerning
change from a single synchronous study which although comparative
is essentially static. The conclusions of Lieberson and Hansen's
study are very important so far as language-conservation is concerned. A commonsense criticism of Pool's paradigm would have been
that the existence of countries like Switzerland refuted his
general conclusion. The Lieberson and Hansen study illustrated how
a stabilising and even gradually increasingly linguistically diverse
polity may develop into what is an impossibility within Pool's
model: that of an increasingly economically developed state. In
Canada similarly stable or increasing language-diversity co-exists
with a rapidly developing economy. The present study has examined
situations more comparable with the conclusions of Lieberson and
Hansen than with those of Pool.

The results are interesting and indicate that an application of
the cross-cultural and international comparisons on the lines of
the above studies might be adapted to comparative studies between
districts and regions within linguistically diverse polities. The
longitudinal comparisons of development and language-diversity in
Highland counties and districts, although limited to two censuses,
might be productive in exemplifying social and economic processes
at a more intimate level than the more general national and international level which has to date been the chief form of investigation of these problems.

The model of the relationship between language, society and the
transmission of culture which has been developed in the present
study can be regarded as being compounded of such elements as

those following.

A process similar to that developed by Durkheim and Mauss(21) may be viewed as operating with regard to language in its societal matrix whereby the social structure is reflected in language usage. Language mirrors society, not only at the level treated by Durkheim and Mauss (namely at the level of classificatory schemata: an essentially lexical aspect of the realisation of social values in the folk-taxonomic structures of language), but more importantly there is a coercively-operating process whereby the exercise of power (in its social or moral as well as in its political and economic forms) is reflected in the differential apportionment of language-varieties to individuals, groups and social situations. Taxonomies of sociolinguistic patterning may be developed here — if the situation described for Harris in the present study might be used to formulate one of the ideal types — a possibility to which these conclusions will subsequently return.

In adult life the coercive character of society has been regarded as operating through such agencies as the impact of communications, including the mass media which a local, peripheral community such as Harris passively receives but does not to any significant degree control, direct nor in any real measure participate in as regards decision-making. Communities such as Harris are remote from the decision-making process of the administrative system and essentially receive administrative decisions taken elsewhere. However, agencies such as institutionalised religion are more local and represent a socialising agency within which the community feels itself to be closely identified and where leading community members do have a decision-making role.

In the unequal power situation of local folk communities such as Harris the coercive character of external political and economic relationships (as well as moral relationships exercised in local religious culture) are reflected locally within language and language-usage and in inter-personal social relationships.

LANGUAGE AND POWER

The study has remarked upon the results of socio-political and economic processes as requiring repertoire-extension within the language-behaviour of their recipients and concomitantly discouraging the repertoire extension of their originating or participating social groups. In the case of groups whose social dialect becomes the standard language of the polity (as the result of the operation of processes involving the exercise of social, political and economic power) there is little instrumental necessity for their members to acquire the vernacular of the dominated groups. These vernaculars may be social or regional dialects or discrete languages. The milieu of the power-exercising groups is urban, metropolitan or international and there is a consonance of code between their various agencies of socialisation: family, school and peer-group so far as the children are concerned. Similar consonance may be held to exist between the individual's speechways and agencies of socialisation within adult society: the administrative system, the communications system and the symbolic value system. Social bonding, however, tends to be organic.

In the case of the dominated and power-recipient groups, these may be encountered in a continuum of milieux from the truly urban to the truly rural in Frankenberg's typology.(22) (Although subsuming some twenty-five characteristics, Frankenberg's typology lacks a 'language-dimension' and sociolinguistic sensitivity in its discussion of social change.) To varying extents then these groups form communities in the sense that Redfield signifies by his concept of the 'folk' or 'little' community. Whether the community is truly urban: a working-class community in a down-town inter-city area or a truly rural isolated small island, its social bonding will be of a more mechanical character. Its range of specialisations may be less than that of a power-effecting group — especially so in the case of the truly rural community. Social solidarity tends to be mechanical — pronouncedly so in the latter case. Power relations with the 'core' society and its power-exercising social groupings will be signified by a linguistic marker. There will be an instrumental necessity for the dominated group to acquire knowledge of, access to and understanding of the speechways of the groups exercising power. There will be the need to acquire an 'other tongue' whether this is another social or regional dialect or discrete language. In certain colonial situations access to the 'other tongue' is partial. Social distance is reinforced by the usage of pidgins, the development of creoles, and the marginal registers of colonial culture-contact which King has described.(23) In any event, code-dissonance opens up between the agencies of socialisation of the child. The speech of the home is not encountered as the language of the school. If language-shift is under way peer-culture may have to accommodate to the fact that its members are of different mother tongue or have access to different speech-varieties. In this way children of dominated cultures may come to have wider speech-repertoires than children of cultures participating in the exercise of power. Code-dissonance may also be considerable between the speechways of the sub-culture and the speech and language norms of the administrative and communication systems. Having noted the 'disruptions' whereby the Gaels set up essentially ethnic churches of their own, separating themselves from the established church and bearing in mind such phenomena as the importance of sect-christianity, pentecostalism and cargo-cults in various 'third-world' contact situations, the field of religion presents itself as an important line of future study.(24) There would seem to be an importance in conserving in-group speechways with regard to moral and symbolic cultural institutions. The reported shift to Gaelic amongst the young in recreational domains may indicate similar tendencies within the. expressive aspects of the culture.

The concept of 'demesne-extension' has been suggested as an index of the social relations between the power-exercising and the power-recipient groups. A continuum of speech-situations has been established in rank-order on the basis of the extent to which one language (or language-variety) is used. A gradation of intensity of usage would be expected to run from the domains of 'official' life through domains of formal, transactional, educational, communal, symbolic and individual social life. Using language and language-

use as criteria of social significance, the placement of particular
social behaviour and domains may be separated from their ostensible
place within local communal patterns of social interaction and may
be placed within the sphere of influence of wider social sanc-
tioning. In the present study such ostensible individual activities
as counting and letter-writing were better understood as ways in
which the values and social patterning of outside society entered
into local life. Similarly the differential language usage between
the bank and the post office were to be regarded as indicative of
differential social significance. One was more and the other less
intrusive into local folkways.

The domains or speech-situations predominantly realised through
the 'other tongue' (the 'language of power' or language-variety of
mass-society or the power-exercising social groupings) provides the
'demesne-extention' of English in Harris. The domains or speech-
situations realised through the 'mother tongue' (the 'language of
solidarity' or language-variety of the local community or power-
recipient social groupings) yields the 'demesne-extension' of Gaelic
in Harris. The concept is distinguishable from Weinreich's
'dominance-configureation' on two counts. First, the concept may
be handled at the level of legitimate occupation of social territory by language. The power-dynamic is not essential to the concept. Second, no assumptions need be made regarding the emic significance of domain. The ordering of the particular domains in
terms of their significance to the local culture are empirically
assessed and are not anterior or 'given'.

A TYPOLOGY OF LANGUAGE CONTACT

The concept 'demesne-extension' may be regarded as possessing
validity in the types of language-contact situation which Fishman
categorises as diglossic and/or bilingual.(25)   In returning to
the problem of typologies of language-contact situations it may be
felt that Fishman's two-by-two schema is inadequate as an exhaustive
typology of types of speech-community or national societies ex-
periencing language-contact. The account lacks a dynamic. For
example, if the concept of power is utilised, various forms of
contact are distinguishable under which language-variation takes
markedly different forms. Another difficulty stems from the way
in which we should understand national polities which are bilingual
or multilingual in the sense that two or more languages are in use
— or even officially recognised — within the polity but whose
members do not acquire effective command or working knowledge of
the other tongue. This has been approximately the case in imperial
forms of political organisation as well as in metropolitan countries such as Belgium. As these situations are neither truly bilingual nor diglossic we are thus brought to regard such cases as
political association of discrete speech-communities. Fishman
somewhat confusingly discusses this problem as being subsumed
under the condition of 'diglossia without bilingualism';(26) we
seem clearly here to need a new term to signify the separation of
speech varieties between distinct social groups: 'schizoglossia'.

Another inadequacy inheres in the limitation of the scheme to
language-variation between discrete standard languages alone. The
principle is capable of extension at least to the level of bidialectism, as readily as it is to bilingualism proper. The criteria
for the distinction of dialect from language include political
considerations. For example, Flemish and Dutch relate together
as a language-cline. Flemish and Dutch as geographical varieties
of Nederlands are separated not by an isogloss but by a political
frontier. Fishman's schema is readily capable of conceptual extension to the point where one of his dimensions may be understood
as bilingualism and/or bidialectism, taken together as language-
variation (i.e. linguistic differentiation). The other dimension,
of diglossia, may be similarly extended in conceptual terms in
that it is concerned with social differentiation (either in terms
of social stratification or individual social behaviour).

Fishman's condition of 'bilingualism without diglossia' appears
to him as a condition of individuals' language-situations rather
than that of communities or national polities.(27) Expressed,
however, in more general terms as language-variation without
socially allocated usages, it is difficult to conceptualise as a
condition of any actual speech-community. But there may be social
circumstances where something of the kind occurs — and this may
be in supra-national organisations. United Nations and OEEC
institutions require effective ambilinguality of their personnel.
Equal regard must be paid to the officially recognised languages.
Officials must use any of the languages when required to do so
throughout the range of social usages encountered within the work
of the organisation. This may be required at any time on demand as
the result of contact with, say, a politician able to use only
one of the organisation's official languages. The case of air-
control as an international institution is contrasted. Diglossic
usage of English and mother tongue occurs here as English is in
widespread international use as the virtual sole medium of the
social situation or domain of ground-to-air control.

Concerning true speech communities or national polities, however,
a typology may be attempted on the basis of patterns of language-
variation in terms of social situation of language-use. These
sociolinguistic patterns may be regarded as being brought about
by a dynamic process of the exercise of power by different forms
of power-effecting groups in societal interaction with different
forms of power-recipient groups within which different principles
of social control are operating. The following typology is
ordered in an increasingly coercive exercise of political power.

The Swiss-German type

Here within a participating democratic polity numbers of speech-
communities co-exist, having associated together freely for such
purposes as mutual defence and exchange. Power is effected by
inter-community administration with which all groups identify.
Social control within such a speech-community as the Swiss-German
is relatively open to achievement norms and does not exhibit
strongly-delineated barriers to mobility. Members of the speech-

community throughout the social spectrum use two dialectal variants
of German: Standard High German in formal, 'high' domains; and a
local dialect Schwyzertüütsch, in relaxed, 'low' domains.

The English type

Here the polity is relatively ethnically homogenous. However, it
is characterised by a fairly well-defined class-system within
which an upper-class or more latterly an establishment group has
functioned as a power-élite. Lower strata within the social spectrum have not always felt themselves effectively to participate in
the exercise of political power. The operation of social control
has tended towards ascription norms hierarchically enforced and
mobility has been of the sponsorship rather than the contest
type.(28) Language-variation is principally in terms of the allocation of distinct sociolects as between the classes. Lower-class
sociolects exhibit considerable geographical variation. Members
of a particular class do not have access to very wide speech-
repertoires, and such variation as there may be for particular
social usages and social situations will be at the level of code,
register and style rather than dialect or discrete language.

The Celtic type

(This type is as exemplified by Harris in the present study.) In
this case the speech-community has been incorporated within a
much larger polity as an ethnic minority. Language-shift is well
advanced but within the relict mother-tongue community there is a
relatively homogenous bilingualism. Power is effected by the dominant group of mainstream society: power that is shared in some
measure amongst the membership of mass-society generally and in
particular by incoming metropolitan settlers or administrators.
Diglossic bilingualism is the predominant pattern of social usage.
Different discrete languages are used by members of the speech-
community throughout the social spectrum (which is truncated owing
to the distortions of the local economy as a kind of 'internal
colony' of the polity) in a well-defined patterning as between
domains. Social control tends towards ascriptive traditional norms.

Imperial or colonial types

With such types, the power-effecting group comprises the repre-
sentatives of a colonising foreign people: whether military,
administrative, commercial or 'settler'. Local speech-communities
may be protected by a 'great tradition' of high culture or a 'little
tradition' of folk culture. It is likely that a policy of 'divide
and rule' will preserve a high degree of linguistic differentiation
between native ethnic and social groups. Admission to or participation in the affairs of the power-effecting group will be strictly
controlled and relatively few of the native groups will gain access
to the educational institutions or the standard language-variety of

the dominating groups. Social control within the power-recipient
groups will be under ascriptive traditional norms. Unlike the
preceding type there is no greatly pronounced ideology or educational process to incorporate these external colonies into the
ethnicity of the imperial power. In other varieties of 'third-
world' contact situations, trade relations encourage the spread
of pidgins after speakers of disparate vernaculars have been brought
together in commercial centres. Processes such as enslavement and
the establishment of plantation-type economic production have resulted in forms of coercive domination whereby power-recipient
groups have lost all of their effective power and have been allocated pidgins as the sole means of intra-group communication and
inter-group communication. The pidgin is subsequently creolised
as the vernacular of the power-recipient group. The allocation of
language variety is now in terms of a less markedly distinct
variety than a discrete language or a pidgin, but the social allocation of the non-standard dialect and the standard variety of the
dominating language is no less strongly bounded between social
groups. Social control ensures within a highly hierarchical caste-
system very strongly ascriptive in character.

–   *Diglossia*   +

	– Diglossia +	
Bilingualism +	1 Both diglossia and bilingualism	2 Bilingualism without diglossia
Bilingualism –	3 Diglossia without bilingualism	4 Neither diglossia nor bilingualism

Figure 8.1 The relationships between bilingualism and diglossia
(After Fishman (1971), Fig. 13, p. 288f.)

Language-differentiation in social use has been delineated as a
response to the operation of processes of power and control. The
above typology is illustrated in Figure 8.2. It is put forward as
a theoretical extension of existing schemata in the hope that it
may contribute further insights concerning language and social
process. Language-planning in the modern world can only be
maximally effective if it is grounded in an adequate understanding of the social matrix. Whether the aim is language-conservation or language-restoration in promoting societal access to a
'language of solidarity' side-by-side with a 'language of power',
or whether the aim is the effective promotion of a 'language of
wider communication', the needs of the individual in society can
be better served only by further theoretical exploration and
informed research.

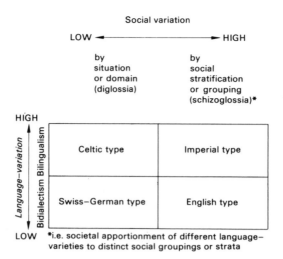

Figure 8.2 A typology of linguistic and social variation

SOME SUGGESTIONS FOR THE FUTURE

The scope and resources of the present study have enabled little
more than an exploration to be undertaken of one small part of an
important problem area in British educational and rural sociology.
Its conclusions can only be tentative and limited but clearly they
point to the need of further and concerted research activity regarding Gaelic speech-communities. It would be most valuable to
develop a more detailed picture of the relationship of socio-
economic and linguistic factors within the Gàidhealtachd. Within
such studies it will be most valuable to consider the development
of attitudes towards language and towards other aspects of the
culture, for example concerning the symbolic value-system and its
mediation through religious institutions, as well as the popular
culture of the Gael and its modes of transmission. It would be a
most welcome development in Scottish academic institutions were the
departments of Celtic studies, linguistics and the various social
studies to be able to effect co-operative and multi-disciplinary
approaches to these problems. The initiation of research on these
lines by such institutions as the School of Scottish Studies,
Edinburgh University, and the Institute for the Study of Sparsely
Settled Regions at Aberdeen might prove feasible originating
centres. The results of the present study of one Gaelic community,
Harris, should indicate the value of comparative and longitudinal
studies of Gaelic communities. The presentation of official
statistics both in the population Census and in Scottish Education
Statistics have not provided data in usable form to help answer
some of the crucial problems and this indicates the need for particular surveys tailor-made for the problems in hand.

The Scottish Council for Research in Education report of 1961
called for a study in depth of the bilingual problem in Highland
education. This still awaits attention. As that report emphasised
survey material cannot just be borrowed or adapted, it must be
specifically made for the purpose. It would be timely to consider
a new start to this endeavour. The news of the initiation of a
bilingual education project shortly after the establishment of the
new Western Isles education authority in mid-1975 gives hope that
such approaches may already be under way. With assistance from the
Scottish Education Department and funding in the order of £68,000,
there now exists the chance that an effective step forward may
occur. The appointment of John Murray (former editor of the Gaelic
Books Council) and in August 1975, the secondment of serving
teachers (as has been done in Wales), may show valuable results
over the forthcoming three years. There exists a rich field today
within the areas of sociology and psychology of education, socio-
linguistics and psycholinguistics, curriculum reform and the
development of media resources and bilingual teaching method which
was not so far developed in 1961. The appointment of Finlay
Macleod as adviser for Gaelic and primary education to the authority
is an additional hopeful indication that the formulation of a truly
bilingual and bicultural education for the Western Isles is on the
way, and one hopes that it may be made available throughout the
Gàidhealtachd.
     The establishment of such a bicultural education must rest
upon a substantial basis of public confidence. Fishman has indicated the value of such an educational opportunity for all, the
monoglot child as much as the bilingual (in his yet unpublished
monograph 'A Sociology of Bilingual Education', 1974). The public
relations of educational innovation — especially within a traditional community — cannot be too strongly stressed. Furthermore
the effectiveness of a bicultural Gaelic education scheme must rest
upon a lot of work which as yet has not been particularly thoroughly
accomplished: individual child studies, especially in those cases
where the equivalence of 'mother tongue', 'first language',
'language of conversational ease', 'immediate conversational
response' and 'familial language' do not necessarily coincide.
Similar depth study of children's attitudes towards language, use
of language varieties, and use of both languages to family members
and peers for different purposes and in different circumstances is
urgent. A recent editorial in the Gaelic quarterly 'Gairm'
(Autumn 1975) cites a Lewis teacher as observing that it was a
cause of worry and sorrow to her concerning how indifferent were
the children regarding their own language. They now get Gaelic
as a school subject but they cast it away as they reach the school
gate. Once it had been the case that English remained inside the
school gate. Now no matter what the teachers tried to do it was
making little difference.
     If it is considered valuable to retain the use of Gaelic as a
community language — and to develop the school as a means of
achieving this (as many Gaels, even the moderately loyal, seem to
feel reasonable) — then the common-sense approaches which individual teachers have persevered with over the years will clearly
be insufficient. In England the Bullock Report has called for a

heightened language awareness amongst teachers and recommends
strengthened language education both within initial and continuing
teacher education. A region of communicational difficulty such as
northwest Scotland calls for the establishment of greatly improved
facilities for teachers. There needs to be a permanently-based
unit within the Gaelic area itself developing audio-visual and
teaching materials for bicultural education, functioning as a
teachers' centre for short residential courses and conferences and
also handling aspects of initial training which enable teachers to
gain their theoretical studies in bilingual and bicultural teaching
methods throughout the range of school subjects and teaching levels,
and where effective supervision of teaching practice may easily be
organised within the ambience of the Gaelic area itself. The unit
might also be staffed so as to be able scientifically to study the
linguistic characteristics of the varieties of Gaelic used by
children and their significant others so that courses in Gaelic
for the non-Gaelic-speaking child as well as for adult learners
might have the chance of really imparting varieties of Gaelic
which their Gaelic-speaking peers actually use. On the other hand,
university departments of Celtic might develop equally important
and complementary work in the formulation of a standard variety
for the language including the provision of a vocabulary of neologisms and technical terminology and standard forms of placenames
in Gaelic (on the lines of the Board of Celtic Studies of the
University of Wales). The Gaelic area — indeed the whole of the
former seven 'crofter counties' — lacks the presence of any form
of advanced educational institution (above the level of technical
colleges handling 'non-advanced further education'). University
initiatives or the intelligent use of 'pooling' arrangements by
local education authorities might enable the financial problems
vitiating these developments to be reversed.(29)
     The present study has also drawn attention to many other
desirable improvements affecting Gaelic-speaking children and their
community. If there is to be a truly bicultural education scheme
it means that teachers not only of Gaelic but of Gaelic-speaking
children should themselves be or become Gaelic-speaking and be
capable of using both languages of their children and of extending
both their Gaelic and their English. This needs explicit policy
to be developed by the local education authorities (now the new
Scottish regions), the Scottish Education Department and the
colleges of education, especially as regards recruitment into the
profession (into which the General Teaching Council will need to be
brought), teaching method, placements and more specific encourage-
ments to serve in the Gaelic areas. In this latter connection
morale, sense of purpose, vocation, intellectual stimulation and
cultural supports are as important as the financial inducements of
the 'remote area' or 'island allowance' type which have operated
in the past. The range of school examinations will need to be
available in Gaelic. A real Gaelic educational broadcasting service handling the range of school and college work will be necessary.
So also will a complete local radio service in Gaelic. Local education authorities could provide much better library facilities for
Gaelic readers. (In 1972 the Harris library carried no Gaelic
books — but it is to be hoped that the new travelling service has

now improved this situation.) Adult education and further education classes should be in Gaelic for Gaelic-speaking people. Even
more vital is the provision of Gaelic playgroups and nursery classes.
    The reorganisation of secondary education gives hope for the
future. If the principle of bringing education to the child rather
than the converse now becomes the keynote of policy a number of
things may follow; first, that the closure of small rural primary
schools on mere economic grounds may be avoided. The value of
family grouping in urban schools shows that the small country
school has some built-in advantages it would be a pity to lose.
Also the common-core comprehensive curriculum should mean that
small secondary schools within the home community may keep younger
children generally at home. As travel and hostels for the oldest
secondary children may be necessary in many cases, it should be
possible to ensure that there are ways in which a Gaelic and homely
atmosphere may be promoted within them and enable young people to
get the best of both their worlds: the stimulation of development
of their own culture and the introduction of the wider culture in
non-alienating ways. The development of new opportunities of
educational and cultural institutions within the *Gàidhealtachd*
(which should go hand-in-hand with the socioeconomic remit which
is laid upon the Highlands and Islands Development Board by Act of
Parliament) ought to mean increasing opportunity for the Gaelic
child at all levels of final educational attainment to have a real
choice as to whether he will seek a future within his own community
or outside of it — or both. If the bilingual policy of the
new Western Isles authority, Comhairle nan Eilean, as adopted in
its own 'Rae Report' is seriously put into practice, there can be
good grounds for optimism.
    These suggestions have focused very much upon action by official
bodies but there is much that non-official activity might achieve.
A great deal of research might be accomplished at individual B.Ed.
and higher-degree level into such areas as the different attitudes
towards language and culture between the sexes at the higher
secondary levels and beyond. Studies of language-attitude and
language-loyalty would be valuable amongst typical sections and
key figures within the local community. Comparable studies to
the present exploration might yield a valuable synchronous sociolinguistic 'map' of the *Gàidhealtachd* and its education system.
Within the area of voluntary associations, the reformulation of a
truly Gaelic youth movement is crucial and the establishment of
COGA (Comhairle Oileanaich Gàidhealaich Alba) co-ordinating the
various student Gaelic societies in late 1974 was timely. The
Gaelic 'renaissance' centring around the establishment of Sabhal
Mór Ostaig, the Gaelic College in Southern Skye, provides another
'growth point' for Gaelic cultural activity. Its initial activities between 1973-5 already indicate that as a community cultural
centre operating through the medium of Gaelic, really every island
and mainland Gaelic community should have one. A number of suggestions have from time to time been made to establish a travelling Gaelic repertory group or entertainment company. The idea was
again raised in June 1975 by the Western Isles Education Committee:
an idea well deserving of joint funding by the Highland and Strath-
clyde Regions and the Scottish Arts Council. Voluntary associations

such as An Comunn Gàidhealach have often been criticised as dissi-
pating their efforts from the lack of a concerted policy and a
practical programme based upon good principles of analysis of the
situation and consistent application of them. As the recipient of
substantial public monies, it might well behove An Comunn to give
more concentrated attention to research and to ensure its policy
statements were made explicit and driven home more vigorously
amongst their own members and the public at large.

However, the suggestions are now proceeding beyond the 'academic'
into the field of public life. The transformation of Gaelic
society is of course a matter for the Gaelic public itself and all
suggestions concerning the Gaelic community (and there is a vast
and various 'literature' of such suggestions) are essentially a
matter for the interplay of choice and public opinion of the
community itself. The final word must be with the Gaels themselves:
'*Is e beul a labhras, ach is e gnìomh a dhearbhas*!'

NOTES

CHAPTER 1 SCOTTISH GAELIC STUDIES — SOCIOLOGICAL PERSPECTIVES

1 For accounts of the place of Gaelic as in the education system
   see: Campbell, J.L. (1950) 'Gaelic in Scottish Education and
   Life', Edinburgh: W.A. & K. Johnston; Macleod, M. (1963)
   Gaelic in Highland Education, in 'Transactions of the Gaelic
   Society of Inverness', vol. XLIII; Thomson, D.S., and Grimble, I.
   (1968) 'The Future of the Highlands', London: Routledge & Kegan
   Paul (esp. chapters on The Position of Gaelic and Gaelic Culture
   in Scottish Education by J.H. Smith, and Literature and the Arts
   by D.S. Thomson); MacKinnon, K.M. (1971) 'A Sociolinguistic
   Study of Scottish Gaelic as an Institution in Social Life and
   Education', unpub. M.A. (Educ.) dissertation, London University
   Institute of Education (esp. chapter 4, pp. 35-44); and,
   MacKinnon, K.M. (1974) 'The Lion's Tongue', Inverness: Club
   Leabhar (esp. chapter 6, pp. 54-74).
2 MacKinnon, L. (ed.)(1956) 'Prose Writings of Donald MacKinnon
   (1839-1914)', Edinburgh: Oliver & Boyd, Introduction (p. xvi).
3 Thompson, F.G. (1970) Gaelic in Politics in 'Transactions of the
   Gaelic Society of Inverness', vol. XCVII (1971-72), and
   Mac a' Ghobhainn, S. (1973) The Second Highland Land League in
   'Stornoway Gazette', vol. LVII, no. 7175, week ending 16 June
   1973, p. 4.
4 Campbell, J.L. (1950) op.cit., p. 19; MacKinnon, K.M. (1971)
   op.cit., pp. 19-20, and MacKinnon, K.M. (1974) op.cit., pp. 24,
   29, 37.
5 Thompson, F.G. (1970) op.cit., pp. 82-7.
6 The only English translation of Saunders Lewis's broadcast
   'Tynged yr Iaith' has been made by Elizabeth Edwards (1971) and
   is published in 'Planet', no. 4, February/March 1971, pp. 13-27.
7 Carter, I. (1972) 'The Highlands of Scotland as an Underdeveloped
   Region' in British Sociological Association Annual Conference
   papers for 1972, reprinted in de Kadt, E., and Williams, G.
   (eds)(1974) 'Sociology and Development', London: Tavistock
   Publications, pp. 279-311.
8 As discussed by Merton, R.K. (1949) On Sociological Theories of
   the Middle Range in 'On Theoretical Sociology' (1967), New York:
   Free Press.

9   A situation which in a generally developed country has led
    to the description of such cases as comprising a 'Fourth World'.
    For a development of this idea see Whittaker, B. (ed.)(1972)
    'Fourth World: Victims of Group Oppression', London: Sidgwick
    & Jackson.
10 Grimble, I. (1962) 'The Trial of Patrick Sellar', London:
    Routledge & Kegan Paul.
11 MacKinnon, K.M., (1971) and (1974) op.cit.
12 Blom, J.P., and Gumperz,J.J., Social Meaning in Linguistic
    Structures: Code Switching in Norway in Gumperz,J.J. and Hymes,
    D. (1972) 'Directions in Sociolinguistics', New York: Holt,
    Rinehart & Winston. Gumperz, J.J. (1961b) 'Religion and Social
    Communication in Village North India', Berkeley: University of
    California, (seminar mimeograph).
13 Labov, W. (1969) 'The Logic of Non-standard English' George-
    town Monographs on Language and Linguistics, vol. 22 (1969),
    pp. 1-31; reprinted in Giglioli, P.P. (ed.)(1972) 'Language
    and Social Context', Harmondsworth: Penguin, pp. 179-216.
14 Fischer,J.L. (1966) Syntax and Social Structure: Truk and
    Ponape in Bright, W. (ed.)(1966) 'Sociolinguistics', Mouton:
    The Hague, pp. 168-82.
15 Registrar-General, Scotland, Census Office (1968) Lewis and
    Harris, Special Survey Areas, Edinburgh: HMSO; School of Town
    and Country Planning (no date) 'Harris Planning Study 1966',
    Edinburgh: College of Art; mainly unpublished studies of
    internal migration but some information in Lawson, U. (1973)
    Di-Sathurn' an Fhuadaich in 'Gairm' no. 85, Winter 1973,
    Glasgow, pp. 24-32; Owen, T.M. (1958) The Role of the Township
    in a Hebridean Crofting Economy in 'Gwerin', vol. 2 (1958-9),
    pp. 147-61; and Owen, T.M. (1956) The Communion Season and
    Presbyterianism in a Hebridean Community in 'Gwerin', vol. 1
    (1956-7), pp. 53-66.
16 See Weinreich, U. (1966) 'Languages in Contact: Findings and
    Problems', The Hague: Mouton, pp. 79-80 for information on the
    derivation of the concept. Fishman has further developed this
    chapter, as in Fishman, J.A. (1971) The Sociology of Language,
    para. 142 in Fishman, J.A. (ed.)(1971) 'Advances in the Sociology
    of Language', vol. I, The Hague: Mouton, p. 307.
17 Scottish Council for Research in Education, Committee on Bi-
    lingualism (1961) 'Gaelic-speaking Children in Highland Schools',
    London: University of London Press.
18 Improvements, for example, in questions regarding occupational
    class, concepts of first and second languages, use of language
    in 'specific situations', concepts of language-function and
    domain.
19 'Media-variance', for definition and description see Fishman,
    J.A. (1966) 'Language Loyalty in the United States', The Hague:
    Mouton, p. 427.
20 'Language-loyalty', see Fishman, J.A. (1971) The Sociology of
    Language in Fishman, J.A. (ed.)(1971) 'Advances in the Socio-
    logy of Language', vol. I, The Hague: Mouton, pp. 312-15,
    331-2.
21 'Dominance-configuration' see Weinreich, U. (1966) 'Languages in
    Contact: Findings and Problems', The Hague: Mouton, pp. 79-80.

22 'Domain': for definition and description see Fishman, J.A.
    (1971) The Relationship between Micro- and Macro-sociolinguis-
    tics. . . in Pride, J.B. and Holmes, J. (eds)(1972) 'Socio-
    linguistics', Harmondsworth: Penguin, pp. 18-28. Fishman,
    J.A. (1971) The Sociology of Language in Fishman (1971)
    'Advances in the Sociology of Language', vol. I, The Hague:
    Mouton, pp. 255f.
23 Campbell, J.L. (1945)(revised 1950) 'Gaelic in Scottish Educa-
    tion and Life: Past, Present, Future', Edinburgh: W. & A.K.
    Johnstone Ltd.
24 Campbell, J.L. (1936) Scottish Gaelic in Canada in 'American
    Speech', vol. II, pp. 128-36 (revised 1948 in 'An Gàidheal',
    vol. XLIII, March 1948, Glasgow).
25 Dunn, C.W. (1953) 'Highland Settler: a Portrait of the Scottish
    Gael in Nova Scotia', Toronto: University of Toronto Press.
26 Campbell, D. and MacLean, R.A. (1974) 'Beyond the Atlantic
    Roar: A Study of the Nova Scotia Scots', Toronto: McClelland
    & Stewart.
27 Ibid., p. 176.
28 Thomson, D.C. (1963) The MacMhuirich Bardic Family in 'Trans-
    actions of the Gaelic Society of Inverness', vol. XLIII,
    1960-63, pp. 276-304; Thomson, D.C. (1967) Gaelic Learned
    Orders and Literati in Medieval Scotland in 'Scottish Studies',
    vol. 12, part I (1968),pp. 57-78; Thomson, D.C. (1970) The
    Poetry of Niall MacMhuirich in 'Transactions of the Gaelic
    Society of Inverness', vol. XLVI, pp. 281-307.
29 Thomson, D.C. (1966) The Role of the Writer in a Minority
    Culture in 'Transactions of.the Gaelic Society of Inverness',
    vol. XLIV (1964-66), pp. 256-71; Thomson, D.C. (1968) Litera-
    ture and the Arts in Thomson, D.C. and Grimble, I. (1968) 'The
    Future of the Highlands', London: Routledge & Kegan Paul,
    pp. 205-40.
30 Deutsch, K.W. (1953) (revised 1966) 'Nationalism and Social
    Communication: an Inquiry into the Foundations of Nationality',
    Cambridge, Mass.: MIT Press, esp. pp. 118-19, 137-8, and
    Appendix IV, pp. 231-4.

CHAPTER 2   LANGUAGE FUNCTION AND SOCIAL CONSTRAINT

1 Durkheim, E. and Mauss, M. (1903) 'Primitive Classification',
   translated by Needham, R. (1970), London: Routledge & Kegan
   Paul.
2 Weber, Max (1948) The Chinese Literati in Gerth, H.H. and Mills,
   C. Wright (1948) 'From Max Weber: Essays in Sociology',
   London: Routledge & Kegan Paul, pp. 416-44, esp. pp. 429-31.
3 Mills, C. Wright (1939) Language, Logic and Culture in 'American
   Sociological Review Note' (October 1939), pp. 670-80: and
   Merton, R.K. (1945) The Sociology of Knowledge in Gurvitch, G.,
   and Moore, W.L. (1945) 'Twentieth Century Sociology', New York:
   Philosophical Library, pp. 366-405.
4 Halliday, M.A.K. (1973) Language as a Social Semiotic: Towards
   a General Sociolinguistic Theory in Makkai, V.B. and Heilmann, L.
   (eds) 'Linguistics at the Crossroads', The Hague and Paris:
   Mouton (in press).

5   Ibid., para. 1.3.
6   Fishman, J.A. (1965) The Relationship between Micro- and Macro-Sociolinguistics in the Study of Who Speaks What Language to Whom and When in 'La Linguistique', vol. 2, pp. 67-88; reproduced with amendments in Pride, J.B. and Holmes, J. (eds)(1972) 'Sociolinguistics', Harmondsworth: Penguin, p. 19.
7   Ogden, C.K. and Richards, I.A. (1923) 'The Meaning of Meaning, A Study of the Influence of Language upon Thought and of the Science of Symbolism', London: Routledge & Kegan Paul, esp. pp. 234f.
8   Malinowski, B. (1923) The Problem of Meaning in Primitive Languages in Ogden, U.C. and Richards, (1925) op.cit., Supplement I, pp. 296-336, esp. pp. 313-16.
9   Ibid., p. 314.
10 Ibid., p. 315.
11 Britton, J. (1971) What's the Use? A Schematic Account of Language Function in 'Educational Review' no. 23(3), pp. 205-19; reprinted in Cashdan, A., et al. (eds)(1972) 'Language in Education: A Source Book', London: Routledge & Kegan Paul, pp. 245-51.
12 Ibid., p. 245.
13 Moffett, J. (1968) 'Teaching the Universe of Discourse', Boston: Houghton, Mifflin, pp. 34-5, 47.
14 Britton (1971) op.cit., p. 251.
15 Hymes, D.H. (1962) The Ethnography of Speaking in Gladwin, T. and Sturtevant, W.O. (eds)(1962) 'Anthropology and Human Behaviour', pp. 13-53; reprinted in Fishman, J.A. (1968) 'Readings in the Sociology of Language', The Hague: Mouton, pp. 99-138.
16 Ibid., p. 115.
17 Ibid., p. 115.
18 Hasan, R. (1973) Code, Register and Social Dialect, chapter 10 of Bernstein, B. (ed.)(1973) 'Class, Codes and Control', vol. 2, London: Routledge & Kegan Paul, pp. 253-92.
19 Halliday, M.A.K. (1973) 'Explorations in the Functions of Language', London: Edward Arnold (esp. chapter 1, Relevant Models of Language, pp. 9-21 and chapter 2, The Functional Basis of Language, pp. 22-47).
20 Ibid., p. 39.
21 Ibid., p. 42.
22 Ibid., p. 44.
23 Ibid., p. 43.
24 Whorf, B.L. (1939) The Relation of Habitual Thought and Behaviour to Language in Spier, L. (ed.)(1941) 'Language, Culture and Personality, Menasha: Winsonsin; reprinted in Carroll, J.B. (ed.)(1966) 'Language, Thought and Reality', Cambridge, Mass.: MIT Press, pp. 134-59, p. 156.
25 See ibid., p. 138, for Whorf's designation 'Standard Average European' ('SAE').
26 Fischer, J.L. (1965) The Stylistic Significance of Consonantal Sandhi in Trukese and Ponapean in 'American Anthropologist', vol. 67, pp. 1495-502; reprinted in Gumperz, J.J. and Hymes, D. (1972) 'Directions in Sociolinguistics', New York: Holt, Rinehart & Winston; and Fischer, J.L. (1966) Syntax and Social

Structure: Truk and Ponape in Bright, W. (ed.)(1966) 'Socio-
linguistics', The Hague: Mouton, pp. 168-82.

27 Greenberg, J.H. (1963) 'Universals of Language', Cambridge,
Mass.: MIT Press.

28 Basso, K.H. (1970) To give up on Words: Silence in Western
Apache Culture in 'Southwestern Journal of Anthropology',
Autumn 1970; reprinted in Giglioli, P.P. (1972) 'Language and
Social Context', Harmondsworth: Penguin, pp. 67-86.

29 Whorf, B.L. (1936) The Punctual and Segmentative Aspects of
Verbs in Hopi in Carroll, J.B. (ed.)(1956) op.cit., p. 55.

30 Whorf, B.L. (1939) The Relation of Habitual Thought and Behaviour to Language in ibid., pp. 134-59.

31 Ibid., pp. 242-43: Whorf, B.L. (1941) Language and Logic in
Carroll, J.B. (ed.)(1950) op.cit., pp. 233-45.

32 See for example, MacGregor, A.A. (1949) 'The Western Isles',
London: Robert Hale, a book which earned itself notoriety in
the Gaelic world on account of its presentation of stereotypes
of the Gael and his alleged behaviour patterns.

33 Brown, R., and Gilman, A. (1960) in Giglioli, P.P. (1972)
op.cit., p. 283.

34 Berger, P.L. and Kellner, H. (1964) Marriage and the Construction of Reality: an Exercise in the Microsociology of Knowledge in 'Diogenes' 46(1), pp. 1-23; reprinted in Cosin, B.R.
et al. (eds)(1971) 'School and Society', London: Routledge &
Kegan Paul and Open University Press, pp. 23-31.

35 Ibid., p. 25.

36 Brown, R. and Gilman, A. (1960) op.cit., pp. 266-9.

37 I suspect that one bright and independently-minded middle-aged
woman reckoned to use — or used — *thu* to numbers of such
officials in order to put them in their place. If so, she was
unique amongst the sample.

38 Macleod, F. (1969) 'Experimental Investigation into some Problems of Bilingualism', unpub. Ph.D. thesis, Aberdeen University,
p. 82.

39 Dorian, N.C. (1970) East Sutherland By-Naming in 'Scottish
Studies', vol. 14, part I, pp. 59-65, also printed as A Sub-
stitute Name-system in the Scottish Highlands in 'American
Anthropologist' (1970).

40 See Dunn, C.W. (1953) 'Highland Settler: a Portrait of the
Scottish Gael in Nova Scotia', Toronto: University of Toronto
Press (1971) Edition, pp. 52-4 and pp. 136-8: and Campbell, D.,
and MacLean, R.A. (1974) 'Beyond the Atlantic Roar: a Study
of the Nova Scotia Scots', Ottawa: McClelland & Stewart, p. 109.

41 Blake, J.L. (1966) Distribution of Surnames in the Isle of
Lewis in 'Scottish Studies', vol. 10, part II, Edinburgh.

42 Dunn, C.W. (1953) op.cit., p. 53.

43 Lawson, U. (1973) Di-Sàthuirn 'an Fhuadaich in 'Gairm', no.
85, Winter 1973, Glasgow, p. 29.

44 Vallee, F.C. (1954) 'Social Structure and Organisation in a
Hebridean Community', unpub. Ph.D. thesis, University of
London, p. 50.

45 Dorian, N.C. (1970) op.cit., p. 62.

46 Ibid., p. 63.

47 Ibid., p. 63.

48 Ibid., p. 63.
49 Ibid., p. 64.
50 Ibid., pp. 64-5.
51 Vallee, F.G. (1954) op.cit., p. 46.
52 Cicourel, A.V. (1972) 'Cognitive Sociology', Harmondsworth:
    Penguin, p. 57.
53 Sapir, E. (1934) The Emergence of the Concept of Personality
    in a Study of Cultures in 'Journal of Social Psychology',
    vol. 5, pp. 408-15; reprinted in Sapir, E. (1966) 'Culture,
    Language and Personality', Berkeley: University of California
    Press, p. 205.
54 Ibid., p. 34.
55 Ibid., p. 68.
56 Ibid., pp. 68-9.
57 King, A.D. (1974) The Language of Colonial Urbanisation in
    'Sociology', vol. 8, no. 1, January 1974, pp. 80-110.
58 There were, however, at least three such incomers in 1972.
59 MacAulay, D. (1972) Studying the Place-names of Bernera in
    'Transactions of the Gaelic Society of Inverness', vol. XLVII,
    1971-2, pp. 313-37.
60 Fraser, I. (1973) The Place-Names of Illeray in 'Scottish
    Studies', vol. 17, part II, Edinburgh, pp. 155-61.
61 Hymes, D. (1964) 'Language in Culture and Society', New York:
    Harper (reference note appended to Boas, F., On the Geographi-
    cal names of the Kwakiutl Indians, p. 176).
62 As in Brookfield, N.C. (1969) On the Environment as Perceived
    in Board, C. et al (eds) 'Progress in Geography', vol. 1,
    London: Edward Arnold.
63 As in Kirk, W. (1951) Historical Geography and the Concept of
    the Behavioural Environment in 'Indian Geographical Society
    Silver Jubilee Volume' (1952), pp. 152-60.
64 As in Frake, C.O. (1962) Cultural Ecology and Ethnography in
    'American Anthropologist', no. 64, pp. 53-9.
65 As in Korzybski, A. (1933) 'Science and Society', Lakeville: Inst.
66 As in Hymes, D. (1962) op.cit., pp. 178-9. [of Gen. Semantics.
67 White, R. (1969) Mental Maps in 'New Society', 2 January 1969;
    and Gould, P., and White, R. (1974) 'Mental Maps', Harmonds-
    worth: Penguin.
68 As in Gaster, T. (1950) 'Thespis: Ritual, Myth and Drama in
    the Ancient Near East', New York: Abelard Schuman.
69 Ibid., pp. 4-5.
70 Owen, Trefor M. (1958-9) The Role of the Township in a
    Hebridean Crofting Economy in 'Gairm', vol. 2, pp. 147-61.
71 White, R. (1969) op.cit., p. 100.
72 Dwelly, E. (1901-11) Illustrated Gaelic to English Dictionary',
    Glasgow: MacLaren (items for names of months); and Ferguson, C.
    (n.d.) 'Sàth: A Gaelic Teaching Course', Glasgow: Caledonian
    Music Co.
73 Brown, R., and Gilman, A. (1960) The Pronouns of Power and
    Solidarity in Giglioli, P.P. (1972) 'Language and Social
    Context', Harmondsworth: Penguin, pp. 252-82.
74 Ibid., p. 254.
75 Bernstein, B. (1971) A Critique of the Concept of Compensatory
    Education, chapter 10 of 'Class, Codes and Control', vol. 1,

Theoretical Studies Towards a Sociology of Language, London: Routledge & Kegan Paul, p. 198.

76 Ibid., p. 198. Also see for example Thomson, D.C. (1968) Gaelic Learned Orders and Literati in Medieval Scotland in 'Scottish Studies', vol. 12, part I, pp. 57-78.

77 Categories adapted from Professor V. Gordon Childe and discussed in Redfield, R. (1953) 'The Primitive World and its Transformations', Penguin edition, 1968, pp. 19-27; also see Redfield, R. (1947) The Folk Society in 'American Journal of Sociology', no. 52, pp. 293-308.

78 Redfield, R. (1953) op.cit., p. 58, also see below chapter 3, p.52, for a recent striking subordination of the technical order to the moral order in Harris.

79 Ibid., p. 55, the reference to Toynbee here cited is to Toynbee, A.J. (1947) 'A Study of History' (abridgement of vols I-VI by Somervell, D.C., New York and London: Oxford University Press, p. 414.

80 Robinson, W.P. (1971) Restricted Codes in Sociolinguistics and the Sociology of Education in Whiteley, W.H. (ed.)(1971) 'Language-use and Social Change', London: Oxford University Press, p. 88.

81 Ibid., p. 89.

82 MacLeod, F. (1969) 'Experimental Investigation into Some Problems of Bilingualism', unpub. Ph.D. thesis, University of Aberdeen.

83 Bernstein, B. (1972) A Sociolinguistic Approach to Socialisation with some Reference to Educability in Gumperz, J. and Hymes, D. (eds)(1972) 'Directions in Sociolinguistics', New York: Holt, Rinehart & Winston, pp. 482-5.

84 Pool, J. (1969) National Development and Language Diversity in Fishman, J.A. (ed.)(1972) 'Advances in the Sociology of Language', vol. II, The Hague and Paris: Mouton, pp. 213-30.

85 Ibid., pp. 225-6.

86 Watson, W.J. (1926) 'The History of the Celtic Place-names of Scotland', Edinburgh and London: Blackwood, pp. 389-90.

87 MacPherson, R. (1971) The Making of a Highland Parish in 'Transactions of the Gaelic Society of Inverness', vol. XLVII, pp. 260f.

88 See Mead, M. (1942-3) Our Educational Emphases in Primitive Perspective in 'American Journal of Sociology', vol. 48, pp. 633-9; reprinted in Keddie, N. (1973) 'Tinker, Tailor . . . the Myth of Cultural Deprivation', Harmondsworth: Penguin, pp. 96-107. 'The school ceased to be chiefly a device by which children were taught accumulated knowledge or skills and became a political device for arousing and maintaining national loyalty through inculcating a language or system of ideas which children did not share with their parents' (ibid., p. 102).

89 Cennard Davies (Lecturer in Welsh and Head of Welsh Language Unit, Barry College of Education) to Annual Conference of An Comunn Gàidhealach, Ayr, April 1973.

CHAPTER 3   DIMENSIONS OF AN ISLAND COMMUNITY

1   Edinburgh College of Art School of Town and Country Planning,
    'Harris: Planning Study 1966', published for Harris Council
    of Social Service (no date), pp. 8-9 and fig. 3.3 following
    p. 12.
2   'Harris 1966', op.cit., p. 49.
3   Western Isles Tourist Organisation Handbook.
4   See Grant, T.S. (1967) 'Crofting', Inverness, An Comunn
    Gàidhealach, and Owen, T.M. (1959) The Role of the Township
    in a Hebridean Crofting Economy in 'Gwerin', vol. 2, 1958-9.
5   The only published account (apart from items in Dwelly, E.
    (1901-11) 'Illustrated Gaelic to English Dictionary', Glasgow:
    MacLaren) is also only in Gaelic: MacArtair, Iain (1953)
    Comharran Chaorach in 'Gairm', no. 5, Foghar, 1953, pp. 75-7.
6   Caird, J.B. and Moisley, H.A. (1961) Leadership and Innovation
    in the Crofting Communities of the Outer Hebrides, in 'Socio-
    logical Review', vol. 9, no. 1, March 1961, pp. 85-101.
7   C.f. MacAskill, Joan C. (1966) The Roads go East, 'Education in
    the North', Aberdeen College of Education.
8   Borgstrøm, C.M. (1940) 'The Dialects of the Outer Hebrides',
    Oslo.
9   'West Highland Free Press', during Spring 1974.
10 In 1973 some 2¾-3 hours per week were broadcast in Gaelic on
    radio, and approximately ½ hour-1 hour per month on television
    depending on the time of year.
11 See MacLeòid, C.I.M. (1969) 'Sgialachdan a Albainn Nuaidh',
    Glasgow: Gairm, p. 43 for a good example in Gaelic, dated
    1802.
12 Something of the uncompromising character of the Free Presby-
    terian attitude to community affairs is gained from the follow-
    ing taken from the 'official' history of the Free Presbyterian
    Church: 'We condemn (a) bazaars, (b) sales of work, (c) social
    meetings. . . raffling. . . and other unscriptural schemes such
    as whist drives. . . in the same category are to be placed
    Boys' Brigades, Boy Scouts, Girl Guides; football, cricket,
    golf, badminton, boxing, dramatic and rambling clubs connected
    with Churches. . . we condemn without hesitation the modern
    movement of Community Drama. . . Burns' Concerts and Dinners. . .
    we also condemn the objectionable practices of the Comunn
    Gàidhealach and the Womens' Rural Institute.' Committee
    Appointed by the Synod of the Free Presbyterian Church (1933)
    'History of the Free Presbyterian Church of Scotland (1893:
    1933)', Glasgow: N. Adshead & Son, pp. 257-8.
13 For good descriptions of the Gaelic style of psalmody see
    Collinson, F. (1966) 'The Traditional and National Music of
    Scotland', London: Routledge & Kegan Paul, ch. X, pp. 261-4;
    and Knudson, T. (no date) 'Musique Celtique, Îles Hébrides:
    Gaelic Music from Scotland', notes of record sleeve, OCR45
    Disques Ocora, Paris, Office de Radiodiffusion Télévision
    Française.
14 See Owen, T.M. (1956) The Communion Season and Presbyterianism
    in a Hebridean Community in 'Gwerin', vol. 1, 1956-7.
15 Whittet, M.M. (1963) Problems of Psychiatry in the Highlands

and Islands in 'Scottish Medical Journal', vol. 8, no. 8, August 1963..

16 Dr M.M. Whittet quoted in the 'Scotsman' of 1 October 1963.

17 Vallee, F.G. (1954) 'Social Structure and Organisation in a Hebridean Community: A Study of Social Change', unpub. Ph.D. thesis, University of London, pp. 46-50.

18 Campbell, D., and MacLean, R.A. (1974) 'Beyond the Atlantic Roar: A Study of the Nova Scotia Scots', Toronto: McClelland & Stewart, p. 190.

19 Ibid., pp. 190-1.

20 Ibid., p. 186.

CHAPTER 4   ETHNIC LANGUAGE IN EDUCATION

1 For a discussion of the objectives and methods of this scheme from a Gaelic point of view, see MacGill 'Eathain, I. (1956) Cothrom na Féinne do'n Sgoil - Ghàidhlig in 'Gairm', no. 16, Samhradh, 1956.

2 Scottish Education Department (1955) 'Junior Secondary Education', ch. 26, pp. 274-84. 1965 'Primary Education in Scotland', ch. 26, pp. 199-201.

3 Inverness County Council Education Committee (Maclean, J.A., Director)(1964) 'Scheme of Instruction in Gaelic', Inverness.

4 Bell, R. and Mackenzie, M. (1974) 'Decision-making in the School', Milton Keynes: Open University Press, p. 29.

5 The nearest implementation of general availability of Gaelic to all in the Higher Secondary schools has been the introduction of Gaelic as well as French as a first-year subject for all pupils at the Nicholson Institute, Stornoway. This was replicated with some public controversy at Oban High School in 1972 after Mr Twatt transferred from Stornoway to Oban as rector.

6 Mackey, W.F. (1970) A Typology of Bilingual Education in Fishman, J.A., (ed.)(1972) 'Advances in the Sociology of Language', vol. II, The Hague and Paris: Mouton, pp. 413-32.

7 See MacGill'Eathain, I. (1956) op.cit., supra, p. 631.

8 Scottish Council for Researches in Education (1961) 'Gaelic-speaking Children in Highland Schools', London: University of London Press, Table III, p. 26.

9 Scottish Education Department (1974) 'Education in Inverness-shire', Report by H.M. Inspector of Schools (1973), Edinburgh: HMSO, esp. p. 26.

10 Ibid., p. 18.

11 Ibid., p. 19.

12 Ibid., p. 20.

13 Ibid., p. 20.

14 Ibid., p. 21.

15 Ibid., p. 21.

16 Bernstein, B. (1971) On the Classification and Framing of Educational Knowledge in 'Class, Codes and Control', vol. I, London: Routledge & Kegan Paul, p. 229, note 8.

17 Ibid., p. 212.

18 SED (1974) op.cit., p. 37.

19 Ibid., p. 6.
20 Ibid., p. 3.
21 Scottish Council for Research in Education, Committee for Bilingualism (1961) 'Gaelic-speaking Children in Highland Schools', London: University of London Press.
22 Ibid., p. 64.
23 Ibid., p. 64.
24 Macleod, F. (1969) 'Experimental Investigation into Some Problems of Bilingualism', unpub. Ph.D. thesis, University of Aberdeen.
25 Vernon, P.E. (1965) Abilities and Attainments in the Western Isles in 'Scottish Education Journal', 8 October 1965; Vernon, P.E. (1965) 'Intelligence and Cultural Development', London: Methuen.
26 Morrison, M. (1961) 'An Investigation into Bilingualism: the Application of a Gaelic Translation of the WISC', unpub. B.Ed. thesis, University of Aberdeen.
27 SCRE (1961) op.cit., p. 64.
28 Ibid., p. 63.
29 Ibid., p. 64.
3O Ibid., p. 63.
31 Ibid., pp. 44-5.
32 Ibid., pp. 28-31.
33 Ibid., p. 46.
34 Ibid., pp. 17-2O.
35 Ibid., p. 64.
36 Ibid., p. 2O.
37 Ibid., p. 64.
38 Ibid., p. 64.
39 In ibid., pp. 67-9.
4O Sharp, D., Thomas, G., Price, E., Francis, G. and Davies, I. (1973) 'Attitudes to Welsh and English in the Schools of Wales', Basingstoke and London: MacMillan Education/University of Wales Press.
41 SCRE (1961) op.cit., p. 64.
42 Sharp, D., et al (1973) op.cit.
43 Ibid., p. 15.
44 Ibid., p. 4O.
45 Ibid., p. 42.
46 Ibid., p. 38
47 Ibid., p. 36.
48 Ibid., pp. 35-6, 76.
49 Ibid., p. 35.
5O Ibid., p. 36.
51 Ibid., p. 57.
52 Ibid., p. 53.
53 Ibid., pp. 53-4 and Fig. 2, p. 54.
54 See ibid., p. 54 and Fig. 4.1 of the present study.
55 See Fig. 4.2 of the present study.
56 Sharp, D. et al. (1973) op.cit., pp. 58, 6O.
57 Ibid., pp. 67, 66.
58 Ibid., p. 67.
59 See chapter 2, p. 28.
6O Ibid., pp. 53-4.

61   Ibid., p. 88.
62   Ibid., p. 98.
63   Ibid., p. 156.
64   Ibid., p. 155.
65   Ibid., p. 156.

CHAPTER 5   GAELIC IN HARRIS PRIMARY SCHOOLS

1   Scottish Council for Research in Education (1961) 'Gaelic-
    speaking Children in Highland Schools', London: University
    of London Press.
2   SCRE report, op.cit., pp. 45-51.
3   Ibid., p. 44.
4   Ibid., p. 45.
5   For fuller details see ibid., p. 44 and Table 5.7 in the
    present study. For the proportion of the two mother-tongue
    groups within each occupational class in the bilingual area
    as a whole see MacKinnon, K.M. (1974) 'The Lion's Tongue',
    Inverness: Club Leabhar, pp. 70-3; MacKinnon, K.M. (1971)
    'A Sociolinguistic Study of Scottish Gaelic as an Institution
    in Scottish Life and Education', unpub. M.A. (Educ.) thesis,
    University of London Institute of Education; SCRE (1961)
    op.cit., Table III, p. 29.

CHAPTER 6   GAELIC IN SECONDARY AND FURTHER EDUCATION

1   Established in 1969 under the aegis of Glasgow University
    Department of Celtic with an annual government grant (in
    1973 increased to £8,000) and a remit of stimulating book
    publication in Gaelic.
2   See Tables 6.4, 6.5 and 6.6 following.
3   MacLeod, M. (1963) Gaelic in Highland Education in 'Trans-
    actions of the Gaelic Society of Inverness', vol. XLIII,
    1960-3, p. 334.
4   Ibid., p. 333.
5   Bernstein, B. (1971) On the Classification and Framing of
    Educational Knowledge in Young, M.F.D. (1971) 'Knowledge and
    Control', London: Collier-Macmillan, pp. 47-69 (in which
    Bernstein explains the concepts 'classification' and 'framing',
    'collection' and 'integration' codes).
6   Ibid., p. 49.
7   Ibid., p. 50.
8   MacLeod, M. (1963) op.cit., p. 334.
9   Inverness-shire Education Authority (1955) Report on 'Teaching
    of Gaelic', p. 5, para. 12 (where, furthermore, instructional
    advantages to non-native-speakers learning Gaelic 'as a foreign
    language' are cited as the learner having ready access in
    Inverness-shire to the background of the language and the
    'spoken word' - as compared with French).
10 Occupation of parents were: minister (4), doctor (1), ship's
    chief engineer (1), county roads supervisor (1), chief light-
    house keeper (1), fishing boat owner (1), county works mechanic
    (1), a bus driver (1).

11 The sources are the schools themselves. The difficulties of obtaining reliable statistics in this field arise from the fact that the local education authority does not handle the transition from school to university or other higher further education. This is a function of the Scottish Education Department. The SED aggregate statistics but has no breakdown to county level - let alone to district level for an area like Harris.

12 MacAskill, J.L. (1966) The Roads go East in 'Education in the North', Aberdeen College of Education, pp. 28-32.

13 Ibid., p. 39.

14 Ibid., p. 30.

15 A pejorative term in Scottish English for a Gaelic-speaker, Gael or Highlander. Probably onomatopoeic as the word contains typical Gaelic sound-combinations not common in English.

16 See MacKinnon, K. (1973) Opportunity in an Educational Backwater in 'West Highland Free Press', no. 68, 27 July 1973, p. 2.

17 SED (1972) 'Scottish Education Statistics', Table 95 (82), pp. 224-5.

18 Registrar General for Scotland Census 1971, County Report for Inverness-shire, Edinburgh: HMSO.

19 Solstad, K.J. (1971) Education in a Highland Region: Geographical Factors in School Progress in 'Scottish Education Studies', vol. 3, no. 1, May 1971, pp. 3-9.

20 Ibid., p. 5.

21 Lee, D.J. (1973) The Regional Factor in the Further Education and Employment of Male School Leavers, research note in 'Sociology', vol. 7, no. 3, September 1973, p. 433 and footnote 15 on p. 436.

22 Synge, J. (1973) Scottish Regional and Sex Differences in School Achievement and Entry to Further Education, research note in 'Sociology', vol. 7, no. 1, January 1973, pp. 106-16.

23 See MacKinnon, K.M. (1975) 'Language, Education and Social Processes: an Exploratory Study in Institutional Sociolinguistics', unpub. Ph.D. thesis, University of London, pp. 316-17.

24 See, for example, MacKinnon, K.M. (1972) Education and Social Control: the Case of Gaelic Scotland in 'Scottish Education Studies', vol. 4, no. 2, November 1972, esp. pp. 125 and 132.

25 A copy of the questionnaire, speech samples and notes on the derivation of the measures will be found in Appendices to MacKinnon, K.M. (1975) 'Language, Education and Social Processes: an Exploratory Study in Institutional Sociolinguistics', unpub. Ph.D. thesis, University of London Institute of Education, pp. 346-51, 500-1.

26 See ibid., pp. 329-30.

27 Giles, H. (1971) Our Reaction to Accent in 'New Society', 14 October 1971, and Giles, H. (1970) Evaluative Reaction to Accents in 'Education Review', vol. 23, 1970, pp. 211-27.

28 Bourhis, R. and Giles, H. (1974) Welsh is Beautiful in 'New Society', 4 April 1974.

29 Ibid., p. 16, col. 2.

30 As in Fishman, J.A. (1966) 'Language-loyalty in the United States', The Hague: Mouton, pp. 424-54.

31 Fishman, J.A. The Sociology of Language in Fishman, J.A.
    (1971) 'Advances in the Sociology of Language', vol. I, The
    Hague: Mouton, pp. 331-3.
32 Ibid., p. 331.
33 Ibid., p. 331.
34 Ibid., p. 332.
35 Ibid., p. 332.
36 Vallee, F.G. (1954) 'Social Structure and Organisation in a
    Hebridean Community: A Study of Social Change', unpub. Ph.D.
    thesis, University of London, pp. 46, 50.
37 See Bernstein, B. (1971) op.cit., pp. 49, 50.

CHAPTER 7 LANGUAGE-CONSERVATION AMONGST THE HARRIS ADULT POPULATION

1 Unpublished Census data for 1971 indicated some 38 individuals
   speaking Gaelic only in Harris. The 1971 Census report for
   Gaelic (Edinburgh: HMSO, 1975) is careful to stress the doubtful reliability of the returns for Gaelic only (paras 1-10,
   pp. viii-x).
2 Fishman, J.A. (1971) The Sociology of Language in Fishman,
   J.A. (ed.) 'Advances in the Sociology of Language', vol. I,
   The Hague: Mouton, p. 304.
3 Fishman, J.A. (1966) 'Language-loyalty in the United States',
   The Hague: Mouton, pp. 424-54.
4 Pike, K.L. (1967) 'Language in Relation to a Unified Theory
   of the Structure of Human Behavior', The Hague: Mouton.
5 Fishman, J.A. (1971) The Sociology of Language: An Interdisciplinary Social Science Approach to Language in Society,
   in Fishman, J.A. (1971)(ed.) 'Advances in the Sociology of
   Language', vol. 1, The Hague: Mouton, p. 255.
6 Ibid., p. 255.
7 Weinreich, U. (1953a) 'Languages in Contact', The Hague:
   Mouton, edition of 1966.
8 Wittgenstein, L. (1921) 'Tractatus Legico-Philosophicus', 5.2
   (English Edition of 1961, London: Routledge & Kegan Paul,
   p. 115).
9 Armitage, P. (1965) Tests for Linear Trends in Proportions
   and Frequencies in 'Biometrics', September 1955, pp. 375-86.
10 Sharp, D., Thomas, G., Price, E., Francis, G. and Davies, I.
   (1973) 'Attitudes to Welsh and English in the Schools of
   Wales', Basingstoke and London: Macmillan Education/University
   of Wales Press, pp. 35-6, 76.
11 Based upon the language-loyalty categories and scores (1)
   'Antipathetic' (below O), (2) 'Low' (O-30), (3) 'Moderate'
   (35-45), (4) 'High' (50-65), and 'Very high' (70+).

CHAPTER 8 CONCLUSION: LANGUAGE IN SOCIAL PROCESS

1 Vallee, F.G. (1954) 'Social Structure and Organisation in a
   Hebridean Community: A Study of Social Change', unpub. Ph.D.
   thesis, University of London.

2 Deutsch, K.W. (1953, 1966) 'Nationalism and Social Communication', Cambridge, Mass.: MIT Press.
3 Marx, K. (1953) The Duchess of Sutherland and Slavery in 'New York Daily Tribune' for 9 February 1853.
4 Houston, S.H. (1971) 'A re-examination of Some Assumptions about the Language of the Disadvantaged Child' in Chees, S. and Thomas, A. (eds)(1971) 'Annual Progress in Child Psychiatry and Child Development', London: Butterworth, pp. 233-50.
5 Robinson, W.P. (1971) Restricted Codes in Socio-linguistics and the Sociology of Education in Whitely, W.A. (ed.)(1971) 'Language-Use and Social Change', London: Oxford University Press, p. 80.
6 Macleod, F. (1969) 'Experimental Investigation into some Problems of Bilingualism', unpub. Ph.D. thesis, University of Aberdeen.
7 Labov, W. (1969) 'The Logic of Non-standard English', Georgetown Monographs on Language and Linguistics, vol. 22 (1969), reprinted in Giglioli, P.P. (ed.)(1972) 'Language and Social Context', Harmondsworth: Penguin, esp. pp. 188-9, 181-92.
8 Houston, S.H. (1971) op.cit., esp. section 3.
9 Chomsky, N. (1968) 'Language and Mind', New York: Harcourt Brace & World, pp. 60-1.
10 Fishman, J.A. (1971) 'Advances in the Sociology of Language', The Hague: Mouton, pp. 286f.
11 Census of Scotland 1961, vol. VII, Gaelic, Edinburgh: HMSO; Census 1971, Scotland, Gaelic Report, Edinburgh: HMSO.
12 Ibid., p. x, para. 9. Yet much the same could have been said in the case of Wales where a decline in Welsh-apeakers occurred between 1961-71.
13 Alasdair MacDhomhnaill(Alasdair MacMhaighistir Alasdair), in Watson, W. (1932) 'Bardachd Gàidhlig', Stirling: Learmouth.
14 Morgan, G. (1966) 'The Dragon's Tongue', Cardiff: Triskel Press, pp. 16-17.
15 See article and maps by MacKinnon, K. (1966) The Little That is Left. . . in 'New Cornwall', vol. 14, no. 1, Spring 1966.
16 Cennard Davies (1973) in an address to the annual conference of An Comunn Gàidhealach, Ayr.
17 Leiberson, S., and Hansen, L.K. (1974) National Development, Mother Tongue Diversity and the Comparative Study of Nations in 'American Sociological Review', vol. 3a, August, pp. 523-41.
18 Pool, H. (1969) National Development and Language Diversity in Fishman, J.A. (1972) 'Advances in the Sociology of Language', vol. II, The Hague: Mouton; discussed in Chapter 4 of the present study.
19 Ibid., p. 225.
20 For which see the discussion in Chapter 3 above.
21 Durkheim, E., and Mauss, M. (1903) 'Primitive Classification', London: Cohen & West.
22 Frankenberg, R. (1966) 'Communities in Britain', Harmondsworth: Penguin, pp. 285-96.
23 King, A.D. (1974) The Language of Colonial Urbanisation in 'Sociology', vol. 8, no. 1, January 1974, pp. 81-110.
24 A useful exposition of the relationships between changes in

social structure and the development of the Free Church in the early nineteenth-century Gaelic-speaking Highlands is in Hunter, J. (1974) The Emergence of the Crofting Community: The Religious Contribution 1798-1843 in 'Scottish Studies', vol. 18, 1974, pp. 95-116.

25 Fishman, J.A. (1971) op.cit., pp. 286f.

26 Ibid., p. 293.

27 Ibid., p. 298.

28 See Turner, R.H. (1960) Sponsored and Contest Mobility in the School System, in 'American Sociological Review', vol. 25, no. 5, December 1960, and Halsey, A.H., Floud, J. and Anderson, C.A. (eds)(1961) 'Education, Economy and Society', New York: Free Press.

29 See MacKinnon, K.M. (1973) Opportunity in an Educational Back-water, in 'West Highland Free Press', Kyleakin, nos 68, 69, July 1973.

BIBLIOGRAPHY

BARKER, G.C. (1947) Social Functions of Language in a Mexican-American Community in 'Acta Americana', no. 5, July/September, pp. 185-202.

BASSO, V.H. (1970) To give up on Words: Silence in Western Apache Culture, in Giglioli, P.P. (1972) pp. 67-86.

BELL, R. and MACKENZIE, M. (1974) 'Decision Making in the School', Milton Keynes: Open University Press.

BERGER, P.L. and KELLNER, H. (1964) Marriage and the Construction of Reality: an Exercise in the Microsociology of Knowledge, in 'Diogenes', no. 46, part I, pp. 1-23.

BERNSTEIN, B. (1965) A Socio-linguistic Approach to Social Learning, in Bernstein, B. (1971).

BERNSTEIN, B. (1967) Open Schools, Open Societies? in 'New Society', September 1967.

BERNSTEIN, B. (1971) 'Class, Codes and Control', vol. 1, London: Routledge & Kegan Paul.

BERNSTEIN, B. (1971) A Critique of the Concept of Compensatory Education, in Bernstein, B. (1971), pp. 198f.

BERNSTEIN, B. (1971) On the Classification and Framing of Educational Knowledge, in Bernstein, B. (1971).

BERNSTEIN, B. (ed.)(1973) 'Class, Codes and Control', vol. 2, London: Routledge & Kegan Paul.

BERNSTEIN, B. (1975) 'Class, Codes and Control', vol. 3, London: Routledge & Kegan Paul.

BLAKE, J.L. (1966) Distribution of Surnames in the Isle of Lewis, in 'Scottish Studies', vol. 10, part II.

BLOM, J.P. and GUMPERZ, J.J. (1972) Social Meaning in Linguistic Structures: Code-Switching in Norway, in Gumperz, J.J. and Hymes, D. (1972).

BOAS, F. (1964) On the Geographical Names of the Kwakiutl Indians, in Hymes, D. (ed.)(1964), p. 176.

BORGSTRØM, C.M. (1940) 'Dialects of the Outer Hebrides', Oslo.

BOURHIS, R. and GILES, H. (1974) Welsh is Beautiful, in 'New Society', 4 April 1974.

BRIGHT, W. (ed.)(1966) 'Sociolinguistics', The Hague: Mouton.

BRITTON, J. (1971) What's the Use? A Schematic Account of Language Function, in Cashdan, A., et al. (eds)(1972), pp. 245-51.

BRITTON, J. (1971) 'Language and Learning', Harmondsworth:
Penguin.
BROOKFIELD, N.C. (1969) On the Environment as Perceived, in
Board, C. et al. (ed.)(1969) 'Progress in Geography', vol. I,
London: Edward Arnold.
BROWN, R., and GILMAN, A. (1960) Pronouns of Power and Solidarity,
in Giglioli, P.P. (ed.)(1972).
CAIRD, J.B. and MOISLEY, H.A. (1961) Leadership and Innovation in
the Crofting Communities of the Outer Hebrides, in 'Sociological
Review', vol. 9, no. 1, March, pp. 85-101.
CAMPBELL, D. and MACLEAN, R.A. (1974) 'Beyond the Atlantic Roar:
a Study of the Nova Scotia Scots', Toronto: McClelland & Stewart.
CAMPBELL, J.L. (1936) Scottish Gaelic in Canada, in 'American
Speech', vol. II, pp. 128-36; revised 1948 in 'An Gàidheal',
Glasgow, vol. XLIII, March 1948.
CAMPBELL, J.L. (1950) 'Gaelic in Scottish Education and Life',
Edinburgh: W.A. & K. Johnston.
CARROLL, J.B. (ed.) (1956) 'Language, Thought and Reality:
Selected Writings of Benjamin Lee Whorf', Cambridge, Mass.:
MIT Press.
CARTER, I. (1972) The Highlands of Scotland as an Underdeveloped
Region, in de Kadt, E. and Williams, G. (eds)(1974) 'Sociology and
Development', London: Tavistock Publications.
CASHDAN, A. et al. (eds)(1972) 'Language in Education. A Source
Book', London: Routledge & Kegan Paul.
CHOMSKY, N. (1968) 'Language and Mind', New York: Harcourt, Brace
& World.
CICOUREL, A.V. (1972) 'Cognitive Sociology', Harmondsworth: Penguin.
COHEN, P.S. (1968) 'Modern Social Theory', London: Heinemann.
COLLINSON, F. (1966) 'The Traditional and National Music of
Scotland', London: Routledge & Kegan Paul.
CREIGHTON, H. and MACLEOD, C. (1964) 'Gaelic Songs in Nova Scotia',
Ottawa: Department of Secretary of State, Canada.
DAY, J.P. (1918) 'Public Administration in the Highlands and
Islands of Scotland', London: Oxford University Press.
DEUTSCH, K.W. (1953, 1966) 'Nationalism and Social Communication',
Cambridge, Mass.: MIT Press.
DORIAN, N.C. (1970) East Sutherland By-naming, in 'Scottish
Studies', vol. 14, part I, pp. 59-65.
DUNN, C.W. (1953) 'Highland Settler: a Portrait of the Scottish
Gaelic in Nova Scotia', Toronto: University of Toronto Press.
DURKHEIM, E. (1915) 'The Elementary Forms of the Religious Life',
(trans. Surain, J.W.), London: Allen & Unwin.
DURKHEIM, E. and MAUSS, M. (1903) 'Primitive Classification,
London: Cohen & West.
DWELLY, E. (1901-11) 'The Illustrated Gaelic-English Dictionary',
Glasgow: MacLaren.
EDINBURGH COLLEGE OF ART, School of Town and Country Planning (no
date) 'Harris Planning Study 1966.
FERGUSON, C. (no date) 'Sàth: A Gaelic Teaching Course', Glasgow:
Caledonian Music Co.
FISCHER, J.L. (1965) The Stylistic Significance of Consonantal
Sandhi in Trukese and Ponapean, in Gumperz, J.J. and Hymes, D.
(1972), pp. 498-511.

FISCHER, J.L. (1966) Syntax and Social Structure: Truk and Ponape, in Bright, W. (ed.)(1966).

FISHMAN, J.A. (1965) 'Yiddish in America: Sociolinguistic Description and Analysis', Bloomington: Indiana University Press.

FISHMAN, J.A. (1966) 'Language-Loyalty in the United States', The Hague: Mouton.

FISHMAN, J.A. (ed.)(1968) 'Readings in the Sociology of Language', The Hague: Mouton.

FISHMAN, J.A. (ed.)(1971) 'Advances in the Sociology of Language', vol. I, The Hague: Mouton.

FISHMAN, J.A. (1971) The Sociology of Language: An Interdisciplinary Social Science Approach to Language in Society, in Fishman, J.A. (ed.)(1971), pp. 255f.

FISHMAN, J.A. (1971) The Relationship between Micro- and Macro-Sociolinguistics in the Study of Who speaks What Language to Whom and When, in Pride, J.B. and Holmes, J. (eds)(1972), pp. 18-28.

FISHMAN, J.A. (ed.)(1972) 'Advances in the Sociology of Language', vol. II, The Hague: Mouton.

FISHMAN, J.A. (1974) 'A Sociology of Bilingual Education', unpub. monograph and research report, New York: Yeshiva University.

FISHMAN, J.A., COOPER, R.L., MA, R. et al. (1971) 'Bilingualism in the Barrio', The Hague: Mouton.

FRAKE, C.O. (1962) Cultural Ecology and Ethnography, in 'American Anthropologist', no. 64, pp. 53-4.

FRANKENBERG, R. (1966) 'Communities in Britain', Harmondsworth: Penguin.

FRASER, I. (1973) The Place-Names of Illeray, in 'Scottish Studies', vol. 17, part II, pp. 155-61.

FREE PRESBYTERIAN CHURCH (Committee of Synod)(1933) 'History of the Free Presbyterian Church of Scotland', Glasgow: N. Adshead & Son.

GASTER, T. (1950)'Thespis: Ritual Myth and Drama in the Ancient Near East', New York: Abelard Schumann.

GERTH, H.H. and MILLS, C.W. (eds)(1948) 'From Max Weber: Essays in Sociology', London: Routledge & Kegan Paul.

GIGLIOLI, P.P. (1972) 'Language and Social Context', Harmondsworth: Penguin.

GILES, H. (1970) Evaluative Reaction to Accents, in 'Educational Review', vol. 23, 1970, pp. 211-27.

GILES, H. (1971) Our Reaction to Accent, in 'New Society', 14 October 1971.

GILES, H., TAYLOR, D.M. and BOURHIS, R. (1973) Towards a Theory of Interpersonal Accommodation through Language: some Canadian Data, in 'Language and Society', vol. 2, no. 2, October, pp. 177-92.

GOFFMAN, E. (1959) 'The Presentation of Self in Everyday Life', Harmondsworth: Penguin.

GOFFMAN, E. (1971) 'Relations in Public', Harmondsworth: Penguin.

GOFFMAN, E. (1971) 'Interaction Ritual', Harmondsworth: Penguin.

GOULD, P. and WHITE, R. (1974) 'Mental Maps', Harmondsworth, Penguin.

GRANT, J.S. (1967) 'Crofting', Inverness: An Comunn Gàidhealach.

GREENBERG, J.A. (1963) 'Universals of Language', Cambridge, Mass.: MIT Press.

GRIMBLE, I. (1962) 'The Trial of Patrick Sellar, London, Routledge & Kegan Paul.

GUMPERZ, J.J. and HYMES, D. (eds)(1972) 'Directions in Socio-linguistics', New York: Holt, Rinehart & Winston.
HALLIDAY, M.A.K. (1964)   The Uses and Users of Language, in Fishman, J.A. (ed.)(1968), pp. 134-69.
HALLIDAY, M.A.K. (1973) 'Explorations in the Function of Language', London: Edward Arnold.
HALLIDAY, M.A.K. (1973) Language as a Social Semiotic: towards a General Sociolinguistic Theory, in Makkai, A., Makkai, V.B. and Heilmann, L. (eds)(1973) 'Linguistics at the Crossroads', The Hague: Mouton.
HANSEN, M.C. (1952) Third Generation in America: A Classic Essay in Immigrant History, in 'Commentary', no. 14, pp. 492-500.
HARDING, D.W. (1937) The Role of the Onlooker, in Cashdan A. et al. (eds)(1972).
HASAN, R. (1973) Code, Register and Social Dialect, in Bernstein, B. (ed.)(1973), pp. 253-92.
HAUGEN, E. (1953) 'The Norwegian Language in America Vol. I: The Bilingual Community', Philadelphia: University of Pennsylvania Press.
HERZLER, J. 'A Sociology of Language', New York: Random House.
HOUSTON, S.H. (1971) A Re-examination of Some Assumptions about the Language of the Disadvantaged Child, in Chess, S. and Thomas, A. (eds)(1971) 'Annual Progress in Child Psychiatry and Child Development', New York: Butterworth.
HUNTER, J. (1974) The Emergence of the Crofting Community: the Religious Contribution 1798-1843, in 'Scottish Studies', vol. 18, 1974, pp. 95-116.
HYMES, D. (ed.)(1964) 'Language in Culture and Society', New York: Harper & Row.
HYMES, D.H. (1962) The Ethnography of Speaking, in Fishman, J.A. (1968), pp. 13-53.
HYMES, D.H. (1967) Models of the Interaction of Language and Social Life, in Gumperz, J.J., and Hymes, D.H. (eds)(1972), pp. 35-71.
INVERNESS COUNTY COUNCIL EDUCATION DEPARTMENT (1964) 'Scheme of Instruction in Gaelic', Inverness: County Offices.
INVERNESS-SHIRE EDUCATION COMMITTEE (1955) 'Report on Teaching of Gaelic', Inverness: County Offices.
KEDDIE, N. (1973) 'Tinker, Tailor . . . the Myth of Cultural Deprivation', Harmondsworth: Penguin.
KING, A.D. (1974) The Language of Colonial Urbanisation, in 'Sociology', vol. 8, no. 1, June 1964, pp. 80-110.
KIRK, W. (1951) Historical Geography and the Concept of the Behavioural Environment, in 'Indian Geographical Society Silver Jubilee Volume', 1952, pp. 152-60.
KNUDSON, T. (no date) 'Musique Celtique, Îsles Hébrides: Gaelic Music from Scotland', Paris: Office de Radiodiffusion Télévision Française (Disques Ocora OCR45).
KORZYBSKI, A. (1933) 'Science and Society',Lakeville: Inst.Gen.Semantics.
LABOV, W. (1969) The Logic of Non-Standard English, in Giglioli, P.P. (1972).
LAWSON, U. (1973) Di-Sàthuirn' an Fhuadaich, in 'Gairm', no. 85, Winter 1973.

LEE, D.J. (1973) The Regional Factor in the Further Education and Employment of Male School-leavers, research note in 'Sociology', vol. 7, no. 3, September 1973, pp. 429-36.

LEWIS, S. (1971) The Fate of the Language (translated by Edwards, E.) in 'Planet', no. 4, February/March 1971, Llangeitho, Dyfed.

LIEBERSON, S. and HANSEN, K. (1974) National Development, Mother Tongue Diversity and the Comparative Study of Nations, in 'American Sociological Review', vol. 39, August 1974, pp. 523-41.

MAC A'GHOBHAINN, S. (1973) The Second Highland Land League, in 'Stornoway Gazette', vol. LVII, no. 7175, 16 June, 1973, p. 4.

MACARTAIR, I. (1953) Comharran Chaorach, in 'Gairm', no. 5, Autumn 1953, pp. 75-7.

MACASKILL, J.L. (1966) The Roads go East, in 'Education in the North' (1966), Aberdeen: College of Education.

MACAULAY, D. (1972) Studying the Place-Names of Bernera, in 'Transactions of the Gaelic Society of Inverness', vol. XLVII, 1971-2, pp. 313-37.

MACGILL'EATHAIN, I. (1956) Cothrom na Féinne do'n Sgoil-Ghàidhlig, in 'Gairm', no. 16, Summer 1956.

MACGREGOR, A.A. (1949) 'The Western Isles', London: Robert Hale.

MACKEY, W.F. (1970) A Typology of Bilingual Education, in Fishman, J.A. (ed.)(1972), pp. 413-32.

MACKINNON, K.M. (1966) The Little that is left. . . , in 'New Cornwall', Hayle, vol. 14, no. 1, Spring 1966.

MACKINNON, K.M. (1971) 'A Sociolinguistic Study of Scottish Gaelic as an Institution in Scottish Life and Education', unpub. M.A. (Educ.) dissertation, London University Institute of Education.

MACKINNON, K.M. (1972) The School in Gaelic Scotland: some Historical and Sociological Perspectives, in 'Transactions of the Gaelic Society of Inverness', vol. XLVII, 1971-2, pp. 374-91.

MACKINNON, K.M. (1972) Education and Social Control: the Case of Gaelic Scotland, in 'Scottish Education Studies', vol. 4, no. 2, November 1972.

MACKINNON, K.M. (1973) Opportunity in an Educational Backwater, in 'West Highland Free Press', Kyleakin, nos 68, 69, July 1973.

MACKINNON, K.M. (1974) 'The Lion's Tongue', Inverness: Club Leabhar.

MACKINNON, K.M. (1975) 'Language, Education and Social Processes: an Exploratory Study in Institutional Sociolinguistics', unpub. Ph.D. thesis, University of London.

MACKINNON, L. (ed.)(1956) 'The Prose Writings of Donald MacKinnon (1839-1914)', Edinburgh: Oliver & Boyd.

MACLEOD, F. (1969) 'Experimental Investigation into some Problems of Bilingualism', unpub. Ph.D. thesis, University of Aberdeen.

MACLEOD, M. (1963) Gaelic in Highland Education, in 'Transactions of the Gaelic Society of Inverness', vol. XLIII, 1960-3, pp. 305-34.

MACLEÒID, C.I.M. (1969) 'Sgialachdan á Albainn Nuaidh', Glasgow: Gairm.

MACNEIL, N. (1948) 'The Highland Heart in Nova Scotia', Toronto: Saunders.

MACPHERSON, R. (1971) The Making of a Highland Parish, in 'Transactions of the Gaelic Society of Inverness', vol. XLVII, pp. 260f.

MACTHOMAIS, S.(1957-8) Na Sgoilean Gàidhlig, in 'Gairm', nos. 22 and 23.

MALINOWSKI, B. (1923) The Problem of Meaning in Primitive Languages, in Ogden, C.K. and Richards, I.A. (1923), pp. 296-336.

MARX, K. (1853) The Duchess of Sutherland and Slavery, in 'New York Daily Tribune', 9 February 1853.

MEAD, M. (1942-3) Our Educational Emphases in Primitive Perspective, reprinted in Keddie, N. (1973), pp. 96-107.

MERTON, R.K. (1945) The Sociology of Knowledge, in Gurvitch, G. and Moore, W.L. (eds.)(1945) 'Twentieth Century Sociology', New York: Philosophical Library, pp. 366-405.

MERTON, R.K. (1949) On Sociological Theories of the Middle Range, in 'Theoretical Sociology' (1967), New York: Free Press.

MOFFETT, J. (1968) 'Teaching the Universe of Discourse', Boston, Mass.: Houghton, Mifflin.

MORGAN, G. (1966) 'The Dragon's Tongue', Cardiff: Triskel Press.

MORRISON, M. (1961) 'An Investigation into Bilingualism: the Application of a Gaelic Translation of the WISC, unpub. B.Ed. thesis, University of Aberdeen.

NISBET, R.A. (1966) 'The Sociological Tradition', London: Heinemann.

OGDEN, C.K. and RICHARDS, I.A. (1923) 'The Meaning of Meaning', London: Routledge & Kegan Paul.

OWEN, T.M. (1956) The Communion Season and Presbyterianism in a Hebridean Community, in 'Gwerin', vol. I, 1956-7, pp. 53-66.

OWEN, T.M. (1958) The Role of the Township in a Hebridean Crofting Economy, in 'Gwerin', vol. 2, 1958-9, pp. 147-61.

PIKE, K.L. (1967) 'Language in Relation to a Unified Theory of the Structure of Human Behaviour', The Hague: Mouton.

POOL, J. (1969) National Development and Language Diversity, in Fishman, J.A. (ed.)(1972), pp. 213-30.

PRIDE, J.B. and HOLMES, J. (eds)(1972) 'Sociolinguistics', Harmondsworth: Penguin.

REDFIELD, R. (1947) The Folk Society, in 'American Journal of Sociology', no. 52, pp. 293-308.

REDFIELD, R. (1953) 'The Primitive World and its Transformation', edition of 1968, Harmondsworth: Penguin.

REGISTRAR GENERAL FOR SCOTLAND (1966) 'Census of Scotland 1961 Vol. VII, Gaelic', Edinburgh: HMSO.

REGISTRAR GENERAL FOR SCOTLAND (Census Office)(1968) 'Lewis and Harris Special Survey Areas', Edinburgh: HMSO.

REGISTRAR GENERAL FOR SCOTLAND (1973) 'Census of Scotland 1971 County Report: Inverness-shire', Edinburgh: HMSO.

REGISTRAR GENERAL FOR SCOTLAND (1975) 'Census of Scotland 1971 Gaelic Report', Edinburgh: HMSO.

REX, J. (1961) 'Key Problems of Sociological Theory', London: Routledge & Kegan Paul.

ROBINSON, W.P. (1971) Restricted Codes in Sociolinguistics and the Sociology of Education, in Whiteley, W.H. (ed.)(1971).

SAPIR, E. (1966) 'Culture Language and Personality', Berkeley: University of California Press.

SCOTTISH COUNCIL FOR RESEARCH IN EDUCATION, Committee on Bilingualism (1961) 'Gaelic-speaking Children in Highland Schools', London: University of London Press.

SCOTTISH EDUCATION DEPARTMENT (1965) 'Primary Education in Scotland', Edinburgh: HMSO.

SCOTTISH EDUCATION DEPARTMENT (1972) 'Scottish Education Statistics', Edinburgh: HMSO.

SCOTTISH EDUCATION DEPARTMENT (1974) 'Education in Inverness-shire (Report by H.M. Inspector of Schools)' (1973), Edinburgh: HMSO.

SEMPLE, S.W. (1964) 'The Problem of Bilingualism in the Schools of Wales and Scotland', University of Toronto.

SHARP, D. et al. (1973) 'Attitudes to Welsh and English in the Schools of Wales', Basingstoke and London: Macmillan Education/ University of Wales Press.

SMITH, C.A. (1948) 'Mental Testing of Hebridean Children', Edinburgh: Scottish Council for Research in Education, Publication no. XLVII.

SOLSTAD, K.J. (1971) Education in a Highland Region: Geographical Factors in School Progress, in 'Scottish Education Studies', vol. 3, no. 1, May 1971, pp. 3-9.

SPOLSKY, B. and KARL, J. (1974) Apache Language Maintenance, in 'International Journal of Sociology of Language', no. 2, 1974, pp. 91-100.

SYNGE, J. (1973) Scottish Regional and Sex Differences in School Achievement and Entry to Further Education, research note in 'Sociology', vol. 7, no. 1, January, pp. 106-16.

THOMPSON, F.G. (1970) Gaelic in Politics, in 'Transactions of the Gaelic Society of Inverness', vol. XLVII, 1971-2.

THOMSON, D.C. (1963) The MacMhuirich Bardic Family, in 'Trans-actions of the Gaelic Society of Inverness', vol. XLIII, 1960-3, pp. 276-304.

THOMSON, D.C. (1966) The Writer in a Minority Culture, in 'Trans-actions of the Gaelic Society of Inverness', vol. XLIV, 1964-6, pp. 256-71.

THOMSON, D.C. (1967) Gaelic Learned Orders and Literati in Medi-eval Scotland, in 'Scottish Studies', vol. 12, part I, 1968.

THOMSON, D.C. (1968) Literature and the Arts, in Thomson, D. and Grimble, I. (1968).

THOMSON, D.C. (1970) The Poetry of Niall MacMhuirich, in 'Trans-actions of the Gaelic Society of Inverness', vol. XLIV, 1964-6, pp. 281-307.

THOMSON, D. and GRIMBLE, I. (1968) 'The Future of the Highlands', London: Routledge & Kegan Paul.

TOYNBEE, A.J. (1947) 'A Study of History', New York and London: Oxford University Press.

TRUDGILL, P. (1972) Sex, Covert Prestige and Linguistic Change in the Urban British English of Norwich, in 'Language in Society', vol. 1, no. 2, October, pp. 179-95.

TURNER, R.H. (1960) Sponsored and Contest Mobility in the School System in 'American Sociological Review', vol. 25, no. 5, December.

VALLEE, F.G. (1954) 'Social Structure and Organisation in a Hebridean Community: A Study of Social Change', unpub. Ph.D. thesis, University of London.

VERNON, P.E. (1965) Abilities and Attainments in the Western Isles, in 'Scottish Education Journal', 8 October.

VERNON, P.E. (1965) 'Intelligence and Cultural Development', London, Methuen.

WATSON, W.J. (1926) 'The History of the Celtic Place-Names of Scotland', Edinburgh and London: Blackwood.

WEBER, M. (1948) The Chinese Literati, in Gerth, H.H. and Mills, C.W. (eds)(1948), pp. 416-44.

WEINREICH, M. (1953) Yiddishkayt and Yiddish, in Fishman, J.A. (ed.)(1968), pp. 382-413.

WEINREICH, U. (1966) 'Languages in Contact: Findings and Problems', The Hague: Mouton.

WHITE, R. (1969) Mental Maps, in 'New Society', 2 January.

WHITELEY, W.H. (ed.)(1971) 'Language Use and Social Change', London: Oxford University Press.

WHITTAKER, B. (ed.)(1972) 'Fourth World: Victims of Group Oppression', London: Sidgwick & Jackson.

WHITTET, M.M. (1963) Problems of Psychiatry in the Highlands and Islands, in 'Scottish Medical Journal', vol. 8, no. 8, August 1963.

WHORF, B.L. (1936) The Punctual and Segmentative Aspects of Verbs in Hopi, in Carroll, J.B. (1956), p. 55.

WHORF, B.L. (1939) The Relation of Habitual Thought and Behaviour to Language, in Carroll, J.B. (1956), pp. 134-59.

WHORF, B.L. (1940) Science and Linguistics, in Carroll, J.B. (1956), pp. 213-14.

WITTGENSTEIN, L. (1921) 'Tractatus Logico-Philosophicus (English edition of 1961), London: Routledge & Kegan Paul.

ZNANIECKI, F. (1919) 'The Polish Peasant in Europe and America', Boston, Mass.: Badger.

INDEX